SUGAR *of the* CROP

SUGAR *of the* CROP

MY JOURNEY TO FIND THE CHILDREN OF SLAVES

Sana Butler

THE LYONS PRESS
Guilford, Connecticut
An Imprint of the Globe Pequot Press

To dad, John Wesley Butler,
who gave us everything we ever wanted
and more than we ever needed.
But he never spoiled us.

~

The Lyons Press is a registered trademark of The Globe Pequot Press.

Text design by Sheryl P. Kober

ISBN 978-1-59921-375-0

Printed in the United States of America

"He'd say, 'she was the Sugar of the Crop because she was the sweetest of the whole family.'"

—HERMAN HOOD ON HIS DAUGHTER'S NICKNAME, GIVEN TO HER BY HER GRANDFATHER, THE REV. JOHN HOOD

CONTENTS

CURIOSITY KILLS THE CAT

The last person I interviewed for this book was ninety-one-year-old Herman Hood. He lived with his daughter and granddaughter in Gastonia, North Carolina, about four hours southwest of the Raleigh-Durham airport. On the passenger seat of my rental car was a front page article from *The Charlotte Observer* about Mr. Hood, who up until the age of ninety had built homes for a Los Angeles real estate company. The reporter mentioned that Mr. Hood's father, Rev. John Hood, was a slave in South Carolina's Lowcountry. When I called to schedule an interview, his daughter Juanita pushed for a meeting sooner rather than later, because Mr. Hood was dying of prostate cancer.

I arrived in Gastonia the week of July 4th to the warm welcome of Juanita, standing and waving on the front steps with a kitchen towel draped over her shoulder, holding open the screen door.

"Welcome, Sana," she said in a soft voice, and hugged me with such excitement I felt as though maybe we had met before.

"I told Dad you were coming and was hoping he would stay with us long enough to talk to you. Looks like he made it," she said, inviting me in.

For the next four hours and every day that week, I sat with a tired Mr. Hood. The cancer had spread to his bones by the time I reached him. His limbs had curved inward at the joints and he dropped in and out of sleep every few minutes. Still, in the quiet of his bedroom, as my knee pressed against the metal rail of the bed and a tape recorder rested on Sesame Street sheets, he talked and I listened. He described his relationship with his parents, the impact of slavery on his family, and its legacy for the first generation of free blacks. We even tackled race relations, as he recounted a driving-while-black story, which ended when he bought a white jacket and black chauffeur cap to fool the police into thinking the Cadillac he was driving was not his.

"That didn't make you mad?" I asked.

"No, I just laughed at the boys," he said. "They didn't pull me over after that."

Several times during my visits I was concerned that Mr. Hood was too weak to talk. He paused at times after one word to catch his breath. When he got a rhythm going in a sentence he struggled sometimes to finish the thought before wheezing for air. When he would hiccup-cough, hallowing dead air from the back of his throat, I would glance at Juanita sitting behind me in the doorway to see if it was okay to ask more questions. Each time Mr. Hood nodded for us to keep going.

"There's so much to tell." I remember him saying.

Soon after I left Gastonia, Juanita called to tell me her father had died. "He stopped talking two days after you left and died three days later," she said.

Everyone I interviewed for this book is now dead, except for one woman. Most died within a year of the interview. Left behind are weeks of tape-recorded conversations that have completely redefined my perspective on American history.

Before these talks, I had my own ideas of how the children of slaves grew up. I expected them to be an angry and frustrated generation. After all, their parents had survived the single most barbaric period in U.S. history. I thought they might have trouble building strong bonds with their children or handing down anything other than the fear and hatred that remained from being considered someone else's property.

After our talks, all those ideas changed. They have been replaced with something more inspirational that has opened the door to an entirely new understanding of human behavior in the face of oppression and the unyielding strength that comes from unconditional love.

Before I started the search, the one person I knew who was a granddaughter of a slave was my own great-grandmother, Larue Johnson. But I had no idea of this until the morning of her funeral. When she died at the age of ninety-eight, my father drove us down to Kipling, North Carolina, to be with my mom's family. The service was held at the AME Zion Church, across the field from her tobacco farm, on a chilly Saturday morning in February 1991, a few days after my nineteenth birthday.

The fact that her grandparents were slaves came out during the service without pause or emphasis. I was busy wrestling for leg room inside the pew with my younger sister Sheria when I heard it. The words stuck in my head the way a song on the radio stays with you hours after it ends. I couldn't stop thinking about it. "Born to freed slaves." Before her grandparents, everyone in my family was a slave. But my great-grandmother was born free.

No one mentioned it again and I didn't bring it up. Other than generic questions of where and when, there didn't seem to be much to discuss. What could I learn that I didn't already know?

I had read the biographies of Harriet Beecher Stowe and Frederick Douglass and learned about underground railroads and runaway slaves. Watched *Roots* on ABC every Black History Month. I still can't bear to look during the scene when Kunte Kinte's master cuts off part of Kunte's foot to keep him from escaping. Maybe I knew enough.

Most of the history written about slavery didn't match my own family. We didn't struggle with many of the problems scholars assert came from slavery—poverty, single-parent households, chronic violent behavior. As far as we knew, there were no Union soldiers in the family tree. No runaway slaves. No abolitionists.

As I watched my great-grandmother's casket being lowered into the cemetery grounds in the woods behind her house, I couldn't connect those images of slaves with the faces around me. And even though it was a funeral, I wasn't sad. I was happy to be together as a family. The day was more of a reunion. Which got me thinking: If the pent-up anger and aggression from slavery carried through from generation to generation, and members of my family had been slaves, where did all our love come from? How did my family raise children who raised children who raised us, who turned out fine? The only way I could explain it to myself at the time was to assume that my family was special: We were the exception to the rule.

Perhaps my curiosity would have ended there if it weren't for President Bill Clinton. By 1997, I'd graduated from Georgetown University in Washington, D.C.; gone on to complete a master's degree in journalism from Columbia University in New York City; and had written for both television and newspapers. That's when I heard about his race idea. President Clinton created what he called the President's Initiative on Race, a committee that would travel the country holding town hall meetings on how to improve race relations. The one topic that kept coming up in discussion was slavery. The sentiment was so strong that U.S. Rep. Tony Hall, a white Democrat from Ohio, and eleven white co-sponsors introduced legislation calling on Congress to issue an official government apology.

I was working for *World News Tonight with Peter Jennings* and thought the apology coalition of all white politicians—six of them Republicans—would be an interesting story idea to pitch to Peter directly.

I called Hall's secretary to find out how many children of slaves were still alive to accept the apology. I figured if my great-grandmother died less than a decade ago and she was the granddaughter of slaves, maybe there was a slight chance there were seniors still alive who had parents who were slaves.

Either way, it didn't matter. The bill was more of a symbolic gesture. No one was tracking down either generation. "All the children are dead unless they're two hundred or something," the press secretary assured me, her sarcasm pouring from the phone.

"I'm sure there are some out there," I said defensively, not quite sure this was true.

Then I became curious. Were any children of slaves still alive?

New York

PEN AND PAPER

Sitting on the bed in my Brooklyn studio, staring at a blank page in my reporter's notebook, I devised a game plan to find out if any children of freed slaves were out there somewhere. I needed access to a central database that listed their names. I needed it to be organized by state, with up-to-date locator information.

All of it was wishful thinking. I knew such records didn't exist. But surely, an expert on African-American history or slavery in the United States had already collected similar primary interviews.

I didn't want to step on anyone's toes, finding people who had already been found, duplicating work that had already been done. So I called all over: a Society of Sons and Daughters of Slave Ancestry in Chicago, Harvard University's W.E.B. Du Bois Institute for African and African American Research in Boston, the American Folklife Center at the Library of Congress which houses the Works Progress Administration Slave Narrative Collection, even historian John Hope Franklin at Duke University in North Carolina. Each time the person on the other end called me crazy. Well, not in so many words. But I was definitely told I was wasting my time. One Virginia historian even laughed at the question. "Do you know what year slavery ended, Miss Butler? You are talking about 1865. Those children are long gone, young lady. Your best bet is to look for grandchildren and hope you get lucky."

I couldn't believe no one had ever tried to track down the children of freed slaves. Over the next couple of days, I asked myself questions about where to find them:

Who was I looking for?

Black people, in their nineties, or even older.

Where do old people live?

Nursing homes and retirement centers.

What do they do?

They go to church. They play bingo at senior citizen centers. They stay at home.

Where do they live in large numbers?

The South.

I started calling Southern states, one by one. I Googled a list of Department of Aging centers and called them in alphabetical order starting with Alabama. I'd ask to speak to a person familiar with the older black population in the state and have them fax me a listing of senior day care centers. If the person had extra time, they'd star the ones in counties with a majority black population. Then I called the director of each senior center to ask about their oldest members. I also asked for popular black churches in the neighborhood.

Then I called each church and spoke to the pastor to see if he could make an announcement or put the information in the Sunday bulletin, saying I was looking for anyone who had a mother or father who had been a slave. One pastor's secretary responded, "I hope you don't mind me asking, but what are you?"

"I am black," I said.

Usually the person on the other end was less direct. They would beat around the bush by asking where I was calling from, or if I had people from the state. Most people were hesitant about helping because of my strong New England Yankee accent. A few hung up. Some decided I was Jewish.

"Really?" I'd say. "What made you think that?"

"You have a funny accent and said something about quitting your job to travel the country. Not many black people have money to do that."

I laughed—because I didn't.

But I must have touched a nerve because when word got around about my search, I started to receive e-mails and phone calls from great-grandchildren, great-great nieces, neighbors down the street, church members, nurses, museum curators. Some were white, most black. All knew or knew of someone who knew a child of a slave. My hunch was right.

I traveled to a home in Cerulean, Kentucky, where the woman didn't know the name of her street. She told me, "When you get into town ask for my husband, James. Everyone knows him." I drove eleven hours from Tennessee to Mississippi on a tip because the 106-year-old I wanted to see was hard of hearing and didn't like to talk on the phone. Once I drove three hours in Kentucky to leave a note on a screen door because the family didn't have a phone. One time I called a family, after having already made travel arrangements, only to be told that the person I was to interview had died the night before.

In the end, this quest stretched on for ten years. It became part of my life, and for many years, as ex-boyfriends will attest, it was my life. I picked up a fleeting Southern accent and would call everyone "Sir" or "Ma'am," or Mr. or Mrs. Last Name, unless they told me it was okay to call them by their first.

I decided early on to do more than collect oral history, letting the tape recorder record as they went on about their lives and what they remembered their parents saying about slavery. I wanted to get opinions on current events, put their stories within a historical context, ask why and what for when I didn't agree with something they said. But most important, I wanted to see how slaves became husbands and wives; mothers and fathers and how they raised their children. Some days, the topic of slavery never came up. Ultimately, spending time reminiscing about their parents helped me see mine in a whole new light.

Talking with the children of slaves also opened my eyes to how much I'd underestimated the everyday person left out of history books. Famous celebrated slaves like Harriet Tubman no longer seemed to be the exception but closer to the norm, making me think these interviews revealed only the tip of the iceberg.

Historians and academics have focused so much attention on the victimization of slaves and the horrors that took place under slavery that they rarely documented the strength that enabled former slaves to overcome long-term disabling trauma in order to function normally as parents, in many cases with stellar success.

It was hard to see the resilience of ex-slaves and their children and not wonder, what happened to us over the years? What did ex-slaves do right that we should be doing now? I have some new thoughts on what went right, and what went wrong, as you'll see.

On a much smaller scale, this book was my personal challenge. It was written almost entirely in chronological order, as I hopped from one state to the next between August 1997 and July 2008. Sometimes I spent a month or a week or one day. I took whatever I could get. I almost always left with or found later, documents proving the parent was born before 1865 such as records kept by the slave owner, Census rolls, Civil War registries.

During our times together, we would laugh about our families. I had fun comparing theirs with mine to see if there were certain parenting techniques that transcended time. And in a country eager to forget and move on, there are still many jewels to be unearthed in remembering: a mom in the kitchen on Sunday morning; a dad who hugs so hard it hurts. We all know what good family feels like. This is a part of our shared past we don't want to forget.

A few months before my first big road trip, my dad checked into the sixth floor of Yale-New Haven Hospital for major surgery. He had had cancer for about twenty years—a rare type called olfactory neuro-blastoma that grew around the nose toward his brain. This time the tumor was growing toward his left eye. For that first week of recovery, Mom, my older sister Kwanza, my younger sister Sheria, and I all slept in chairs and on the windowsill in his hospital room, keeping him company.

Staying in that room was hard. I went into the bathroom often during the day to cry while flushing the toilet so no one could hear the sniffles. Once or twice an hour, he opened his eyes to look around. We would all stop what we were doing to say, "Hi Dad," one by one. And then he would go back to sleep. But most of the time we sat in silence with our necks tilted up watching a television that was too far over our heads, trying to read lips with the volume muted.

After a week of watching Dad, I couldn't take it anymore. There was nothing new about who we were together. But in such a small room—it couldn't have been more than fifteen paces by ten—I started to notice little things in his behavior that reminded me of myself. And I'll be honest, the resemblance was scary.

It began only a few hours after surgery, when he asked a nurse for a pad and pen so he could write a note to Mom. He was at the time breathing through a hole in his throat. His mouth was wired shut and his nose had cotton in it to stop the bleeding.

"Are you okay with this?" he wrote.

When he started to feel better, he wrote notes to nurses about what pain medication to give him. The notes weren't long—just enough to make sure he knew that the nurse knew what she was doing. I couldn't help but notice because I sat in the chair blocking the door and had to move each time they left to double-check his medical chart. The scenes had become bittersweet entertainment for me, and not because my dad seemed to know more, though I admit I was impressed that even in his ailing condition he almost always did.

But because here I was in front of myself: the person who second-guessed everyone to keep them on their toes. The person who needed to be in control to make others feel comfortable and safe. All the defining parts of my personality I thought I got from me, or from my friends or my travels or my life experiences. Did I really just get them from my dad? How much is each of us a mirror of our parents?

When he started to feel better and was able to leave the hospital, I went back to planning a trip. My ticket was to California to interview a millionaire. When I first heard of lawyer Crispus Attucks Wright, I said to myself, that's impossible. How did the son of a slave become a millionaire? So I started with him, because if I turned out to be a lot like my dad, maybe the self-made millionaire son of a former slave was something like his.

2

California

SIPPING ON DOM PÉRIGNON

A year ago I received a fax about Crispus Attucks Wright from the University of Southern California (USC) Law School. The press release announced that Mr. Wright had recently donated $2 million to his alma mater to create a scholarship fund for minority students. The cash gift was the largest to USC by an African American. But more remarkable was the headline that mentioned the donation was made by the retired 85-year old lawyer whose father was born a slave in southern Louisiana.

I flew out to Los Angeles on the second Tuesday of November in 1999. A morning thunderstorm had washed away the smog caked over the city. Cars on the freeway, under construction from Lake Forest Drive to the mall off of the Bristol Street exit, inched along bumper to bumper in both the northbound and southbound lanes, newly paved and now slippery wet.

When I spoke to Mr. Wright on the phone a couple days earlier, he invited me to his house and gave me directions, which I wrote down on a yellow Post-it and pasted to the dashboard. He listed freeway names all beginning with the word Santa: Santa Clara, Santa Monica, Santa Ana, Santa Barbara. But the map I purchased at Los Angeles International Airport used numbers, not words, to identify exits. I must have called Mr. Wright two or three times that first day from the highway, lost.

"Where are you?" he'd ask

"Trying to find the exit to I-10 West."

"Are you talking about Santa Monica?"

"I don't really know, Mr. Wright. Thanks for walking me through this. This is my first time in California."

"Don't worry about it, young lady. I cleared my schedule for the day and am just sitting here waiting on you. You came out here by yourself?"

"Just to see you, Mr. Wright."

"Well, then. Come on and take your time."

Finally, the rain stopped and traffic started to lighten up. I turned off the air conditioner to save money on gas and rolled down the windows. When the directions began to agree with the freeway signs, I found exit 11, Washington Boulevard, four traffic lights from his house. There was a man standing on the front lawn, waving as I turned the corner. I stopped the car along the sidewalk, leaned across the dashboard, and stuck my head out the passenger window.

"Mr. Wright?"

"So you made it," he said. He had been standing outside since our last phone call fifteen minutes ago to make sure a gray four-door Taurus didn't drive by the house. I pulled up the driveway to park in front of a three-car garage. A black BMW sports car sat on the left, a black Rolls Royce with red interior in the middle, and a fitness center with dumbbells and a treadmill was on the right.

I got out of the car and we introduced ourselves with a handshake. Mr. Wright was wearing a khaki cotton linen suit with a crisp white oxford shirt. No tie. He had a smaller frame than I'd expected. His phone voice projected big and tall in a charming baritone kind of way. But as it turned out, he was about my five-foot-eight height.

I asked for a minute to grab some things out of the car, though I really wanted time to pick up the litter before he could see it. An empty soda can, paper bag, Styrofoam coffee cup, and a half-eaten blueberry Danish from the morning were scattered over the seat and floor on the passenger side. Not a good first impression.

As I turned to duck inside to reach across the driver's seat, I saw Mr. Wright out of the corner of my eye, through the window, walking in front of the hood to the other side. He opened the passenger door and grabbed my purse and tape recorder from the floor, ignoring the junk. "Thank you," he said as he carried them to the house, as if I were doing him a favor instead of the other way around.

Mr. Wright lived in a two-story peach colonial home with a pool on the corner of a street lined with palm trees. He had it built in 1952 on a then dead-end road and was the first black person to move into the neighborhood. While the house was being built, a white neighbor walked up to him and begged him not to finish construction.

I followed Mr. Wright inside. The carpet in the living room had fresh vacuum lines. Unopened envelopes and supermarket flyers covered the dining room table. The kitchen had a single plate, fork, and plastic container in the sink. There were no recent photos on the refrigerator or walls, just an old one in the hallway leading upstairs. It was of him with his wife and his then five-year-old son, all smiles, huddled together on the front steps.

Mr. Wright lived by himself now. His wife, Helen, had passed away some years ago and the son, Warner III, lived across town on Wilshire.

After a brief tour of the first floor, we walked to his study on the side of the house that faced the pool. It was a blood-maroon room much like an Ivy League alumni club with little direct sunlight, dark hardwood floors, and a topographical globe as tall as the coffee table next to it.

Mr. Wright pointed to one of the two high-backed leather chairs for me. He sat on a gold camelback sofa placed against the wall that squeaked when he crossed his legs. I sank into the chair and leaned my head against the side as I grabbed a notebook from my pocketbook, then scrounged for a piece of candy. I had a horrible stress headache. The three-hour detour on the Santa Monica had sucked away all my energy, and Mr. Wright could tell.

"Los Angeles is a peculiar place," he said when I looked up. "It's built haphazardly. There are about a hundred towns around here. I think you've done very well. Incidentally, were you born in the Carolinas?"

I had mentioned on the phone that my mother was from North Carolina and my dad from South Carolina.

"No, I was born in Connecticut," I said.

"Oh, that's where the accent is from." His response came with a broad, double-dimple smile and an arresting pit-of-the-stomach laugh much like a mix of jolly St. Nick and Don Cornelius.

After we spent a few minutes discussing what my dad does for a living (he's an engineer) and how lucky we were that mom was able to stay home to raise us, Mr. Wright stood up and walked toward the only three pictures in the room. The first was a framed photo of him and Tom Tomlinson, an associate dean of USC Law School. It was taken the year Mr. Wright made the scholarship donation. The other two hung on the wall, facing the couch: large head shots of his parents, Gertrude and Warner Wright, in antique bronze frames the size of oval tea trays.

Mr. Wright reached inside a cabinet underneath the picture of his father to pick up a stack of papers. "These are copies of things I thought might be useful in your research on my father." Under a color photocopy of his parents' portraits was a bulky stack of 11x17 pages, stapled and folded. The pages were handwritten.

"Is this your handwriting?" I asked.

"No. Those are my father's notes on his life."

His what? Mr. Wright hadn't mentioned that his father kept a journal when we spoke on the phone. The family itself, it turned out, had forgotten the journal existed until a couple years ago, when Mr. Wright's grandson was asked to write about the family history for a college paper. "I went to my sister who was alive then and she said, 'I've got some stuff here that you may be interested in,' and she started digging," Mr. Wright explained.

And here it was, in my hands.

No one knew where the original was anymore. Mr. Wright only had a copy with wide, yellowed, unlined pages handwritten with perfectly even cursive. The journal had fifteen pages but no dated entries, and much of the ink had faded. The only reference to time appeared on the first page in the upper-right-hand corner, where Warner had simply written, "1891." Below, in the center of the first page, was a manufacturer preprinted poem, titled "Home Sweet Home":

> I remember, I remember
> The House where I was born,
> The little Window where the Sun
> Came peeping in at Morn.

The journal didn't duplicate well. In spots the original ink was too light to copy legibly. Faded writing left holes in the middle of sentences, and missing pages cut adrift in the middle of thoughts. I struggled in silence through the beginning few pages of Warner's childhood in southern Louisiana, trying to guess what went in the blanks. On the first page, he wrote that he was born on the Woodlawn Plantation, some five or six miles south of the town of Houma. "It was 26 of February of 1864 that I first saw the [illegible]. My father was also born on the above named plantation," he wrote.

In my excitement to have found Mr. Wright, I forgot to ask the most important question before making the cross-country journey to meet him: How old was your father when slavery ended? I was somewhat disappointed to learn that Warner was just a baby then. Still, I wanted to keep going.

True, the early entries in Warner's journal weren't earth-shattering. A birthdate. The name of the plantation where he was born. The location. As much as I was moved by hearing about his life, in his own words, I was drawn to everyday information as to have been found on a map or birth certificate. Often in my travels more journals turned up, kept safe in a foyer or attic or in a kitchen drawer. Enough to believe that an undocumented number of freed slaves felt inspired to record every aspect of their lives for family members to have, as if they knew later generations of great-great-greats would want to know what had happened to them long after they were gone.

I was able to figure out the basics from the first couple pages of the journal. Mr. Wright's father and his father's father, at one time, were owned by the same family whose last name was Pugh. They lived on the Woodlawn Plantation where Warner was born and was a baby when the Civil War ended. But when Warner was freed was less clear. "My father said his owner kept them as slaves years after the war ended" Mr. Wright said. Warner's memory of slavery—not sharecropping—continuing past 1865 is a point of contention among a small number of historians. Everyone knows that 1865 was the year the Civil War ended and the Thirteenth Amendment abolishing slavery was ratified by the requisite number of state legislatures. But Congress didn't vote on the Fourteenth Amendment granting black Americans citizenship until 1868. For those three years blacks were constitutionally undefined. Stuck in limbo, they were no longer enslaved but not yet citizens with inalienable rights to freedom.

Harsh, restrictive state laws known as Black Codes were passed by Confederate states in the early months following the war to restrict civil and legal rights of newly freed slaves. Enforced at the request of former slave owners who could no longer maintain profitable plantations without free labor, the Codes also coerced the population to work as farmers for little or nothing.

Warner later described activities on Woodlawn in 1869 that appeared to be more in line with what a very young slave would have done, rather than what a free slave would have accepted. Looking back to when he was five years old, Warner wrote that he was responsible for entertaining the Pugh family after dinner. He put together a courtly strut he called the "city walk."

"Imagine that you have before you a boy of not more than five summers with hat on one side of his head, wad in jacket and short britches strutting as he imagined how the men and women carried themselves in New Orleans, or Houma, or Thibodaux," Warner wrote.

The skit was likely a suggestion made by the Pughs. For amusement, plantation owners would organize similar dance performances on Sundays called the cakewalk, where they would order their slaves to dress up in hand-me-downs and imitate the way whites waltzed at ballroom formals. Slaves did little more than stumble and humiliate themselves to which as a reward owners would hand out slices of cake. "I almost burst into a fit of laughter now as I think of it," he added.

Many considered the slave minstrels as a power play between master and servant, begging the question, Whom was making fun of whom? Was Warner laughing at the way his owners walked or did his owners use the city walk skit to laugh at themselves at his expense?

I couldn't tell by the entries. But what was obvious was that his thoughts showed a charming and refreshingly clever side. His words were filled with sarcasm and quick wit, combinations I didn't expect from a child growing up during this period. I had imagined someone more in line with reenactments in which actors limp along using broken English like "dere," "de," "fust," and "dat" instead of saying "there," "the," "first," and "that," as if poor enunciation by slave characters added to the drama.

Warner's grasp of the English language was a moneymaker for him as he sought to be a public speaker as a boy, trading in his hat and cane for a Bible and a tractor that doubled as a podium. Whites and blacks paid to hear him speak on the street, dropping coins in a collection plate for the show. He wrote that on a good day he didn't speak for long, "How could I when the plate of nice dimes sat just over there on the table?"

At times he called himself John the Baptist, "not in the wilderness, but standing in a big armed chair in the white folks' tractor." He recited from the Bible verse of Matthew, chapter three, which he memorized. He prided himself at always being brief but to the point. And he never spoke for free. "The dimes I enjoyed immensely. Sometimes I would refuse to preach until they had brought the dime and placed it in sight. Then I would mount a chair and put forth my best effort."

By the time Mr. Wright's father was making his career as a public speaker, the United States was moving toward the peak of a unique social and political movement the likes of which would never again be seen in this country. Like immigrants lured to the New World for its offer of freedom, fresh off the boat with little more than the clothes on their backs, newly freed slaves, inspired by Civil War's end, walked off plantations to a new free world, carrying confidence in the future.

First on their agenda was to get an education. As early as 1866, there were more black students than whites enrolled in schools throughout the South. Adults and children of all ages went to school during the day, at night, and on the weekends. It wasn't unusual for student ages to range from four to seventy in the same classroom.

In Louisiana the Freedmen's Bureau, funded by Congress to help former slaves make the transition to free men and women, couldn't build schools fast enough. When overcrowding became an issue, many didn't wait for new schools to be built and a large number enrolled in regular public schools—a practice that became so widespread, according to a Pugh family letter dated August 1867, that parents started to send their children away to "paying" schools because Louisiana blacks were not only going to Freedmen's schools but also schools whites attended.

Although funds for the program started to run out in Louisiana only a year after the Bureau was established, one Northern abolitionist observed the push to build schools in the state only picked up in pace. "Private schools for Negroes sprung up outside Bureau control. Enrollment in such schools grew from 150 in February to nearly 3,000 in December."

The newly educated former slaves wasted no time in designing grand plans for a new life and the education revolution paid off almost immediately. By 1877, two thousand black men actively participated in local, state, and federal government, becoming everything from U.S. Senators and state Supreme Court judges to lieutenant governors and mayors. Louisiana alone employed more than two hundred officeholders. The new leadership made up half of South Carolina's House of Representatives, claiming three out of six seats. In all, twenty-two blacks were elected to Congress, most just out of slavery. The new regime immediately repealed all the Black Codes. With slavery over and the Codes in the past, free men and women looked to the future believing, in many ways, that the worst was behind them.

Mr. Wright's father did too. In his journal he talked about his attendance record in school and that he wanted to be a doctor when he grew up. Encouraged by a teacher who saw serious potential in Warner, he wrote that she had arranged a parent teacher meeting to push "my father to give me a medical education. It was always my ambition to stand first in my class both when in public school and also at college. But it was not always my lot to be first. Sometimes others outstrip[p]ed me in the race. But I studied hard never the less believing that victory would finally be granted to the studious and determined." He went on to say that he loved to play with friends at school but "loved books more." When I read that, I looked up at Mr. Wright, tempted to make a sarcastic comment. What kid loves reading, writing, and arithmetic over recess? But I didn't. I kept the comment to myself.

That page came close to the end of the journal and, I wondered if it referred to a time before or shortly after the end of Reconstruction. My guess was that it was written before Reconstruction's end because Warner wrote about the future with such blind excitement and unbridled enthusiasm. His teachers felt the same way. There was a new optimism throughout the South that southern whites hated, shocked that freed slaves actually believed in equality, that they could rise from servitude to achieve so much in such a short period. This bitter resentment was epitomized by a Georgia Democrat, who destroyed any historical record that included the name of elected officials or as he wrote, "men who were but yesterday our slaves."

Leading up to the overthrow of Reconstruction, southern whites made it no secret of their hatred of blacks and made it their mission to squash the momentum by any means necessary. They tortured and killed political incumbents as well as voters to send a message to stay out of politics and away from the polls on election day. Intimidation also reigned from Democratic rifle clubs, where members would schedule target practice near the black sections of Republican rallies. Eventually it worked. State by state, beginning as early as 1870, Democrats regained control of state and federal legislative houses, immediately writing new laws to reduce black voting, claiming black voters were electing candidates who were not qualified to hold their positions. New legal barriers to black voter registration, such as Mississippi's "grandfather" clause, which allowed registration only for those whose grandfathers had voted previously, cut the voting population from over 90 percent during Reconstruction to less than 6 percent by 1892. In Louisiana, the number of voters fell from 130,334 in 1896 to 1,342 in 1904. Moses Sterrett, who served two consecutive terms in the Louisiana legislature, could only get work cleaning courthouse toilets once Reconstruction had come to an end. The country's promise of a new beginning also ended.

"It was an interesting period," said Wright. "My father wrote that we had a number of legislators, a number of congressmen during those periods. There was a vast advancement and then it all stopped. The South was still the South. It was an issue of race."

I hadn't heard the word "Reconstruction" since high school. Still, I didn't remember feeling this riled up the first time around. I found myself reading and rooting for a young Warner, who sincerely believed the country would be fair to "the studious and determined." I badly wanted it to be true, even though I knew the history of the future he faced.

I shook my head. Warner's journal also brought to light an assumption I'd made about freed slaves that I was now disappointed in myself to have made. Because by the 1880s a majority were sharecroppers, farming the land of their former owners for a tiny percent of the profit, I assumed they'd settled for this life because most didn't know anything else but how to farm. Now I saw that they wanted more, had longed to better themselves, to participate fully in the newly equal society they briefly believed they'd become a part of. From wide-eyed voters to book-smart seventy-year-olds, how many wanted to be doctors? Politicians? Lawyers? How many dreamed big?

In the late nineteenth century, Warner started to build his family. He graduated from Leland College in Baker, Louisiana, an institution of higher learning for blacks founded by northern Baptists in 1870. He became a principal in Alexandria, where he got married and where his children were born. Mr. Wright's father also owned a pharmacy, but he never became a doctor. Jim Crow segregation laws made it impossible for him to enroll in a credible public medical school decades following slavery. While there were at least fourteen black medical schools established in the South over a thirty year period, by 1918, twelve of them had closed their doors. The two in Louisiana and others received a healthy number of student applications but failed because of questionable administrative practices.

Mr. Wright had to let go of his dream. In order to operate as a drug store, filling prescriptions, Mr. Wright said "he couldn't be a doctor so he hired a white one."

No birth records were kept for blacks when the Wrights started to have children. "So my father, he wrote notes in a Bible about us."

"What did he say?"

"Notations of when we were born. He would give the name of the child and say a few things about them."

"What did he write when you were born?"

"As you know the original Crispus Attucks was a free black man and the first man killed in the Revolutionary War. I was, of course, named after him."

Some years before Mr. Wright was born in 1914, his father was diagnosed with diabetes, and by the time he was born, his father was very sick. Mr. Wright's mother started to think about a healthier place for the family to live. California had distributed flyers along the railroads in Louisiana to encourage people to move West, where the air is dry and the sun always shines. The family knew Booker T. Washington's eldest son, a real estate broker in Los Angeles. Gertrude contacted him for advice. A former student of Warner's who went on to become one of the original founders of the National Association for the Advancement of Colored People (NAACP), Dr. H. Claude Hudson, also lived in Los Angeles and advised Gertrude and the family to come out and join them. In 1920 the family bought a home in South Central Los Angeles.

Six months after the move, Mr. Wright's father died. Much of what his father wrote in the journal Mr. Wright didn't know until he read it himself a couple years ago. "I didn't know my father was a speaker until recently," said Mr. Wright. "I was an excellent debater and speaker in school and my brother was also a debater. See, I took after my father. I did not know him well; I was too young to really remember many things, but I remember some. I remember that he was so interested in education."

As the youngest of seven, Mr. Wright was born smack in the middle of the Jim Crow era, so his memories are strongly connected to that time. "I mean when [progress] stopped, it stopped. They just cut off what we had. It's like 209."

I put the journal down. The reference he made was to Proposition 209, the controversial 1996 referendum that barred public institutions in California—including universities—from giving preferential treatment on the basis of race. I knew 209 would come up sometime in our conversation because it was the reason why Mr. Wright made the donation to create a scholarship in his name the following year. But I was very surprised to hear the topic come up in relation to his father and Reconstruction. More than 140 years have passed, but still Mr. Wright saw a connection between then and now?

The issue for Mr. Wright was access to opportunities—who got it and who didn't. "All these years we've been fighting to get into professional schools, and now they want to turn back the clock," he told a magazine reporter in 1998. At the heart of the argument put forward by 209 supporters was the belief that too many unqualified minorities were getting university acceptance letters. The long version of the argument was that white students with lower-than-average test scores were more likely to be rejected than minority students with the same scores because of a race-conscious admissions policy.

Mr. Wright anticipated the effect of the proposition and the results he foresaw were immediate. A year later after the law passed, the University of California (UC) reported an 80 percent drop in the admission of black students to law school. The year before 209, UC's three law schools accepted eighty-eight black freshmen. The year after, the first-year class had one. A headline in the *Boston Globe* in 1998, read, UC's FALL CLASS IS WHITE, ASIAN. After a decade the numbers were still plunging, with black enrollment at UCLA, where Mr. Wright went as an undergraduate, at its lowest level since the late 1960s.

Concerned that he was seeing signs of history repeating itself, Mr. Wright made a gift as an incentive for USC Law School to continue to actively recruit minorities. USC, a private university, was not affected by 209, but the idea was to send a message that affirmative outreach to minority students was a good thing and was going to continue.

At the same time, the tide was turning across the country. The University of Texas and University of Michigan later went in the opposite direction with two Prop 209-like lawsuits stemming from rejections of white law school applicants. The plaintiffs, in essence, blamed blacks (and Hispanics and Native Americans) for their rejection letters.

Ultimately, they lost the Supreme Court argument, but not before a little-known fact in the education field was revealed: University presidents from Columbia, Harvard, Princeton, and other Ivy League schools testified as Friends of the Court that their schools accepted a larger number of white applicants with lower-than-average test scores than minorities. This meant that for every black student accepted with a low score there were, say, ten whites accepted with the same or lower scores, which Mr. Wright didn't need the Supreme Court to tell him. "Whites, as you know, have had their own programs in place for years. These of course don't raise a red flag. They donate money to schools to get their kids accepted when they wouldn't otherwise have been. They have a student apply to a school a parent went to, to receive special alumni privileges as a legacy. They will tell us those programs are different, but the results are the same."

He articulated a theme in the debate I had been aware of but never thought about. People complain when blacks get accepted with lower test scores but don't care when unqualified whites get accepted. "Of course you are living in a time when people have more guts to discuss the weaknesses of other races and do it openly," he said. "They won't acknowledge it as a black thing, but they know exactly what they are talking about and we know what they are talking about."

The year California passed 209, Mr. Wright toured the USC campus for the first time in almost sixty years, happily surprised when the law school admissions told him seventy-five blacks were enrolled. At one point while he was in school in the late 1930s, he was the only black person on the law campus. USC didn't have the best reputation then; it was considered a school for wealthy whites. Now that he's seen a change in his lifetime, he wanted it to stay that way if he could help it. "Someone has to stand up," he said. "Race is just as difficult as it was during Reconstruction, in my view. Those feelings I can't help but believe are still there, even among the liberal whites."

The more we talked about the donation, the clearer it became that paying for tuition was only half of the story. The other part was his view of life after his wife was murdered in 1985. During a botched robbery attempt at a funeral home the Wrights owned, a new employee watched Mr. Wright leave to go to the supermarket and walked into the office, thinking it was empty, to steal the safe. Startled to see Mr. Wright's wife, he shot her. "When my wife died, I didn't want to go on living. I was supposed to be the one killed that night. I just didn't know why God took her and not me. It took some time for me to realize that He wasn't done with me yet."

Mr. Wright considered the gift to USC his calling. A *People* magazine story shows his picture with four out of the nine scholarship recipients in 1998, hugging in a circle with him in the middle, smiling wide. Mr. Wright called the students "his kids."

To Mr. Wright, educational access to USC in particular was an issue long before he was old enough to apply to the school. His big brother, Dr. Warner Jr., was accepted to medical school there in 1953, years before there was a race box to check on the application. As far as the admissions office knew, Mr. Wright's older brother was white.

"I was very proud of him because he had overcome so much. When he arrived for the first day, admissions told him he would feel more comfortable going to a black school and made arrangements for him to attend Howard University School of Medicine in Washington, D.C."

"And he went?" I asked.

"Yes."

"And you still wanted to apply to a school that didn't want your brother?" I expected a response about paving the way or breaking the race barrier.

"It was the best school in California and I didn't want to leave the West Coast," he said, adding that his brother returned to Los Angeles after graduation, opening a private practice in South Central. The first millionaire in the family, Dr. Warner Jr. earned seven figures by age forty-eight.

It was midday now and we had been talking nonstop. Mr. Wright looked at his watch, which I pretended not to see because I had yet to ask the money question: "How in the world did you go from a child of a slave to a rich man?"

For a few minutes we talked about his career, which I have to admit was like the story of any hard-working person and not unique to him. He juggled three jobs to pay for the $350 law school tuition.

SUGAR *of the* CROP

"I sold shoes on the weekend on Central Avenue, and after school for three hours, I worked in the drugstore right on the corner of Vernon and Central," he recounted, adding that he was studying in the school library one day when he overheard a conversation between two lawyers about a job opening up that paid $30 a month to retrieve court cases from the library archives. Later that day, it became his third job.

I continued to listen, nodding through job titles and positions as they might read on a resume. Then he started to talk about his friends. The names he mentioned sounded like a *Who's Who* volume. Like Rev. Martin Luther King Jr.—he'd host the Civil Rights leader at his house when he was in town and made arrangements to have one of his funeral cars chauffeur him around. Or Thurgood Marshall— Wright threw a birthday party for the first African American Supreme Court Justice and invited Rev. King and longtime buddy Rep. Adam Clayton Powell Jr., the first black congressman from New York. Or the Jackson Five—they held rehearsals in his living room when the family didn't want to use Hollywood recording studios. Or classmate Arthur Groman, the trial lawyer whose entertainment and business clients included major Hollywood studios, Howard Hughes, and Judy Garland. "I thought I was a pretty good public speaker until I debated against him, and then I came down to my normal self." Or schoolmate Thomas Price, son of a leading department store who as Mr. Wright pointed out, "never practiced a day in his life but today is a billionaire."

By the time he graduated from law school, most of the civil court judges recognized him from the bench. "I had no experience to start off with, so I would go down to the courthouse and listen to some of the cases. Judges got to know me pretty well. I mean they saw me down there everyday and wondered who I was. I sat through cases and I met people." And they introduced him to other people who introduced him to yet more people, many of whom wanted to do business with him. Mr. Wright didn't hang around just anyone, only with people as smart or smarter than he was. "You don't learn anything from dummies," he joked. He carried a confidence and conviction that attracted people to him. "That's really how I started. I would meet people and they gave me a little opportunity to work with them."

After 20 years, he started a general practice from his second office in Beverly Hills, representing the supermarket chain, Boys Market, Independent Retailers Association, and old Rapid Transit District.

"You make it all sound so easy, Mr. Wright," I commented, half joking.

"I've led a blessed life, but I never forgot who I was. Still haven't forgotten, young lady," he responded defensively. "I don't know what it was. Maybe spiritually there was someone with me."

With a click, the tape recorder stopped. We had been talking in the study for close to five hours. We decided to call it a day. As he walked me to my car, we made plans to meet on Sunday for brunch.

The drive back to Laguna Beach, where I was staying with the mother of a friend, took about half the time it took on the way over, leaving enough daylight to transcribe the tapes while sitting outside. After ordering a stuffed green pepper with mushrooms to go from Zinc's deli, I sat on the sand until well after sunset with the laptop resting between my legs and the tape recorder clipped to the top of my fluorescent-orange bathing suit. That way I could listen to the interview and still hear the ocean.

We had covered a lot that day, but I was particularly fascinated with the issue of opportunity Mr. Wright brought up. While I tried to hide my feelings during the interview, I agreed with much of what he had to say. I most wanted to share a personal story from my high school days that played out exactly the way Mr. Wright described it: a father pulling strings for his son to get into college. It wasn't until Mr. Wright used that example that I thought there was anything wrong with it. I was a senior at Loomis Chaffee and acceptance letters started to arrive, everyone was gossiping about who got into where. A boy who sat next to me in calculus, who was always surprised that I consistently got better test grades, got into Dartmouth, early. I got into Georgetown, my first choice. But there was one senior, rumor had it, who didn't get in anywhere. Not even his safeties. That's how bad his grades were. Then, close to graduation, a letter came from Dartmouth. He got in. Apparently his father, a Big Green alumnus, was on the board of trustees.

I remember that rumor after all these years because after I heard it, I thought: Wouldn't it have been great if my parents had Georgetown connections? Then I wouldn't have had to work my behind off all these years to get in.

I took the recorder from under my chin to watch seagulls ride the waves to shore. The screen saver swiped the screen blue with red letters, scrolling, "Where do you want to go today?"

Mr. Wright and I were a great couple. He loved to eat and I was always hungry. I was shy at first about admitting it, but he saw right through me. Our talks, after that first day, always started with the same question: "Are you hungry, Miss Butler?"

After a time he stopped waiting for an answer and would just continue on: "I made reservations at such and such a place," he'd say. The first one was at The Belvedere, a five-star restaurant, inside the Peninsula Hotel in Beverly Hills—"to celebrate your visit," as he put it.

We pulled up to the front of the hotel behind a procession of black Cadillac Town Cars and stretch limousines with black-tinted windows. The restaurant was on the first floor, past the front desk and lounge bar. Guided by Mr. Wright, we walked up to a hostess who greeted him with a hug. As we were escorted to our table, the entire room, no kidding, turned around to watch us sit down. It was like dominos. One person facing the door would stare, then the other people at the table turned around to see what was so interesting.

The hostess seated us near the dessert table, stocked high with French pastries, tiramisu, crème brûlée, fresh melons, and a personal favorite—a three-tiered, chocolate-dipped strawberry pyramid.

"What kind of champagne would you like?" Mr. Wright asked.

"I don't really drink. I'll have whatever you order."

"How do you like the place so far?"

"Very impressive, Mr. Wright. I have to tell my mom that you took me here." Since I arrived, she had been ringing my cell phone nonstop to make sure Mr. Wright, or as far as she knew "the stranger I was spending so much time with," was safe to be around. Between checking in and the constant reminders not to drive around Los Angeles at night, I felt like I was in high school all over again.

When I told Mr. Wright this was my first time at a restaurant with stars after the name, he asked the concierge to bring something with the hotel name on it for me and Mom. Ten minutes later, the concierge returned with a gold-plated Tiffany key chain for me and a black leather notebook for Mom, which I loved so much, I kept it for myself.

"You are really popular around here, Mr. Wright."

"You know, the Peninsula is the only five-star restaurant in Beverly Hills. It is where Ovitz and Eisner have their meetings. And I would come here on occasion for business lunches because my last office, before I retired, was right across the street."

"Where?"

"We passed it right before turning into the hotel—the building in between the BMW and Mercedes car dealerships."

"Wasn't this area all white? They let a black lawyer practice here then?"

I couldn't believe I used the word "let" as if he needed to fill out a permission slip.

"I was the second black lawyer in Beverly Hills," said Mr. Wright, adding that the first was Martha Louis, the third wife of the heavyweight champion boxer Joe Louis.

"What year are we talking about?"

"I opened it after I ran against FDR's son for the congressional seat here in Los Angeles," in 1958.

"Wasn't FDR a Democrat?"

"His son, too. But I ran as a Republican." He laughed at the look of confusion on my face. "I have always been sort of a rebel and you will see the same spirit throughout my life."

As far as I knew, blacks had voted overwhelmingly Democratic since 1932, when everyone changed from the party of President Lincoln to support Franklin D. Roosevelt. Which was precisely why Mr. Wright wanted to shake things up. "The Democrats felt they had us in their back pocket so I joined the Republican Party, but I didn't change my thinking."

The Tribune, a local pro-Roosevelt black newspaper, called the GOP decision to nominate Mr. Wright "deceitful and crafty" because he was the kind of "militant" candidate who'd attract black Democrats. He didn't "bow over the white people," the columnist wrote. And it was true. Mr. Wright never embraced his party's conservative platform. Instead his campaign outlined a Democratic agenda, supporting organized labor to recommending greater authority for the Justice Department to prevent civil rights violations. A Los Angeles Times editorial reported that his nomination influenced the GOP County Chairman to launch an "aggressive program" to further the party's civil rights record. But when it came to convincing black voters to listen, Mr. Wright ran into problems.

"What did they say?"

"They were sold on the Democratic Party and that was all there was."

Incumbent James Roosevelt, FDR's oldest son, was running for re-election to the House of Representatives from the Twenty-sixth Congressional District. In a campaign statement criticizing Rep. Roosevelt's term in office, Mr. Writght said his opponent had shown a blatant disregard for the community he serves, adding that "It takes more than a good family name to build a leader."

For his part, Mr. Wright had been serving the community since he was a teenager. As a USC student, he, along with Leon Washington Jr., the publisher of the Los Angeles Sentinel, came up with the idea of protesting against department stores and pharmacies that refused to hire blacks: Woolworth, Kress, furniture stores, dental offices. The two organized a boycott with picket signs reading, DON'T SPEND YOUR MONEY WHERE YOU CAN'T WORK. "This was well before the '60s," Mr. Wright said proudly.

"So everybody stopped shopping there?"

"Yes, everybody stopped shopping and we finally broke down the star, the Kress store. That was the first one."

"How long did it take?"

"It took about six months. After that all the other stores started hiring," he said. "See, I was active in the civil rights movement before the civil rights era, long before Martin Luther King."

In 1940, Mr. Wright opened his first law office on Central and Vernon near the Hotel Somerville where he met W. E. B. DuBois selling newspaper in front as a boy. Excluded from the Los Angeles County Bar Association because of race, three years later he co-founded the John M. Langston Bar Association for African Americans, which still exists today.

He belonged to a network of lawyers from the South, who together took on civil rights issues long before the media called it a movement. Along with then NAACP staff attorney Thurgood Marshall, Mr. Wright helped the nonprofit prepare the *Shelley v. Kraemer* 1948 Supreme Court case that led to the High Court striking down real estate covenants, private contracts between brokers and white homeowners to agree not to sell their house to blacks as a precondition to purchasing the property.

So, when he tried, albeit unsuccessfully, to unseat Rep. Roosevelt, he had the backing of other black Democrats who had similar views. One was friend Rep. Powell Jr., who served in the House of Representatives from 1945-1971. During the 1956 presidential race, the New York congressman told a Republican dinner party that he had withdrawn his support for Adlai Stevenson because the Democratic Party candidate selected a segregationist Senator as his running mate.

In the eleventh hour, a month before the general election, Powell endorsed the GOP ticket to re-elect Dwight D. Eisenhower. When a reporter asked Rep. Powell Jr. if his constituents would see him as a sell-out, the congressman responded, "Before you're a democrat or republican, you must be interested in your race and before that, in your country."

The food started to arrive. Instead of individual appetizer plates, the waiter placed a silver four-tier stand on the table, layered with shrimp, chicken, quiche, and beef. As Mr. Wright popped a bottle of Dom Pérignon he talked about winning the GOP nomination with unanimous support, defeating a white cnadidate who ran in the last election. "I got money from the corporations. They bought billboards with my face and name on it. But Roosevelt in the election beat me by a landslide."

We decided to meet early the next morning at his house and drive to the campus of UCLA, where he went to college. After a month of afternoon lunches and Sunday brunches, today was our last day together. He wanted to show me the building that the school had dedicated to his friend, James "Jimmy" Lu Valle. Mr. Wright had talked about him since our first day. The two used to catch the city bus to the campus together. And when they stayed late, after the buses had stopped running, they would hitchhike home. "The black janitors and cleaning ladies from school were the only ones who stopped to pick us up."

Jimmy received a bachelor of arts in chemistry, graduating Phi Beta Kappa from UCLA in 1936. The same year he won three bronze medals in the Berlin Olympics for the 100, 200, and 400-meter races. He returned to his alma mater to receive a masters in chemistry and physics the following year and a doctorate in chemistry from Cal Tech in 1940, under the direction of Dr. Linus Pauling who later received the Nobel Prize in chemistry in 1954 and the Nobel Peace Prize in 1962. "He wouldn't have won that prize [in chemistry] if it wasn't for James," argued Mr. Wright, insisting the relationship between Linus and Jimmy was very similar to that of the Johns Hopkins pioneering open heart surgeon Dr. Alfred Blalock who learned the surgical procedure from his research assistant.

Mr. Wright was very proud of Jimmy and his dedication. He talked about the building in the same way that he talked about his scholarship recipients, as a reflection of him and the potential of others. And though that last day I wanted to stay home and pack, I opted to go.

But I made a mistake. I let him drive his BMW. I didn't know this at the time and neither did Mr. Wright care to divulge it, but for ten years his doctor had been urging him not to drive because of his failing eyesight. The first sign that something was wrong occurred a few blocks from his house, at a four-way stop. Mr. Wright pulled up to the stop sign first and had the right of way. But instead of continuing through, he let the oncoming car go. Then the car to the right. Then the left. Then the oncoming car again, then the car to the right. I had to say something.

"Mr. Wright, it's your turn to go."

"Oh, yes it is."

I didn't think anything of it because I sometimes lose track of traffic right-off-way. Maybe he was distracted. To keep his mind on the road I asked questions about the campus.

"Have you been back since you graduated, Mr. Wright?"

"Plenty of times, young lady. Wilshire goes straight to campus. Can't miss it."

Confident that he knew where he was going after all, I took a quick nap. The next thing I knew, horns were beeping and Mr. Wright was pulling into a supermarket parking lot.

"Where are we, Mr. Wright? Where's UCLA?"

A Rolls Royce drove by, beeping.

"We must have missed it. I'm going to pull around here."

"Maybe I should drive."

"I think that might be best, Miss Butler."

"But I don't know how to drive stick."

"That's okay. Let's switch."

He then pulled up to the one-way exit of the parking lot. The car started to roll as he unbuckled his seat belt.

"Mr. Wright, the emergency brake!"

"Oh yes. Thank you."

We switched sides. A Bentley rolled up right behind us. "Okay, now take your time. Don't take your foot off the clutch too fast."

The car jerked and stalled. It happened again. And again. Then three more times. I inched the car forward far enough so that the Bentley had room to squeeze by. There was a long line behind us.

"Get out of the way if you can't drive," yelled one guy in a Mercedes.

"Just wait until all the cars pass, Sana, then you can go."

I finally caught the rhythm of the clutch and we pulled out going back the way we came.

"Where was that?" I asked, now that things were calming down.

"Brentwood. You know O. J.? That's where he lived."

We backtracked a couple of miles, and sure enough there was a UCLA banner hanging on a pole on Wilshire Boulevard, just as he'd said there would be.

Once we got near UCLA's campus, we went straight to Mr. Wright's favorite Thai restaurant near campus. We joked and laughed about the ordeal and ordered more than enough food for us both to take home for dinner. I even convinced him to try some of the fried chicken wings, which he hadn't had in years because of his high cholesterol.

"What the heck," he said before grabbing a second and a third wing.

Carrying our to-go orders in my bag, we headed to campus to look for Jimmy's building.

"What does the building look like, Mr. Wright?"

"It has a statue in the front."

I stopped a student walking by. Mr. Wright asked where the building for Jimmy Lu Valle was. The student was clueless.

"Maybe it was the chemistry building? I know you mentioned the Nobel Prize in physics."

We found a directory in the middle of a quadrangle and discovered that the chemistry building was on the west campus. We were on the east campus. So we walked, and stopped students along the way to see if anyone knew about the building. No one did. We got to the chemistry building, which was named after William Gould Young, a UCLA chemistry professor and dean in the College of Science.

After determing that it also wasn't the physics building, I asked Mr. Wright if it could possibly be near the athletic center.

We looked at the map. The athletic center was nowhere nearby.

"Heck no, Mr. Wright. I'm not walking all the way over there."

"I'm not either," he agreed.

"Let's ask a teacher or a professor or something."

We continued to move in no particular direction until we came across an administrator. Mr. Wright asked the question because I was getting tired.

"You mean the student center. Yes, you go past the statue, take a right, and you'll see a big sign."

As we got closer, Mr. Wright said the turns and corners were starting to look familiar. I believed it was because we were in the area about an hour earlier but took a left at the statue instead of a right.

"Oh yes, here it is."

"Where?"

"Right here."

I looked up to see a pink fluorescent sign flashing JIMMY's. It was a diner.

"Are you joking?" I asked as we walked inside.

"No, this is it."

I didn't hear Mr. Wright's excitement. I could only focus on the flashing lights, hamburgers, and french fries.

"I guess if you weren't born in our generation, it might be hard to understand what this means. They dedicated it during the civil rights movement. They felt like they had to give us something."

I later did my own research on UCLA and found that the restaurant was part of the graduate student center named Lu Valle Commons, after Jimmy. The university was honoring him for being the first president of the graduate student association.

I tried to shrug off my disappointment as I followed Mr. Wright to the parking garage. We didn't say anything else about the diner. But once we got back in the car, the conversation picked up again. On the ride home Mr. Wright got me to talk about my dad.

"He used to brag about his spotless attendance record in college. He said he never skipped a class except to go to civil rights demonstrations and sit-ins. He is such a numbers geek, I can imagine him not skipping any classes."

"Well, Miss Butler, it sounds like your father is a smart man. Sometimes, I wish my wife and I had more children so I could have a daughter and she could talk about me the way you talk about your father."

In the months following my visit, I decided to drive to Thibodaux, Louisiana, to visit the grounds where Mr. Wright's father was born. The Woodlawn Plantation was destroyed in a fire set by Union soldiers, but the Madewood Plantation up the road, once owned by a Pugh brother, was not. Legend has it that Madewood still stands because a Union soldier took pity on a younger Confederate widow living there.

Madewood was abandoned by the Pugh family in the early 1930s because it was too expensive to keep up. In 1964 the estate was purchased by the daughter of a wealthy slave owner from Mississippi and is now a bed-and-breakfast.

When Mr. Wright stayed at the twenty-one-room mansion and toured the plantation two years before, he got into a conversation with the tour guide about who he was and why he was there. Within minutes he was introduced to the great-granddaughter of a Madewood slave who was working at the plantation house as a cook.

"She had an interest in my relationship to the place and was kind enough to take me to Woodlawn," Mr. Wright had told me. "It's nothing but weeds and grass now, but behind this big tree in the back, there is a cemetery where the slaves were buried."

When word spread at Madewood that Mr. Wright was a descendant of a Woodlawn slave, he was given the phone number of Robert Pugh, a descendant of the slave owner who built the plantation. Mr. Wright remembered that he enjoyed the phone conversation with Robert. He too was a lawyer "so we talked about that. I told him I was in town to visit what was left of Woodlawn. He put me in contact with a library where most of his family's papers are."

When I told Mr. Wright I'd decided to make the trip to Louisiana, he gave me Robert's phone number. I called him and told him about my project. He sounded eager to help and opened his family Rolodex to put me in contact with a cousin and the Pugh librarian at the Ellender Memorial Library at Nicholls State University in Thibodaux.

I decided to visit the library first to read more about the Pughs because I knew nothing other than their first names and the names of their plantations. The collection was on the first floor of the university's main library, located across from the student center on Madewood Drive. One-third of the 300,000 papers in the Pugh collection are housed here for preservation and public use. The others are divided between Louisiana State University in Baton Rouge and the University of Texas in Austin where some of the Pughs settled after the Civil War.

The librarian, Carol, with whom I had scheduled an appointment the day before to view the papers, greeted me at the door and gestured for me to come in. Spread across two picnic-sized tables were twelve file boxes with lids tilted open; five neat stacks of stapled papers; a three-ring binder holding a thesis titled, "Pugh Plantations, 1850–1865: A Study of Life in Lower Louisiana," by Evelyn L. Pugh; and an array of black, red, and brown legal-size ledgers. "We weren't sure what you needed so we just pulled everything. What are you looking for?" Carol asked as she introduced me around to Cliff, her assistant, and a volunteer researcher and archivist. I told her I wanted to know general information about the family and the plantation because I knew very little other than what was in Warner's journal. Then I sat down in front of one of the boxes and started reading.

Warner's owner was William Whitmell Pugh, the first Superintendent of Schools in Louisiana and later the Speaker of the Louisiana House of Representatives from 1854-1858. Everyone knew him as W. W. Built in 1840, his Woodlawn sugar plantation in Napoleonville ran into younger brother Thomas's land and was a couple of miles from his youngest brother Augustin in Houma. The three brothers were descendants of a Welsh squire whose family had lived along the North Carolina-Virginia border for more than a century. Augustin and W. W. were two of the first four Americans to settle in Assumption Parish along the bayou in 1823.

The year Warner was born, the Woodlawn mansion was completed and the Pughs had branched off into three separate plantations. Each brother had his own rice and sugar plantation extending along both sides of the bayou. W. W. owned Woodlawn—800 acres of crop land, 1,550 acres of swamp, and 162 slaves.

Augustin had his seventy slaves build a small cottage, while Thomas sank a lot of money into Madewood, competing with W. W. to construct the biggest. Known as the "Queen of the Bayou," Madewood was built with 300 slaves. In all the Pughs owned some ten thousand acres. The Pugh holdings were so large there used to be an old Louisiana saying: "Why is Bayou Lafourche like the aisle of a church? Because there are Pughs on both sides."

On the wall near the window of the librarian's office were several legal-size papers taped together that drew my attention because it looked like a sketched map of the area along the bayou. Cliff, in his spare time, had drawn an outline of all of the plantations between Madewood at the top of the bayou and New Hope, owned by W. W.'s father, at the bottom. For a stretch of about ten miles, there were sixty-three plantations aligned side by side perpendicular to the bayou in order to use the waterway as their source of trade. I asked Cliff, a former Madewood tour guide, for directions to his old stomping grounds so I could go on the last tour of the day, which started at 5:00 p.m. "Cross over the bayou, take a left. You'll pass CVS, a McDonald's, an Applebee's. Then all you see is land for miles. Keep going until you see a white house. You can't miss it. It's the only house out in the middle of nowhere."

The bayou runs like a railroad track parallel to the main road with stoplights every other mile for cars to cross bridges over and back. I hugged the bayou for five miles, driving alongside a flat cleared field of brown grass deep as three football fields with a line of trees so far in the distance its color blurred black and green. No sign of the house. My eyes started to feel heavy. I shrugged it off by blasting the air conditioner, but a few minutes later, I was fading in and out again. I reached to the back seat to grab a bottle of water. When I turned back around, there it was: a white mansion half a mile in, surrounded by nothing but a blue horizon, penciled with treetops.

In the driveway I pressed my forehead against the windshield to look at the six fluted Ionic columns. They grew in size as I approached, the way a building seen from an airplane grows larger the closer you get to the ground. I pulled around the back, where a woman was unpacking groceries from a station wagon. She told me where to join the tour. It had already started.

I raced up the stairs. Two couples staying at the B&B were listening to a guide in the grand living room near the spiral walnut staircase. I couldn't see from where I was standing and excused myself as I moved to the front of the line. I stood next to Lenny, our guide, who was wearing a taxicab-yellow Madewood T-shirt. As we passed under the doorframe connecting the living room to the three-story ceiling dining room, I thought, this was a good life the Pughs had. I wondered if this was the kind of room Warner talked about in his journal where he had to entertain with his city walk. The floors were of heart pine, door frames and moldings of cypress, painted to resemble oak.

The house took six thousand cypress trees and this was how it got its name—because it was "made" from "wood."

The grounds today included the main house and attached kitchen, and in the rear, the carriage house, and the Pugh family cemetery. Brad Pitt apparently stayed in one of the old slave quarters when he was in town to film the 1994 movie *Interview with a Vampire*.

We went outside to the kitchen and Lenny pointed to the outside staircase that led up to a balcony running the length of the house. That was how slaves traveled from one end of the house to the other, because they weren't allowed to walk inside.

The tour didn't take more than thirty minutes and ended at the family cemetery in the back where the original owner is buried under the only cypress tree left in the world, according to Lenny, who before he went home introduced me to another Madewood employee who had worked on the estate all his life and just happened to be walking by on the way to his pickup.

"You know, a man from California was here a couple years back who wanted to know about Woodlawn."

"Do you remember his name?"

"No, I don't, but he said that his father was a slave under W. W. My sister took him to the cemetery in the back there so he could see where the slaves were buried."

"I know the guy from California your sister showed around. He mentioned that you had family who were slaves on this plantation."

"That's right. My great-grandmother and grandfather helped build this house. It took them eight years. Eight years."

That night, I called the cousin Robert suggested I talk to. The cousin, who asked that I not mention his name, only wanted to talk about Mr. Wright and my visit to California.

"What kind of person is he?" he asked.

"He's a lawyer, like you. He just donated two million dollars to fund a scholarship at USC—,"

"No," he said, stopping me mid-sentence. "I mean how did he turn out? Is he a happy person?"

3

Virginia

ONE LIFE TO LIVE

I flew back to Connecticut the night before Thanksgiving. The next morning, Mom was up at 7:30, cooking dinner. She'd seasoned the turkey before going to bed, and had it stuffed and in the oven within the hour. She had moved on to the side dishes and four pies by the time Dad came downstairs to make pancakes and bacon for breakfast.

While all the cooking was going on downstairs, my sisters and I were never told to get out of bed and help. I enjoyed staying warm under the covers, allowed to sleep until Dad walked up the stairs, slowly going from room to room, turning on the lights, saying the same thing over and over as if we didn't hear him tell the other sister a second ago down the hall: "Go brush your teeth and come downstairs. Breakfast is ready."

As we filed downstairs one by one, Mom commented that she was getting too old to cook big dinners by herself. Dad grinned and asked what she needed done and then he did it. He never made us feel guilty for not pitching in (I might point out sons are almost never asked to help out in the kitchen on Thanksgiving) because I don't think he really wanted us to. He liked taking care of us. They both did. And even as a grown-up, I still wanted to be their little girl.

Later in the evening, Dad drove me, carrying a Stop & Shop bag packed with leftovers to last a week, to the bus station to catch the 11:00 p.m. back to Brooklyn. On the way he asked when I would be back. "You know your mother likes it when you girls come home." As he got sicker, he started to ask that question more often as if to get me to believe it was Mom who wanted to see us more. "I don't know, Dad. I haven't even left yet." He watched as I boarded the bus,

followed down the aisle as I looked for a seat, and stood in the freezing cold, waving so I could see him.

"Is that your dad?" The passenger sitting next to the window
asked.

"Yeah," I said, almost embarrassed for reaching over her to wave
back. "He'll be there until the bus pulls off."

"That's cute."

I didn't think the send-off was anything special because that was
how my parents always said goodbye at the bus or train station, rain
or shine. I do think it was a little neurotic that they also wanted me to
call at 2:00 a.m. to let them know I was home, but it was their obses-
sive attention that stopped me from needing validation from other
people. I already had it from them. Their smothering set me free into
a world that didn't seem so big and bad because there was always a
safe place to run home to.

And while I wanted to stay in Connecticut longer, I was in a
rush to get back to my apartment to get things in order for the next
trip. There were a few good leads saved on my voice mail. The most
promising came from Catherine Scott of Brooklyn. We met on a Sunday after service at Abyssinian Baptist Church in Harlem—thanks to
Reverend Calvin Butts. I'd faxed him about my search and asked for
his help. He agreed to make two announcements to the congregation
during both early morning and regular worship services.

"This young woman—can you stand so people can see who you
are?" Rev. Butts said from the pulpit. I stood. "Miss Butler is looking
to interview children of slaves. She believes there are some still alive. I
know most of you are from down South. If anyone can help her out,
please talk to her after service so she can tell our story."

Catherine Scott was sitting four pews in front of me and turned
around to pass a note during the benediction. "I have someone you
may want to meet," she wrote. After the service she told me that her
great grandparents, Robert Henry Scott and Alice Gilliam Carrington-
Scott, were slaves. They had nine children. "Everyone is dead except

my uncle, Walter, and my grandfather, Robert James. You should come down to Virginia for a visit."

Months passed before I was able to schedule a visit in the summer of 1997. Robert James had gotten sick and suddenly died as a result of a bowel obstruction at the age of 102. The younger son, Walter, 99, had been living by himself but had recently checked himself into a nursing home after coming down with pneumonia. I told myself if Walter got better, I would take a weekend off to drive down to spend some time with him.

On paper Mr. Scott was the perfect interview. Both his parents were slaves, a situation that was very hard to find. Based on what I had seen so far, the freed slave was usually the father, who married a much younger wife born somtimes decades after 1865. More important was the fact that Mr. Scott's father grew up to be an adult under slavery. Born in 1838, Robert Henry was almost thirty when the Civil War ended. Because both parents were old enough to know what it meant to be a slave (Mr. Scott's mother Alice was seven when the war ended), I thought he would be a great person to offer an opinion on the apology and reparations debates that had been in the news recently.

The timing couldn't have been better. A seven-member panel of experts, appointed by President Clinton, just spent the past year hosting town hall meetings around the country on race relations in general, and problems between whites and blacks in particular. The public forums provoked a national debate on reparations and called for a government apology from the president. Coupled with the release of the new movie *Amistad*, about an 1839 slave-ship revolt, the public's attention to the controversy was so strong, rumor had it Clinton, who said no to both reparations and a formal apology, told his aides he was concerned the panel was getting sidetracked.

Almost everyone had an opinion one way or the other. The opposition argued, among other things, that slavery was so long ago that neither idea made sense anymore. Supporters felt that slavery wasn't that far in the past, and that its economic and cultural legacy are still with us today. Curious to hear Mr. Scott's side, though I thought I could pretty much guess what it would be, I jotted down two pages of notes from the debates to take with me. I had also spent hours in the library researching conversation topics about slave culture and the American construct of race and took along those notes as well.

I made arrangements to meet Mr. Scott in the family church on the last day of a Scott-Carrington family reunion in Prospect, an old tobacco farming town along the North Carolina border in Prince Edward County. Those active in the civil rights movement may recognize the county name from the 1954 *Brown v. Board of Education* Supreme Court case. It was home to one of the five public schools in the separate but equal class action suit that led to desegregation. The Prince Edward County school board gained national attention because it refused to enforce the ruling and, in protest, shut down the entire public school system from 1959 to 1964. The county's eighteen hundred black students were locked out of an education for five years. But with the help of emergency funds designated by the Virginia legislature, the Prince Edward school board created private tax-supported schools for the 1,450 white students, complete with new baseball and football fields guaranteed in three weeks and funds to pay for school buses to carry students to and from. The state even allocated school buses. "The white students would spit at us out the window and throw spit balls," said Catherine, who in 1960 was supposed to be in the fifth grade.

She, too, had come down from New York to attend the family reunion and gave me directions to the church from my motel in a way that made me question whether to buy a map. "These are country roads. We don't use street signs like you do in the city," she said after I asked the name of the cross streets. "I will get you there, don't worry. You won't get lost." The verbal directions were simple enough for a fourth grader. Take a right at the white church with the cemetery in front. After the second gas station, make the next left. Just keep going straight. Along the route, I looked for two landmarks. The first was a weatherworn stop sign, mounted on a rusty, hunched-over metal pole right before a fork where the road splits in two. If I missed the stop sign, the backup was a penny candy store that turned out to be like a rotted wooden lean-to with a chicken coop in the back and a doghouse in the front. Only a few more miles to go.

Sulphur Spring Baptist was a brick church that sat in a forest clearing with nothing around but grass, dirt, and three big trees members parked under to keep their cars cool in the shade, away from the sweltering hot August sun. I walked to the back of the church and opened the screen door to the smell of sizzling bacon and sausage. Mr. Scott was waiting for me in the fellowship hall, sitting at the end of a collapsible picnic table covered with a checkered red-and-white plastic cloth, surrounded by women in white usher uniforms carrying grits and scrambled eggs in black iron skillets. One hand rested on top of his walking cane, the other held a black Bible in his lap. He was dressed in a black suit that fit big, black tie and white shirt. His smile opened to a mouth full of gums and three teeth on the bottom.

I introduced myself and sat down. The format of the meeting was not set in stone, but I was planning to start current and work backward to the civil rights movement and then spend the rest of the time on his parents' lives as slaves. The first question went something like: "A lot of people today are calling for reparations for slavery. Do you think reparations are a good idea?"

"I can't gather that," Mr. Scott answered.

I reworded the question. Maybe he didn't understand the question. "Do you think you should be given money because your parents were slaves?"

"They made a lot of money off of them. They didn't get paid. I gather we should get something," he said.

"You knew your parents were slaves?"

"Yes, we knew."

"Did they talk about what happened during that time?" No response. I tried to coax something out of him. Anything. "Did they pick tobacco, cotton?" To which he simply replied, "Chewing tobacco."

His attention was no longer focused in my direction but on the sound of the black rubber knob on the bottom of the cane as it tapped between his shoes, hitting the soles: Right, left. Left, right.

"Do you think your parents should have been told, 'I'm sorry', that they were slaves?"

"It would have been a nice thing to do."

The conversation was slow. Though I was asking him yes or no questions, I left enough of a pause in between for him to elaborate. At one point I was talking so slowly that when I finally completed a sentence I forgot what the question was.

After about thirty minutes of this back-and-forth, my excitement for the day faded, replaced with a fear that he was too old to remember much about anything. Then there were larger questions: Would everyone I interview have a faded memory? Was I too late? Most would likely fall within the same age range as Mr. Scott—one hundred and older. No matter what the age, I thought if I sat with someone long enough, the person would remember something. I guess I was wrong. I turned the tape recorder off, picked up my pocketbook from under the table, and laid it in my lap. I was ready to go.

Church was about to begin. The senior choir lined up at the side door that opened to the sanctuary behind the pulpit. The single file had started to wrap around the table, past the backs of the folding chairs, when Catherine walked in through the screen door. She had picked Mr. Scott up that morning at the nursing home, and dropped him off at church before going to her cousin's house down the road to get dressed for morning service. I waved. She sat next to Mr. Scott and looked at the closed notebook on the table. I turned my attention to her for a minute to grab an interview tape of Mr. Scott's now deceased oldest brother Otis that she'd brought. The forty-minute tape, recorded in 1979 by Mr. Scott's niece Doris, was selling for $5.00 at the reunion.

"What did you guys talk about, Uncle Walter?" She brushed a piece of lint off his shoulder as she made small talk while digging in her bag. "Did you tell her about how Grandma wanted you guys to be big people?"

"She wanted her kids to be what?" I questioned Catherine, puzzled. Overweight?

"Grandma Alice used to say you had to be somebody, right, Uncle Walter?" He turned from looking at Catherine to look at me but let her continue to talk. "That you had to go to school. You had to be intelligent. You needed to marry somebody intelligent. Right?" Mr. Scott nodded in her direction.

The cool air from the window unit no longer circulated around the room. Sitting at the table, we were now inside a human circle of blue and white robes as they waited for the signal from the organist to start the processional hymn. The kitchen was getting hot and sticky. Gooey patches of deodorant sweat started to cake under my armpits, dripping down the side of my writing hand.

"You didn't tell me that about your parents, Mr. Scott." I put my bag back down on the floor and we both looked at him.

"You didn't ask, young lady. You wanted to know if they were slaves." He didn't look in my direction until the last word, and then only because he was turning his hips toward me in order to get his legs out from under the table. Catherine stood behind him as he started to push on the table to get up.

I smiled. This guy was holding out on me. Here I was thinking he didn't understand the questions when really he didn't want to answer them. They were awkwardly leading and overly predictable. I only wanted to know his parents as slaves. He was right and I was embarrassed.

Catherine picked up the Bible on the table, holding Mr. Scott's bent arm under the elbow for balance while he used his free hand to grab the cane. I too stood up, unsure what to say next.

"Can you stay until after service?" Catherine asked. Mr. Scott started to follow the choir into the church.

"Unfortunately, I'm not dressed for it. But I would love to come back." I trailed behind Mr. Scott into the chapel, wearing black pants and a white T-shirt. "Is that okay with you, Mr. Scott?"

He sat down on the first row, as I quickly explained that I needed to go home today but would love to come back.

"That would be fine. I'll be here."

I stopped at Shoney's for the all-you-can-eat breakfast buffet before getting on the highway for the eight-hour drive back to Brooklyn where I had to work the next morning. That was the moment I knew I had to choose. Either I was going to continue to work full-time and travel only on the weekends or quit in order to find and interview people full time. There was no way I could do both, so with no money in the bank, I chose to throw caution to the wind. I said grace over a plate of french toast, bacon, grits, and a free refill of sweet tea, adding an extra thank-you for Catherine's small talk. If she wasn't there, I never would have known I was asking the wrong questions. Yes, Mr. Scott's parents were slaves, but the way Catherine and Mr. Scott spoke about Alice and Robert made them sound the same as my parents or my friend's parents or even the Huxtables. Where was the posttraumatic slave syndrome? Go to school. Get an education. Study hard. Get good grades. Marry somebody intelligent. What happened to the sense of inferiority? Where was the shame? The debilitating depression and humiliation? The questions I asked steered the interview to what I wanted to hear, completely ignoring the simple fact that Mr. Scott didn't really care to talk about reparations or an apology or any of the history-book jargon.

It was an ugly rainy Wednesday afternoon in March 2000 when I visited Mr. Scott for the second time at his nursing home in Keysville, Virginia. The sky was dark, almost nightlike. I unfolded the road map on the dashboard above the steering wheel so I could use the reflection of the car's overhead lights to read the small print. When I finally made it to the facility, the parking lot was empty. I pulled into the spot closest to the entrance that didn't have a handicap sign. In front of the door were two old men, one black, one white, playing Go Fish. They watched as I got out of the car and stopped me as I reached for the screen door. They wanted to know my name and whom I was there to see.

"Do you know if Walter Scott is inside?" I asked, even though I knew he was.

One of the men turned around, pointing for me to go on in. "He's in the back, in front of the TV near the window."

Mr. Scott was sitting in a brown recliner watching One Life to Live. He didn't see me coming until I was standing next to his chair. Catherine let me know that a lot had changed since I saw Mr. Scott last. His mind was strong the last time I saw him, so I thought it would be okay to squeeze in the Los Angeles trip before seeing him again. I hope I didn't make a mistake by waiting to long. His body had started to shut down. He no longer used a cane because his knees were too weak to hold him up. He couldn't work a wheelchair because his fingers curled at the knuckles from arthritis. He sat all day next to an electrical outlet so his portable oxygen machine could stay plugged in and charged.

"I thought you weren't coming. You said 2:00 p.m."

"I apologize, Mr. Scott. It is raining really hard outside."

"Take a seat."

As I grabbed the back of a chair to pull up to his recliner, I felt like a schoolgirl caught by the teacher without her homework. Phew, I wasn't too late.

"Are you staying in the area?"

"No. I am staying in Appomattox, about an hour southeast." I had booked a room in the town because it was down hill from a historic railroad station and close to the national park where Lee surrendered to Grant. I was planning on visiting later that month.

"I know where it is," Mr. Scott said. "My father was there in the war."

One of the first things Catherine had told me when we met in Harlem was that Mr. Scott's father was volunteered by his owner, Tom Treadway, to join a Colonel Carter with the Confederate Army of Northern Virginia in Richmond in 1864, and that Robert had told his family that he was near the Appomattox Railroad Station at the time of the surrender on April 9. Neither he nor other slaves were officially allowed to serve as armed military soldiers until March 1865, weeks before the surrender. The vast majority were forced to enlist as laborers, manservants, cooks, musicians, and bodyguards. According to Robert's pension application, he served as a "breast worker."

"My father walked ahead of everyone to cut bushes and tree limbs to make a path for the soldiers on horses." Robert's unit was likely forced to retreat from the station after losing crucial supplies to the Union line in a battle the day before. After the surrender, Mr. Scott's father left Appomattox with another slave. "After the war he walked home to Prospect with William Bell," who in 1925 was questioned by a Virginia pension clerk as the only one known to be living who had personal knowledge of Robert's service on Confederate breast works.

I admit to having only a cursory knowledge of black Confederates prior to Mr. Scott's introduction to the subject. The extent to what I knew didn't go beyond quotes and television interviews by Civil War buffs who've said the estimated 60,000 joined of their own free will or as one historian wrote in the magazine *America's Civil War*, "volunteered to defend their homes against the new threat from the North." The theory seemed consistent with descendants today who continue to pledge an allegiance to the South, signing up for local membership in fraternal and memorial groups; donning the gray uniform of the Republic for civil war re-enactments. I've always thought it to be strange that a slave would see anything other than slavery as his worst personal threat. But what did I know?

Maybe more than I thought. Because Robert's presence in the war contradicted with the notion that he volunteered on his own.

Robert told his children that his owner forced him to serve, reminiscent of the scene in the movie *The Patriot* where a white man signs over his slave to fight in his place in the militia. Swaps like this were common during the Revolutionary War and maybe more in the Confederate ranks near the end than previously thought, because there was no record of a soldier named Treadway signed up for the same regiment.

Before the war, Mr. Scott's father was owned by two different families in Prospect. The first owner was a small-time farmer whose last name was Burrell. "My father never knew his first name." The population of Prospect at that time was made up of mainly poor farming families, many of whom were forced to auction slaves farther south after 1840, as the productivity of the soil in the region declined, making it more difficult to grow tobacco. In 1845, cash-strapped Burrell decided to sell a young Robert. "My father said [Burrell] owned him until he was around six, when he wanted to sell him down South to pick tobacco down there," Mr. Scott said.

Robert's mother was a slave on a nearby farm owned by the Scott family and heard the news about her son going on the auction block. She asked a slave she was friends with on the farm to "talk to the owner about buying my father," Mr. Scott said. The friend did and Robert stayed in Farmville. "Scott was his last name—that's all I know. We never knew my father's people."

"Did you know your mother's?"

"My mother was owned by the Gilliams, old man Wylie Gilliam. She was written in a will to go to him when his father died." Along with a one-year-old Alice, Wylie's father also left his son two barrels of corn, a red no-horn heifer, a tablecloth, a blanket, a parcel of soap, and farm tools, in a will dated August 6, 1850. Alice's mother Jinny was already owned by Wylie. I asked Mr. Scott if his mother talked about her experiences as a slave.

"She told us about how she had to go get fresh water from the well one winter before she was free." The story went that Alice's mother, sick in bed, told her not to get water that morning because she didn't have any shoes to wear in the snow. "Old Gilliam came in and asked her why she hadn't been to the house that morning and her mother said what she had said." Gilliam then took Alice outside and told her to take her clothes off and roll in the snow. Then "he hit her with an iron skillet until she said she would bring water every morning and not mind weather or clothes." Later that week, Gilliam sent Jinny off the plantation to a place where sick slaves went to die.

The story seemed to bother me more than Mr. Scott, who showed no emotion. Or maybe I showed too much of it, with my mouth open, shaking my head. I had read the stories before, but to hear a son tell what happened to his mother brings a different level of sensibility. But I think for Mr. Scott, the story was less a novelty. Most of the adults he knew growing up were former slaves who likely had experienced the same treatment, if not worse.

I, on the other hand, had a childhood a lot different than Mr. Scott's. When I was growing up I stood at the bottom of the driveway waiting for the school bus, twirling around in circles hoping for lightning to turn me into Wonder Woman. The sad and bad happened on television, and my most emotional memory was of overhearing twin sisters in summer camp asking my only friend why she was friends with a nigger. As I got older, I heard similar stories from other blacks about the first time they were called the n-word. Once I knew the name-calling wasn't personal, there was no sense in getting upset. But I had to wonder if that complacency was wrong. Mr. Scott reminded me of this by saying, "That's just how it was back then."

After the Civil War, Alice stayed on the Gilliam farm to work but wasted no time to redefine her relationship with her former master. "She used to tell us that one day old Gilliam asked her to get a chair from the house to bring to him in the barn. She went to the house and went up to Missus Gilliam and said, 'Mister Gilliam says to send a chair to the barn.'"

He stopped talking, smiled, and rolled his eyes to the left to look at my reaction without moving his head so to keep the oxygen tube in his nose. I looked back at him with a blank stare, waiting for more. I must have missed something.

"I'm not sure of the punchline, Mr. Scott. Your mom said what?"

"My mother called him Mister Gilliam, not Master Gilliam." The wife didn't like the way Alice addressed her husband and later on in the day Alice overheard her telling a friend, "Niggers have lost their minds since they got free." We both laughed.

Mr. Scott continued. "My mother said slavery was over. She didn't have to call him master no more."

"Did she see much of the Gilliams after the war?"

"I know she loaned him money one time and I remember her going to his funeral."

"Why would she lend him money?"

"She thought it was funny how things turned out."

As much as the thought of Alice handing money to Wylie is a shocker, the power shift was an example of the change in post emancipation relationships between freed slave and former owner. Granted the economic role reversal Alice enjoyed as an adult was far from the norm. For most in the South, race relations got worse. Lynchings and torture of blacks by white Southerners, once limited to scare tactics to discourage slaves from running away, had now become adventurous Main Street fun and games with newspaper ads and flyers encouraging participation. The Jim Crow call for never-ending terrorism hardly seemed like the time for blacks to attempt to make new white friends.

Yet it happened. In Prospect Mr. Scott remembered that there was one white family his father liked, the Lindseys. Tom Lindsey, a rich landowner about ten years Robert's senior, owned so much land that even today deeds in the area refer to Lindsey property boundaries. Tom inherited his father's land after his father died in 1870, and he and his mom would "only let black people have the land and build on it." I asked Mr. Scott why. "He acted like he liked black people more."

Robert purchased his first twenty-five acres from Tom in 1876. "They were friends," remembered Mr. Scott. "Father would always go up the road to visit him. And he would come to visit, and they would sit on the porch and talk for hours." And eventually he became family because Tom's sister's daughter married one of Robert's sons.

Almost every black person who owned land in Farmville bought it from Tom. "He was willing to work with you if you expressed interest." Land was very important to former slaves and that was who Tom was selling his to. Owning land gave freed men the opportunity to be independent farmers with a permanent stake in the community and its future.

Mr. Scott's father owned seventy acres by the time he married Alice in 1887. On this he built a second home because his two children from his first marriage were living in his first home. The Scotts met at Sulphur Spring Baptist church when she was twenty-eight and he was forty-nine. Together they had nine children, five boys and four girls.

"My father used to have all of us sit around him so he could sing to us. He would sing every night and we would just listen." Robert watched for land near their home going up for sale "so we could live together." The firstborn son, Otis, was the first to buy seventeen acres by working on the railroad. All total the Scott boys purchased 150 acres, all of which is still in the family today. "But what did the girls do," I asked Mr. Scott, "when their brothers were working in the fields?"

"My mother sent my sisters away to boarding school."

"What? Really?" I responded. I didn't know blacks sent their kids away to school as early as 1899. "Were parents doing that then?"

"No. This was a big thing for back then."

The Scotts weren't wealthy but they saved enough to be able to send three daughters away to continue their education after local public schools stopped educating black children after eight years. Pearl, the oldest girl, was the first to enroll in private school for what today would be high school. Her tuition was $5.00 a month. The second was Della Althea who attended Christiansburg Academy, an eighty-five acre campus 130 miles from Prospect. The boarding school was built on an old plantation that remodeled the former slaveholder's mansion along with several slave cabins into classrooms. The decision to build the school where it would be located was symbolic, as the principal described in a letter in 1905: "Owning this farm, we had the 'Big House' where the master once lived. . . . It is a remarkable and significant fact that where the master once lived is [now] a recitation building for colored boys and girls, and where the slaves once huddled around the flickering light of a pine-knot, young Negro students are quartered daily, preparing for the duties of tomorrow."

Della Althea graduated as valedictorian of her class, and went on to the Institute for Colored Youth in Pennsylvania, known today as Cheyney University of Pennsylvania, the oldest of the Historically Black Colleges founded in 1839. The next daughter to go to Christiansburg was Ola, who spent her first month at the academy homesick before leaving to go back to her parents.'

"My mother was always pushing us to do stuff. Do this, do that."

"And your father?"

"He didn't say much. He was quiet like me."

At the age of 101, Mr. Scott had a good memory, though it needed time to warm up, and allowing him to do so was a technique I had down cold by the end of the month. A question like, "Tell me about yourself," was too much all at once. He would answer, "I went to church every Sunday," and that was it, as if overwhelmed into silence by all of the things he could possibly say. Many times I found myself asking a similar question three different ways. He would answer it all three times, but each answer provided new information.

"Did you live in Virginia all of your life?"

"I moved to New Jersey in the '30s to work for a white family."

I asked what year and he said he didn't remember.

"How old were you when you left Virginia to go to New Jersey?" This time, not only did he know his age, he added that he went to New Jersey with his wife Esther. She was the cook for the family and he was the driver. They went to New Jersey together to make money to build their house on his land in Virginia. But he didn't know the name of the town in New Jersey.

"Did you like living in New Jersey?" He said he lived in East Orange and thought life in the North was too fast. After two years, they moved back to Prospect.

After a couple weeks of visiting Mr. Scott everyday, I kind of felt that I got as much as out of him as I could. But I continued our daily visits because he asked me to. We would sit and watch television and I wouldn't ask any questions, just keep him company. By having a regular visitor for a month, he had become kind of a celebrity in the nursing home. Nosy residents often joined us. One day, two men wheeled over to talk to us.

"Are you his daughter?"

"No."

"Granddaughter?"

"No."

"Why are you wearing a baseball cap?"

"Because it was raining outside."

"Are you a boy or a girl?"

"You tell me," I said, playing along.

"You don't have lipstick on. And you aren't wearing earrings." And my hair was cut short and I wasn't wearing a dress and I didn't have heels on— I had heard it all before from Mom and my grandmothers.

"Shut up, man," Mr. Scott jumped in. "Leave her alone," Mr. Scott said, in such a soft, raspy voice, I could barely hear him and doubt the other two did either. But I smiled to let Mr. Scott know it was okay.

"I am a girl."

"We knew you were a girl," the two said as they wheeled off.

Mr. Scott turned back around. The two plastic oxygen tubes resting on the bottom of his nose had come out. I readjusted the plastic tube from around his ear, down his jawline in one nostril and back into the other.

I skipped a Sunday visit with Mr. Scott to go to church. It just so happened to be fourth Sunday, which meant, to my delight, the youth choir was singing. A tall lanky boy with a long skinny neck in the third row looked just like my first love, Eric Midder, whom I met in church and giggled with every Wednesday during choir rehearsal. To be thirteen again.

I sat in the last pew by the door. I didn't want to miss a Scott if one left before the service was over. I thought it would be a good idea to get all of the local family together for a meeting. After service, I followed each one in and out of the pews trying not to interrupt conversations but making sure that everyone knew I wanted to talk with them before they left.

I remembered most of the faces from the family reunion. Warren was Mr. Scott's nephew. His father was Robert James. Flossie and her younger brother James were on the lighter side. They were Mr. Scott's niece and nephew. Their father was Otis. Wilsie wore glasses and was Warren's sister. All together I recruited four. We made plans to go home, change clothes, grab a bite, and come back out for a family meeting.

That evening we sat at the kitchen table at Wilsie's house around a plate of green grapes, celery sticks, and cheese. The table was open to talk about anything anyone wanted.

"Did Uncle Walter tell you about the patty roller story?" Warren asked.

"The what?"

"The patty rollers."

Wilsie said, "They patrolled plantations at night to make sure no one escaped. Like security guards, I guess you would call them today."

"No, Mr. Scott didn't mention them."

"One night a group of slaves got together to pray in the woods. Grandma said they would turn a pot down to keep the sound out but a patty roller came and walked up on them. He told everyone to line up so he could whip them and send them on back because you know they weren't allowed to pray. Grandma's brother was on the end of the line. He looked like he was taking his clothes off, but then he went up and hit the man and ran."

Flossie jumped in. "Has she heard the mister and master story? Tell that one," she said, addressing no one in particular.

"I think she already heard it," said James. "You heard it, right?"

"That's a good one," agreed Wilsie.

"Mr. Scott told me a couple days ago."

"He told you that Missus Gilliam said Alice had some nerve calling him Mister Gilliam," said Flossie. "She said those niggers have lost their minds since they got free."

"Lost their minds," said Wilsie, starting the chain of laughter that circled around the table, released in both directions.

"She had a lot of shunts, talking about Mister Gilliam."

"She said those niggers have gone crazy."

"She called him Mister, not Master," said Warren.

"Mister Gilliam, says he wanted her to bring a chair to the barn."

"Ain't that something. She said Mister Gilliam."

The story had become a family legend to the degree it empowered everyone in the room, laughing at an angry and powerless Missus Gilliam who was shocked by a resilient little girl who at the first opportunity playfully reminded her former owner of her status as an equal. Alice likely enjoyed the reaction then as much as her grandchildren and great-grands were enjoying it now. Every Scott loved to tell the story, perhaps as a way to claim the fight in Alice as their own. One of her sons said that his mother was "like many women today, outspoken and forward." The ease with which she made the shift from slave to outspoken mom set the tone for her family.

Robert, "he was very supportive," said Warren. "But he was the quiet type. He let Alice do the talking."

I must have heard the mister-master story at least twice again that week, maybe more.

Before I left that night, I took a phone number with me as a reminder to call Doris, Warren's other sister. Everyone thought I should try to schedule a meeting with her because she had spent a lot of time with Alice, listening to her grandmother's stories.

Admittedly, I wanted Mr. Scott to be the one with all the answers, for him to know everything—every story, every memory, date and time of any significance, and all of the conversations with his parents plus the why, when, and where. He didn't, and that became okay, too. What he didn't know, the family thought Doris would. She lived in Kentucky, but we made plans to meet at her Dad's house when she got into town to visit that Saturday.

As I drove back to Appomattox, I called my sister Kwanza to borrow money. She immediately rolled her eyes (I know she did even though I couldn't see her) and sighed before responding, "How much do you need?" She was a big-time lawyer at a big-name corporate law firm making big bucks right out of law school. She graduated from Columbia University with honors, and had been sworn into the New York State Bar Association a couple of months ago.

Mom came down from Connecticut for the ceremony though Kwanza told her it would only last ten minutes. Dad wanted to come but he was sick. He was in the third, and last, round of chemo for the tumor in his nose that grew back again. But he made sure Mom packed a camera and a camcorder and called to tell both Kwanza and me what bus she was taking and what time to meet her at Port Authority. I knew he was having a hard time with the chemo because my parents always traveled together to Butler girl events. They moved us in and out of the dorms every year without fail and made it to every parents' weekend, even when I told them not to come.

As I watched Mom through the camcorder, desperately trying to find the button to push on the camera after reading the manual five minutes before (Dad was always in charge of taking pictures), I understood why she had traveled three hours to be here and Dad wished he was. Kwanza was the first lawyer in the Butler family. It took five generations to get here and it wasn't by accident. When we were young, after Mom put us to bed, Dad would come into our room to read to Kwanza a book all about questions. She would pick a page and ask why the sky is blue or why dogs have four legs. And Dad would read her the answer. She credits that time with Dad for part of the reason she became a lawyer. She was always full of questions and knew all the answers.

And that was what Dad wanted. He was preparing her for the future. While Kwanza was still too young to see it on her own, he saw her at twenty and at thirty. Who she could be when she grew up. What she could do. (Even my grandmother used to say Kwanza was the smartest of all of us as a toddler. I'm not sure what type of test goes into making that distinction, but I can say without hesitation that she was.)

Over the course of the month, I had come to understand that there did need to be someone in our lives who had a vision of our potential—a person who saw beyond today to who you could become. For us that was our dad. The more I talked to Mr. Scott and other family members, the more I realized that for the Scotts, it was their mom.

Situated where virgin woods bordered cut lawn on a dead end, Doris's house, a two-story, seven room farm house, was the last one built along the developed part of Scott family property. It was down the dirt road from Wilsie, who lived down the road from two other Scotts who lived up North but were coming back to retire. All of the Scotts live together, just as Robert wanted.

When I pulled up to the house, Doris was sitting in the screen-enclosed front porch with Wilsie and Flossie, sipping lemonade. I started to introduce myself, but they had already given her a rundown of my time there. After taking Doris up on the offer for a glass of lemonade, I asked her if she knew why her grandmother stayed in contact with her owner. I was still stuck on the image of Alice loaning Wylie money. What irony.

Doris said her grandmother didn't hold onto any ill will toward the Gilliams. "Grandma told us it's all about how you get above your circumstances and what you and your children become."

Doris was quick to say that her grandmother was very protective of her children. She said that Alice wanted the best for them and out of them. Her uncles used to kid that it was their mother that kept them in line. "Their father gave off the message that I love all of my children. I love them—they don't have to be way up big people. But that wasn't good enough for Grandma. She said you needed to have something, you needed to *be* somebody."

Word got around Prospect that Alice was going to send her oldest daughter to boarding school, and she was criticized by the neighbors. If anyone in the family was going to go, Alice should send the boys, they thought. Some called the idea of sending a girl away to school the most ridiculous thing in the world. "Grandma said that people came from far and near, 'to tell me I ought not to send my child to school,'" Doris recalled. She gave the example of a man named Harry White who "left his home from way down yonder early one morning" to tell Alice she was being foolish. Harry thought she was wasting her money on her daughters because they were going to get married and stay at home to raise children. What he didn't know was that Alice had a bigger plan in store. She wanted them to learn how to be critical thinkers so when they graduated, they could return to the farm to teach their brothers the same skills. "Look here, a fool cannot command business," Alice said before kicking Harry out of her kitchen.

I asked what the line meant. "Have you listened to the tape?" Doris asked me, referring to the interview she did with her Uncle

Otis. "If you listen to it, you'll understand that Grandma had plans for all of them. She never saw her children not being leaders."

Otis's name had come up a lot in the conversation in the past couple hours. I particularly liked the story of the time Alice sent him to pick peas at a white man's farm to make money to buy schoolbooks. At lunchtime the farmer brought food to Otis and pointed to the walkway to the back of the house where he could eat on the cement. The next day, Otis didn't want to go back. "And when Grandmother asked him why he said because the man made him eat outside."

Two days later, the man paid a visit to the Scott farm, looking for Otis. Alice told him why Otis never returned to work. "My children don't eat outdoors," she said. "They eat at the table like folk."

She said the man was taken aback and said, "Well, Alice, let him come back. He can eat at the table with us."

For our last meeting, I brought a surprise for Mr. Scott—the interview Doris recorded of his brother Otis about a year before he died. I played the tape and Mr. Scott's face lit up when he heard Otis's voice. He was the most outspoken of all the siblings and testified against the Prince Edward County board of education in a school desegregation lawsuit that would later become part of *Brown v. Board of Education.*

Years before the landmark Supreme Court ruling, one of the original cases was *Dorothy E. Davis v. County School Board of Prince Edward County.* The lawsuit was filed in federal district court in Richmond by NAACP lawyers Spottswood Robinson and Oliver Hill. It charged that the state law requiring segregated schools should be struck down. Dorothy's name was listed first in the 1951 lawsuit brought on behalf of 117 students who attended the all-black Moton High School, and their parents. The Virginia State Department of Education was not ashamed to play favorites in the public school system. The black schools were made out of wood, used coal, kerosene, or wood stoves for heat and had no bathroom facilities—two thousand students had to use outhouses. During the same period, the white schools had a solid brick construction, indoor toilets, sinks, and steam or hot water heat kept the fourteen hundred students warm during the winter. According to the state's own DOE assessments, the per capita school property value for white students was estimated at $817 and for each black student it was $194.

A two week walkout was started by Moton fifteen-year-old junior Barbara Rose Johns, niece of famous civil rights activist Vernon Johns, after her friends visited a white school and came back to tell everyone how nice the whole school was. Moton on the other hand was described as three shacks covered in tar paper. No gym. No cafeteria. And the overflow of students was sent to an old school bus for classes. Local black parents had repeatedly sought improvements from the school board without success.

Otis testified in the Richmond case at the last minute. Listening to the tape, there was an excitement in his voice as he described the tension-filled hours leading up to his testimony which helped clear the way for the case to be included in Brown.

The story went that when it came time for Moton parents to testify in court, no one who signed the NAACP petition wanted to speak out against the school board's refusal to treat both schools equally. "A whole lot didn't act like they should have acted," Otis reported. "[The school board] brainwashed several folks and told them to go down into Richmond and tell them they didn't know what they were doing, saying all they wanted was a good school and they didn't know it was for segregation at all."

The case to challenge Virginia's separate-but-equal law was falling apart. If no one testified that the schools were separate but not equal, the case was going to be thrown out. After a day of failed testimony, the NAACP lawyers asked leaders in Prince Edward County to hold an emergency meeting to find more people who signed the school petition to drive to Richmond that night to testify in court the next day. Otis, who had three sons in school at the time, and two other parents volunteered and left after the meeting ended. When they got to Richmond on a Wednesday night, the NAACP lawyers were waiting for them in their office to tell them what to expect the next morning.

Otis was the first to take the witness stand at 9:00 a.m. "They called me up and I told them, 'Yeah, I signed it' and I knew just what I was doing and my mind hadn't changed since that time." The defense had no questions.

When the federal district case was cleared to go on the Supreme Court docket, Otis said, the high court sent clerks to Prince Edward County to ask more questions. The NAACP lawyers again turned to him to speak out. He described the gross differences between the white and black school buildings to the clerks. After he finished, one clerk asked him how integration would fix the problem. "I answered it so quick, I said, 'every time we went to the school board, the school said they didn't have no money. We decided to send our children to a school where they could get money.' "

I turned toward the kitchen, hearing the sound of glasses clanging and rattling silverware. There was a mass exodus of residents with canes and walking sticks from their rooms. Holding onto the rails along the walls in the hallway, they headed toward the kitchen tables that had been used for checkers an hour ago. I turned the tape recorder off. A nurse walked towards us with a food tray, sectioned into applesauce, ground chicken, and mashed potatoes. I left as the aide was putting a napkin around Mr. Scott's neck.

On my last day in Virginia, I went to the Appomattox Court House National Historic Park. I'd heard so much about the final days of the war, I thought this would be a good time as any to see where it ended.

I got directions from the owners of the Longacre Bed and Breakfast where I had been staying, but wrote them on the back of a yellow sticky note that kept falling off the dashboard, face down. Every time it did, I missed a turn. I made several illegal U-turns before stopping at a gas station to ask directions. The attendant told me to head north.

"I have no clue where north is."

He looked me up and down. "Go out here to the main road you just got off of. Keep heading in the same direction your car is parked in now. You are going to go about a mile until the road opens to a field of mountains. That's it. You'll see signs."

The Appomattox Court House National Historic Park is a replica of the way the village stood in 1865, with tour guides dressed as if they were extras from *Gone with the Wind*. A busload of Boy Scouts beat me to the visitor center, where I found a mob scene of laughter, yelling and pushing and shoving. I held the door for a mother pushing a stroller with a crying baby, telling her husband that after they dropped by the gift shop, it was time to go home.

I went in. A bell rang. I walked up to the information desk where a park ranger with a Smokey the Bear hat was quick to explain the sudden crowd. "That was the two-minute warning bell. We show two Civil War documentaries upstairs, at the top and the bottom of the hour." The one that was coming up now was a narrative collection of the letters written by Confederate and Union soldiers who were here at the time of the surrender. The second one was a twenty-four-hour timeline of events leading up to the surrender. "You should see them both. They are excellent. You will enjoy them."

"You aren't from around here?" she added.

"No."

"Do you know a little bit about the town?"

"The basics."

"Do you remember those fields you passed near the parking lot?"

In the morning of the day Lee and Grant met to sign surrender terms at the Wilmer McLean house, Lee ordered his troops to try to escape one last time, she told me. The escape plan was to try to break through the Union troops encircling them and join General Joseph Johnston's forces in North Carolina. "A battle ensued and as you know they didn't make it," she said. "The meeting between the two generals happened about two hours later."

I grabbed a map as I walked away from the information desk to head upstairs. The second floor was dark and cramped and felt like a haunted house. Glass exhibits extended the length of the walls, eating up much of the hallway with displays of bloodstained uniforms. Most of what was in the exhibits came from right outside, from digging around in the fields. Other items were gifts from locals. Winona Floyd, according to the index card in the display case, found Confederate letters in her attic when her grandfather died and the house was ready to be sold. In someone else's basement, a rummage for a tag sale turned up a manila-colored doll that Wallace Quarterman's great-grandfather's daughter gave to her father when she came to visit him in the infantry hospital. Bloody fingerprints still stained its dress and yellow yarn hair.

The documentaries were short, but long enough that I felt confused after seeing them. Something was missing. I picked up on it in the middle of the second film. The narrator was describing the defeated soldiers returning home to start a new life, filled with honor and dignity. But weren't these some of the same Southerners who went home to lynch, torture and murder blacks? Was the museum working from the same social studies book I read in class? Nobody mentioned slavery. I never once heard the word. Nor black, colored, or even Negro.

The lights came back on and everyone walked out with today's lesson. I sat there until everyone else had gone. Finally, when the last boy skipped up the velvet-purple aisle, followed by his mother yelling at him to slow down, I picked up my pocketbook and followed the trail of laughter to the exit sign.

I looked for the women's restroom on the map. It was a few yards away, near a slave house I wanted to check out on the way. There was a line for the stalls that gave me just enough time to figure out how I could have missed the slave quarters in the short walk from the visitor center. After asking the woman in front to save my spot, I walked outside and looked in both directions. Every building on the map was accounted for in the area—the county jail, three storehouses, a tavern, a stable. I turned around to face the bathroom, slowly looking at the map to make sure. The slave quarters had been turned into public restrooms.

4

Kentucky

Master in the Family

A few months after I returned from Virginia my research was put on hold indefinitely. September 11, 2001 hit. The world was coming to an end or so a friend, who called that morning in a panic before running scared over to my house, and I thought as we watched the news coverage. Before phones went dead, Dad called from work to make sure I was home. I told him Kwanza had to be in court in downtown Brooklyn at 9:00 a.m.—she was safe across the river too. We talked for a few minutes and I reported that I could see the tower smoke from my apartment window. But all I remember from the conversation was him saying "Thank you" before he hung up. It was the first time I heard him say it.

The year flew by, punctuated by several odd writing jobs. I sold used books on half.com to make extra change to pay for subway tokens. I even interviewed for full-time positions in a quest for health benefits because I could no longer afford the luxury of self-employment co-pays.

I rarely kept track of what day it was; they all seemed to be the same. Even weekends had lost their place. The dead had made a home in the air around the city, drowning our souls and suffocating our thoughts. Time seemed to pass slowly as I drove around in no particular direction looking for guidance. And still I was lost.

E-mail leads that worked one day bounced back undeliverable the next. Cold calls weren't returned. People I had been bugging for months let me know I could stop calling because the person I'd inquired about had died or didn't have a parent born before 1865.

The sound of my voice going on and on about my research started to annoy even me. On any given morning I made at least ten phone calls that led nowhere—except to ten more.

Those who did return my calls seemed interested but didn't commit to a meeting. People post–9/11 didn't have extra time. I played phone tag with one Pennsylvania woman for a couple of weeks. By the time I got her on the phone to ask about her father, she was about to get married. She suggested I call back in four months when she returned from her honeymoon, but we never got back in touch.

I hired two college interns as research assistants to help with calls a couple hours a day for two months. I paid each a $250 stipend and invited them out to eat when they wanted to talk about a lead. To make up for the low pay, I always insisted they order a to-go item to take back to the dorm.

I was desperate. After a couple years I barely made a dent in the twenty-page list of Department of Aging centers. I'd completed a run-through of senior centers, nursing homes, and black churches in only four states, and even in those there were still a few I hadn't reached. But more important, I needed a mental buffer from the cross-offs that were filling my notebook.

Out of the blue one day, I got an E-mail from one of Mr. Scott's nephews, Khalid, whom I'd met at the family reunion. He sent me a 1959 newspaper article from the *Norfolk Journal & Guide* about his great-grandmother, Alice, on her one hundredth birthday. It had been forwarded to him by a genealogist friend who was doing research on another family in Prince Edward County and had stumbled upon the clip. Khalid sent it along with a nice note asking how my research was going.

The article was actually written by Doris and sent to the *Journal* as a tribute to her grandmother who was living in Norfolk at the time with one of her daughters. There were a few events Alice vividly remembered about her early years that were new to me, such as the time the Gilliams were about to have dinner and Alice was told to go get milk for the table. She turned to the master's daughter she'd been playing with and said, "Come on, Betty, and go with me," ignoring the rule of the house that the master's children were only to be addressed in a formal manner: Missus Betty. For that, she received a beating.

Reading the article gave me an idea. What if I looked for newspaper articles on black centenarians? There would be a good chance these people would fit my criteria. And then it hit me: Look for old articles mentioning the specific word combinations I used in my inquiries on the phone.

I pushed the used tea bags and pile of phone numbers, lists, faxes, and cover letters to the side of the desk; logged on to Nexis, a database of local newspapers around the country, and started typing phrases in the query box. "Child of a slave." Enter. "Daughter of former slave." Return. "Father was slave." Click. It took several tries to find a few articles.

I printed everything and started reading the most recent datelines because they offered a better chance the person would still be alive.

When I came across the article in The Courier-Journal about one-hundred-and-two-year-old Charlie Hayden, I dropped the page like a hot plate and dialed 411 for the Kentucky newspaper. Three years had passed since the 1998 piece ran with an accompanying photo of Mr. Hayden driving a lawn tractor, cutting grass in his hometown of Danville. The street Mr. Hayden had lived on for seventy-five years was being renamed in his honor by the mayor. In the article there was a brief mention that Mr. Hayden's father, Austin, was born a slave in Lebanon in 1852. (Later on I learned Jay Leno read the same article and invited Mr. Hayden to be a guest on NBC's The Tonight Show in Los Angeles, but Mr. Hayden turned down the offer because he didn't know who Leno was and hated to fly).

Columnist Bryan Crawford's secretary picked up the line and explained that her boss worked from home. I left a detailed message on his voice mail explaining who I was and what I was doing. He called back three days later and gave me the number of a man named James Johnson, a next door neighbor to Mr. Hayden for twenty years and the best person to contact. The columnist told me that James had been something of an adopted son to Mr. Hayden and his late wife, who never had children.

When I finally reached James, he told me that Mr. Hayden had become far less mobile since that article. About a year after the column ran Mr. Hayden went into the hospital for a bad cold. When he left the hospital, he could no longer walk and didn't want to live at home alone so he agreed to check into the Danville Center for Health and Rehabilitation.

"Can he talk?" I asked.

"Talk your ear off. I go to visit him every Saturday to carry him a chicken plate from Lee's."

I booked my ticket.

I used a Delta voucher for the flight to Louisville and Priceline to rent a car at the airport. Next to toothpaste and a toothbrush in the side pocket of my suitcase, I stuffed a fifty-one-page booklet of Kentucky centenarians put out by the state's Office of Aging Services in 1999.

I took a late flight and for the first time felt scared driving at night by myself. After I took the Versailles/Frankfort exit off I-64 East, a gray two-door revved by to make the yellow light before disappearing into total darkness. Even the rolling landscape vanished in the night, hiding, in the distance, thousands of acres of multimillion-dollar horse farms in this self-proclaimed "Horse Capital of the World." I made a right in the same direction. The long stretches between traffic lights made it hard to stay awake. I hugged the center lane, following the raised yellow reflective markers like a guiding light until I reached the bed and breakfast.

The next morning I went to see Mr. Hayden. On my way, I pretended I was looking for an estate I wanted to buy and imagined the number of horses on it. This car game, picked up from Mom, who liked to sightsee in fancy neighborhoods when she and her college roommate got together, occupied me until something else caught my eye: stone fences, a layered jigsaw puzzle seamlessly assembled from thousands of different rocks dry-laid together without mortar. The fence ran along the right side of the road as if it were following me. The fences looked a lot like what Dad put up around the edges of our property as a border. The Bluegrass Region is home to an extensive collection of such structures. Built by Irish and black stone masons as early as 1790, these original rock fences are historic markers in Kentucky, making them illegal to disassemble in public rights-of-way.

The entrance hallway of the rehabilitation center was long, white, and silent. A wooden handicap railing lined both sides of the corridor with a circular nurse's station farther ahead. The door to the director's office was open. I knocked. When no one answered, I stepped inside. Two women eating lunch looked up.

"You must be Miss Butler," said the one behind the desk as she reached out her hand. "Mr. Hayden is all ready for you. We set him up in the lounge. Come with me."

As she walked out of the office, she turned around to tell the other woman to page his nurse to meet us. "How long has he been here?" I asked, drumming up a conversation to distract myself from looking into the rooms where catheter bags were visible from the hallway.

"He checked in about two years ago—pulled up in a white stretch Cadillac. We all ran to the door to see who was getting out, and there was Mr. Hayden in a three-piece maroon suit and white patent leather shoes, waiting for someone to come around with a wheelchair."

We reached an empty lounge at the end of a hall where a nurse dressed in a yellow shirt and khakis introduced herself as Beth Ann. The director thought that it would be a good idea to have a familiar face in the room because Mr. Hayden seemed to respond better to people he knew. In the corner was a tall man with a big head asleep on a portable hospital bed. A white sheet and cotton blanket were tucked over his shoulders and his feet dangled off the end of the bed. Beth Ann walked over and leaned toward his ear.

"Wake up, Mr. Hayden. This young lady is here to see you." The nurse turned to ask my name, then leaned in again to Mr. Hayden. "Miss Butler is here to see you, Mr. Hayden."

"If he's sleeping, I can come back," I said.

"He's not sleeping. He just fades in and out sometimes."

He opened his eyes, blue and partly blind from cataracts. Beth Ann stopped tapping his shoulder, then pointed to me.

I explained to him that I had spoken to his friend James.

"I phoned him a couple weeks ago to see if it was okay to come to talk to you about your mother and father."

He smiled. "How long have you known him?"

"I don't really."

"You want to know about my father and my what?"

"Your mother. Do you remember them?"

"I don't know what you are saying," he said.

Beth Ann stepped in. She repeated the question for me.

In our first five minutes together, I identified several key problems that would make daily conversations like the ones I'd had with Mr. Wright and Mr. Scott almost impossible. Mr. Hayden couldn't hear me. He could barely see me. He didn't understand my questions. And I couldn't understand his answers. When he did say something his mouth opened a little but his lips didn't move. Usually, the first couple words made sense, but then the sentence trailed off into mumbo-jumbo.

Each time I asked a question, Mr. Hayden would look at Beth Ann to repeat it as if I were speaking Pig Latin and she was my translator. Mr. Hayden did seem to respond better to Beth Ann's voice. When I tried to mimic her intonations and enunciations, my throat started to get scratchy. I sat back in the chair, silently discouraged. This back-and-forth wasn't going to work.

"Ask him about his parents. When were they born? How many brothers and sisters did he have?"

"Mr. Hayden, do you know what your father's name was?"

"His name was Austin."

"What was your mother's name?" she asked

"Carrie. We all lived down in Lebanon."

"Ask him if his parents were slaves," I said. She did a double take, turning back around to look at me.

"I read that his parents were slaves in Lebanon," I explained.

Actually, I'd read a lot more than that on his parents' history. Mr. Hayden's father, Austin, was thirteen when slavery ended. He had one sister and two brothers living on the same plantation owned by Guster "Gus" Hayden. Gus also owned Austin's father—Mr. Hayden's grandfather—who ran away to join the Union Army and later was killed in battle in North Carolina.

According to the newspaper interview, Austin told Mr. Hayden that after the war was over, Gus called all the slaves together and told them he couldn't work them any longer; they were free to leave if they wanted. Then he went back in the house and the newly freed slaves "all went back to work," Austin reportedly said. "They had nowhere else to go."

Mr. Hayden's mom, Carrie, never knew the year she was born, only that she was a few years younger than Austin. After the war they got married and stayed on fifty plus acres that Gus owned. As sharecroppers, Austin and Carrie raised six children on 60 cents a day.

Beth Ann turned to Mr. Hayden.

"Mr. Hayden, do you know if your parents were slaves?"

"Oh yes, they were slaves," he said in a strong, clear voice. "Gus Hayden down in Lebanon owned my mother and father. 'Old Gussie' was what we called him. I had five brothers and four sisters. I am the firstborn and the oldest. Did you know my parents?"

I politely said no and ended the interview soon after that. Mr. Hayden's mind was gone. While it didn't make much sense for me to come back, the director's description of Mr. Hayden arriving in a Cadillac, unable to walk but dressed to impress, spiked my curiosity to learn more about him. But I had to go to someone else to do so. I made a date with James at the end of the week to talk about Mr. Hayden, as well as find out if any of his younger brothers and sisters were still alive.

I had the next day to myself. I spent it looking for a lunch place that served homemade fresh-from-the-batter fried chicken—no easy task given that all over the South drive-thru fast-food chains and buffet Chinese restaurants have run local mom-and-pop diners out of business. My hour-long search ended on the outskirts of town. Yards from a car junkyard, M&J, a tin-roof diner had a sign posted on the door: TUESDAY SPECIAL: FRIED CHICKEN AND GRITS. After I stuffed my face, I introduced myself to the cook in the kitchen to sweet-talk her into making enough fried chicken breasts for me to take away in aluminum foil to rewarm for dinner that night.

On the drive back to my room for a nap, I saw the famed Kentucky Saddlebreds for the first time. There were two together, side by side, in the middle of a wide-open green pasture. I pulled off to the side of the road to stare. The breed, chiseled in shades of dark brown, graceful and tall, became popular during the Civil War as the mount of choice of Generals Lee, Grant, and Stonewall Jackson.

The horses had black fly masks covering their eyes and their heads were down. They looked sad just standing there, or maybe I was sad for them because they were trained not to run and play. They no longer cared about the freedom of the open field.

James lived on a short dead-end street on the edge of town. His home had been recently renovated with a brick fence in front and an above-ground Jacuzzi in back. A white picket fence separated his backyard from the cow pasture behind it. Boarded up across the street was Mr. Hayden's cozy, faded white house. His lawn was crisp and well-kept as if someone had just mowed it and trimmed the hedges.

I met James at the front steps. "The slave lady," he joked, which was kind of funny considering all the voice mail messages I left, reintroducing myself each time. A carpenter with jeans and Timberlands covered in sawdust, pencil behind his ear, and a measuring tape attached to his belt, James, in his mid-fifties, owned a one-man wood shop across the field on Hayden Avenue. He was hard to catch up with because he was putting the finishing touches on a $15,000 custom kitchen cabinet set scheduled for customer pickup the following week.

Sitting in his living room, I reported on my rehab interview and asked if Mr. Hayden had any siblings still alive.

"You mean the white boys?" James said.

The comment caught me off-guard. What'chu talkin' 'bout, Willis? was my gut reaction. "His brothers are white?" I asked. This was the first time I had heard this.

James had met them when he brought Mr. Hayden to the hospital a few years ago. Mr. Hayden didn't think he was going to make it, and asked James to contact his brothers. "Don't be shocked because they are white," Mr. Hayden told James. "I didn't even know he had brothers. Sure enough they came in and they looked white with red hair."

I wasn't too surprised by the idea that Mr. Hayden's family included Caucasians. I joked that James himself was on the light side with freckles, and that somewhere in his line he likely had a white relative. When you have a light complexion, the natural assumption is you have a drop of white blood in the family. Then James told me how much Mr. Hayden said his family had. Now that shocked me.

When they were packing up Mr. Hayden's house into boxes before checking him into the rehab center, he showed James some photos of his parents. His mother was "a real light lady," to use Mr. Hayden's words. But his father was "a dark fella."

"You think this man could make the people you saw in that hospital?" Mr. Hayden said at the time. He went on to talk with James about his parents' owner. "He said Gus treated Mr. Hayden and his siblings well. It was as if they were his own family."

I had heard of slave owners fathering children with slaves, Thomas Jefferson and Sally Hemings being one of the most often-cited and often disputed examples. But nothing had been said about this practice continuing after the war. I had never heard of a former owner fathering children with a freed slave, and a married one at that. "Willie and Ezra never told me that," said James, referring to Mr. Hayden's younger siblings. "Charlie was the only one who said that."

"Are Willie and Ezra still alive?"

"All are dead except Ezra. He lives in Indianapolis."

James turned out to know far more about Mr. Hayden than I'd realized when we first talked on the phone. And while I'd already decided to drive to Indianapolis to meet Ezra, I couldn't help wanting to know more about Mr. Hayden's life.

I remembered from the column that he had only $1.50 to his name when he married in 1918. "But he would soon earn a fortune," James said. When they moved from Lebanon to Danville, Mr. Hayden started contracting work— building homes, digging basements, and drilling wells. He had a gift for finding underground streams with a forked switch from a peach tree—a practice called water witching. James told me that Mr. Hayden also owned a tobacco business with his wife for a while. "He pulled up the grass and his wife rode the tobacco setter," James said, referring to the machine people used to plant tobacco.

Mr. Hayden was drafted into the army near the end of World War I. When he returned home, he got into real estate. He bought old houses in the area and rented them out, making enough money to write a check for $10,000 to his church to buy a new furnace in the early 1950s. Though he had money, he and his wife remained incredibly frugal. For seventy years he wrote in a daily journal the number of eggs, milk, and loaves of bread bought or sold and to whom. "He cooked one egg for breakfast for the two of them. They'd take turns eating the yolk and the egg white," said James.

James and I walked to his garage to go through some of Mr. Hayden's boxes. As he searched for what he was looking for, I heard his white poodle, tied up in back, barking nonstop. I walked over to see what was wrong and looked up at the fence to see nine white-and-brown cows standing a few feet away on the other side. Staring directly at me and the apple in my hand, the cow in front inched closer to me. I took a bite of the apple and threw the rest just as James called me back into the garage. He handed me two stacks of old newspaper clippings, browned and brittle, tied together with string. James didn't want to throw them away, but didn't know what to do with them, so he gave them to me.

Mr. Hayden saved newspaper clippings of articles that were relevant to him. Like a 1978 article from a Lexington paper of a recently discovered rare tintype portrait of a Confederate guerilla soldier, Sue Munday, who was known to disguise himself as a woman. At the bottom of the last column, Mr. Hayden wrote "My father saw Munday many times." On top of the pile was a 1913 black-and-white photo from the Lebanon Enterprise of people dressed up as if going to a party. The women had on fancy, frilly dresses and were holding umbrellas with white gloved hands and the men wore suit jackets. In the foreground was the public hanging for a black man named Jim Buckner. The caption mentioned that photos of the execution were sold as souvenirs.

This led us into a conversation about helplessness and anger. In a state that begged to squeeze in the last public execution in the United States in 1938, blacks were executed for many more crimes than whites for no reason at all other than skin color. Whites were hanged only for murder, while blacks were hanged for murder, attempted murder, rape, attempted rape, and arson. Not to mention the question of whether the trials were fair because justice was certainly not color-blind.

I don't think I will ever be able to fully understand the terror of growing up in a country that proudly celebrated and publicly sanctioned torture. But even as I say it, I know that is a naive comment. Because Muslim Americans today can say they have seen that side of this country. Was I emotionally blind to such sick violence this time around because it wasn't happening to black people?

I don't know how Mr. Hayden and the generations that came before him did it. I would have been mad as hell if I was forced to accept a life in free America where citizens actually had fun cutting out a man's heart and cutting off his penis. What kind of country was this? The hypocrisy alone would've filled me with rage. How Mr. Hayden didn't let the anger control him makes him and his generation stronger than I could ever hope to be. What impressed me most is that they channeled the aggression into outsmarting Southern whites.

"Charlie was very smart about white people," James said as he told the story of a time when Mr. Hayden tricked a farmer at a live stock auction into buying his mules at a higher than average price. "He'd stand in front of a white buyer, pretending to be an employee of a white man interested in buying mules." The competitive buyer paid asking price for the mules because Mr. Hayden gave him the impression that a white person owned them. If he had known that a black man put them up for sale, he would have negotiated their worth to half the asking price. "He had a business mind," James said, laughing.

Where did these smart, gutsy, strong-minded, hard-working humble men come from? Were they still out there? Did parents make them like that anymore? Did James think Mr. Hayden's mother and father had anything to do with how he turned out?

"There is no formula to calculate what kids take from their parents and what they don't. Charlie's theory was that you get a job and save your money and then you'll be who you want to be."

We walked back inside and I asked James for Ezra's son's phone number. While I was there, I called Thomas from the house to ask about coming up to visit his father. The son said it would be okay. On to Indy.

5

Indiana

BLACK MAN'S PROTECTION

During the drive north on I-65 to Indianapolis, I played highway leapfrog with eighteen-wheelers. I was in a hurry to get to where I was going. Thirty minutes into the three-and-a-half-hour ride to Ezra Hayden's house, the local radio forecast snow around Chicago headed toward Indianapolis in the early evening.

I took exit 75 for three miles, then drove around in a circle because the directions didn't mention that Mr. Hayden's street dead-ended at a sidewalk to a new semigated community. When I finally pulled up in front of his one-car garage, I sat for a few minutes trying to decide how long to stay before heading back through what the forecasters were now fearing might be a blizzard. Drained from the traffic and with a slight headache from staring at the road, I took a deep breath, exhaled, and opened the car door.

As I walked up the front steps, Mr. Hayden's wife, Freddie, pressed the screen latch to let me in. Behind her stood Mr. Hayden, holding a cane, and an old, blind black dog with a graying muzzle at his ankles. Except for a dead left eye, Mr. Hayden's features were much like those of his older brother Charlie—thin, curly light brown hair that looked a lot like graying red in the light. He had a long, pale face the color of the palm of a hand after a hot shower. Weak with age, he slouched forward a little as if someone was pushing down on his head. He wore a long-sleeve, brown-and-green flannel shirt tucked into khakis that were too big even with a belt. He seemed quiet, withdrawn.

I followed them both into the dining room, and sat at the end of a table surrounded by ten sturdy wooden chairs. Freddie sat across from me with her back to the kitchen. I sat near the dog, two chairs from Mr. Hayden.

I decided not to ask him the Gus question, whether he thought his parents' former owner was his biological father, as James had told me. Whether it was true wasn't as important as how the story affected the family. I admit I wanted to know if Mr. Hayden was half white, but I wasn't going to discuss a family secret if he didn't bring it up first, though I admit I was still curious. I already felt as if I were intruding in some way when I talked about my research. His wife certainly gave me that impression. Before I could even get a question out, she stopped to correct me.

"Why are you speaking to him?" she asked, as if I were insulting them both by making a family connection to slavery. "He isn't a child of a slave. His parents weren't slaves." She was his new second wife, and younger by at least a decade, so maybe she didn't know. But now she had me confused: Did I have the wrong person? Was I in the wrong place? Why was she saying this? I looked at Mr. Hayden.

"Yes, my mother and father were slaves," he jumped in, affirming his family's past, sounding almost offended that his wife had suggested otherwise. His brother had taken the same proud, boastful tone in the rehab center when his nurse asked the same question. I remember because it struck me as odd at the time. Not that he said his parents were slaves, but that he had such a positive attitude about it. I couldn't put my finger on the source until listening to Mr. Hayden claim his own connection like a badge of honor.

Most people don't brag about being a descendant of a slave. The mere mention of the word makes some cringe, as if it were a five-letter curse. I got a taste of this censorship when I made my research calls. I noticed that people were less defensive in the beginning of the conversation if I told them I was looking for people whose parents were born before 1865, rather than people whose parents were born slaves. Mistake a person whose father was a freed man for a slave, as I did once, and the daughter all but demanded an apology. Why was coming from a family of ex-slaves such an awful thing? Wasn't it a good thing to have survived slavery?

"My father said they went over to Africa and bought them and towed them here on a boat, whupping them, kicking them, and beating them. And they kept on going back and getting more. He couldn't read or write his name, but that's what he told us."

"Did your dad talk about the people who owned him?" I asked.

"He was given the name Hayden by the white people. He talked about one of the Haydens that owned him. I remember one he called Gus Hayden. I hate talking about him a whole lot—all the Haydens."

His answer was probably the most honest and genuine response I'd heard from anyone—he said the word hate. And while there is a lot to be said about taking the high road, not everyone has to take it.

"What would your father say about Gus?" I asked.

"I can't remember none of that. Can't go into that."

"It's not stuff you want to talk about?"

"No. If Charlie was true to himself he could tell a whole lot about it, but I can't."

At that point the interview looked to be over. While I really wanted to know the source of the hate he referred to, I respected his request to change the subject. At least that was what I thought he wanted to do. But when I started to ask him other questions that had nothing to do with Gus, he didn't respond. He had already shut down.

For those next few minutes, he didn't want to talk to me at all. Not about him. Not about his parents. Not about growing up. He gave one-word answers, mainly "no," "yeah," "huh," with the blank look of a cop listening to a driver beg not to be given a speeding ticket. There was no budging him. And I tried as hard as I could, not knowing anything about him except the stuff he didn't want to discuss.

"How far is downtown Indianapolis from here?"

"Not far."

"There seems to be a lot of development in the area."

"Yeah, this area has changed a lot."

"I had a nice conversation with your son Thomas on the phone. Does he live around here?"

"He lives in Minneapolis."

I had nothing else to give. Frustrated, I stopped trying. My only choices were either to sit there in silence and wait for a turning point or wrap it up. I chose the latter, partly because of my anxiety about the blizzard, but mainly because his short answers made me realize I was too burnt out—with everything—to try to pull information from him.

I didn't want to ask questions anymore. I didn't want to be in Indianapolis. I didn't want to drive in the snow back to Kentucky. I didn't want to charge a hotel room with an overcharged credit card I couldn't pay. I wanted to be home with the boyfriend I would have if I wasn't traveling up and down the country, looking for strangers, spending time in other people's lives, with their families.

I was tired of prying and asking and absorbing and listening to other people's hard lives after driving around in circles to get to their houses. I was tired of the past. I missed my own life. And in that split second, as I sat across the dining room table with the black dog the size of a fat cat, peeing near my feet on the rug because he couldn't control his bladder, I felt a tear.

Freddie got up to get paper towels to mop up the puddle. I dropped my pen on the floor, and when I leaned down to pick it up, I grabbed the top of my T-shirt to wipe my eyes. While I was down there, I pet the dog, then sat back up and started talking about my own dog, Spot, the best dog in the whole world. Spot lived in the backyard, under a tree, in the doghouse Dad built for Spot's mother, a beagle named Princess, and father Samson, a collie. I couldn't help myself. I needed to make myself smile or laugh or think happy thoughts or I was going to break down in tears and Mr. Hayden and his wife would think I was some crazy woman.

I turned the tape recorder off and for a short time just talked about Spot, a white mutt with brown spots, who was the first of a litter born under the porch at our house when I was seven. He had five or six brothers and sisters that Dad gave away to people in town. Mr. Hayden and his wife listened to me go on and on about Samson, who was hit by a car, and Princess, who ran away the next day to look for her husband and never came back.

Right away I started to feel better. While I was rambling, I'd had my head down, fidgeting through a notebook. When I looked up, to my surprise, not only was Freddie smiling at me, but Mr. Hayden was, too.

"Where is he now?" he asked.

"He died in the backyard my senior year in high school."

The tables had turned. A few minutes ago, I was ready to pack my stuff and go. But now I sensed it was okay to stay. Mr. Hayden seemed more relaxed with me. I was relaxed. The next thing I knew, we were back to the interview.

"You want to know about my life?" Mr. Hayden asked.

"If you don't mind, Mr. Hayden. I would love to hear about your life."

We talked about easy stuff first like what his family planted on their farm and then he started talking about how hard life was on the farm growing up in Lebanon.

"Papa struggled his entire life. He just made enough to get by," Mr. Hayden said about his father, who planted mainly corn and tobacco, and raised livestock for a family of seven on thirty acres. He remembered his father running a tab at the local store to charge the family groceries for a year and at the end of December paying the bill off only to start racking up more back charges. "He worked all year just to get us enough to live and eat," said Mr. Hayden. "He worked awfully hard."

What the family didn't eat, they sold. The hogs on the farm were some of the most sought after in town. Mr. Hayden was nine when he first saw "Papa being pushed around by a white farmer" who wanted to buy a hog and wouldn't take no for an answer. "Papa told him that he didn't want to sell the hog. He refused to sell it to him." But the man kept pushing for a price quote, maneuvering Austin into saying how much the hog was worth. Not knowing he was being tricked, Austin came up with a figure, essentially giving the buyer an amount to pay. The man slapped the cash down and took the hog. "I'll never forget that." He paused for a minute, "That's where I get my strength from."

The exchange between his father and the farmer that day changed Mr. Hayden's outlook on business. "If it was me, he wouldn't have walked away with the hog."

"What would you have done?" I asked with a bit of sarcasm, questioning what options a nine-year-old boy could have had. "I don't know, but he wouldn't have walked away with the hog." Mr. Hayden didn't want to be like his father. He didn't want to sweat to make ends meet, hated the idea of being outsmarted. There are different ways to gain strength from a parent—sometimes from the obvious encouragement of them saying, "I want more for you." But other times a child can look at his parents and say, "I want more for myself."

At twelve, Mr. Hayden started what he called his investment business. He bought and sold hogs and calves for a profit. In the evening, after he got home from school, he rode a horse to bale hay around town, and at the same time kept his eye open for sick calves and hogs to buy. "I'd wash them in boiled tobacco juice to get the lice and things off and they'd be jumping in two days. Then I'd sell them for double what I paid for them."

"Wasn't it strange that farmers didn't know how to take care of sick animals?" I asked.

"Maybe they thought it wasn't worth it."

I wondered if farmers he bought the pigs from were former slave owners who had relied on slave labor and were unable to function without it.

"I've had a business mind all my life," he said. "I've been alert all my days."

"Did some of it come from your dad?"

"No, my father didn't know them white guys. I knew them."

I rewound the conversation to talk about the school that he had mentioned in passing. The push to educate black children was strong in Kentucky even before the end of the war, with parents holding meetings across the state to encourage freedmen to open schools. Overwhelmed by the call for public education, a black federal official wrote in January 1865 that, "The Colored people are Sending for us in Every Direction...they want Schools Started." But some parents didn't appreciate the value of an education. Others didn't trust white Northerners as teachers and opted not to send their children to school for that reason alone. Mr. Hayden's father didn't think much of education, taking at least one son out of school after he finished the equivalent of third grade writing. Though Charlie begged to continue the following school year, his father told him no. "All you ever need to know is 'git up' and 'whoa.'"

At first I thought it was a shame that Mr. Hayden's father didn't see the importance of an education. But Austin was just doing what he knew best. His father didn't have an education and he turned out fine, so that meant his sons didn't need one to run a farm, either. He wanted his boys to be farmers. That was all he knew, and that was all he thought his boys needed to know.

Does every parent want the best for their children? Do parents always want to give their kids access to opportunities they didn't have? Are you a bad parent if you don't? Is it the children's responsibility to know what is best for them when their parents don't? Is "best" a universal term with every parent having the same checklist of what it includes? This was the first time in my interviews that these questions had come up, and I carried them with me to later interviews, hoping to get the answers.

As a teenager Mr. Hayden had a hot temper, "quick to fly off. Got it from my dad," he said. The first time someone called him a nigger, "the white boy hit the ground."

"What does that mean?" I asked.

"I hit him in the stomach and he passed out. Then he got up and walked on home."

I thought of the newspaper clippings his brother Charlie had kept. "You weren't afraid the boy's father or the KKK would come after you?"

"No."

"Why?" I sensed the answer had nothing to do with the name-calling.

"Tell you what," he started. "My daddy talked me up so that I would kill a white man in a minute. He brought me up to be that way. He said the slave owners would take a bunch of men to one place and take a girl to another, and they would give you stuff to do so you had to stay out in the fields all day while they stayed with her all day. He'd tell me that over and over. And that pumped me up. He did the wrong thing—I just hated white people. But I'm not that way now."

By the time he was ready to marry his first wife, Mr. Hayden had amassed a small fortune through his investments. He was able to build a two-story house with eight bedrooms, four downstairs and four upstairs. He did all the plumbing, electrical work, and the carpentry; dug the basement four feet in the ground to lay a solid foundation. "I had drawn up in my mind that I wanted to be able to see all the way around. So I had four windows in front and back, and four windows on the sides. When I was finished, you could see south, north, east, and west."

"Wasn't that a big house for the time?" I asked. "Eight bedrooms seems large even for today"

He said it was but he had nine children and wanted to give them each their own room if they wanted it. The big house made the neighbors jealous. "White people hated me on account of what I had. Talked about me like a dog."

They often had issues with Mr. Hayden in Lebanon, usually having to do with something he did that they didn't like. He seemed to delight in telling those stories as if they happened yesterday. He often cut me off when I tried to ask a question so that I didn't mess up the momentum building to the climax of another story that ended the same way: with his neighbors organizing against him.

"A nice white boy come and told me that people were running around saying not to give me no work because I'm too empty."

"What's that mean?" I asked.

"Said I was too into things or something like that," he answered.

For Mr. Hayden this kind of oppression forced him to be creative and come up with more side jobs for himself. In August of 1933, he got into buying and selling hogs. President Roosevelt's new economic relief package during the Great Depression called for the slaughter of 5 million hogs when market prices had bottomed out to as low as two cents a pound. The government agreed to purchase all the hogs at five to 9.5 cents a pound. The emergency plan was designed to give aide to corn-belt farms experiencing the worst feed shortage in fifty years due to drought. The goal was to significantly reduce supply in order to trigger an artificial increase in hog prices for the 1934 spring crop.

"When Roosevelt announced he was going to buy up all the hogs and dump them into the sea to feed the fishes," he remembered jokingly, "I said, 'Oh, good. I better go buy all the hogs I can.' So I went up to the old farmers when they were feeding their hogs, and I told them, 'You got some nice hogs there.' 'Yeah, I sell them to you,' they would say."

Mr. Hayden went from one farm to another, negotiating a price a little more than the going rate and buying up all the hogs he could. "Wife raised Cain, said, 'What are you doing with all those hogs? They ain't worth nothing.'" He told her to mark his words. "They are going be worth something."

After eight months, hogs jumped up to 35 cents a pound. "People went wild hunting for hogs. Wasn't none in the area." What local farmers hadn't sold to the government, they'd sold to Mr. Hayden. "I'd bought all the hogs around and nobody had them but me. And when prices skyrocketed, they come around. They almost worried me to death, calling me."

"What would they say?" I asked.

"I want to buy hogs. I want to buy hogs. 'Uh huh,' I'd say. "

"Pretty smart, Mr. Hayden. You made your own way."

"Right. They didn't want to give me no work to help me out. They tried to put me in a ditch. But they can't put you in no ditch unless they get down there with you."

After twenty years of farming in Lebanon, his wife got sick. They moved to Indianapolis at the request of their oldest daughter who was living there and wanted to take care of her mother. He was close to retirement age by then, and had enough money in the bank to live. He bought a new two-family house for his daughter to live on one side.

But retirement didn't suit Mr. Hayden. He wanted to keep busy. "I had no right to play around. I wanted to work, make that money." He was hired at a local bank as a shipping clerk and although his hours were 9 to 5, he still woke up at 3:00 a.m.—farmer's hours. He'd spend hours staring out the bedroom window and noticed one day that the local hospital was building a new addition, tearing down residential houses to make room.

This observation led him to open a real estate business. He knew that the people who used to live in the demolished homes had to have somewhere to live. He started buying houses and managing the properties as a landlord. "I'd get up, ride around, and find a run-down house. When I saw sales signs, I'd buy them, fix them up, and rent them out. I'd buy one house and pay for it; and next year make that one pay for the next." In all, he had twenty-three tenants.

I asked Mr. Hayden what he thought was the key to his success. He started to describe what he called a "black man's protection," a term he created when he was young, watching his father work just to eat. "You can't do nothing with one job. You can work on one income the rest of your days and you won't get no farther than when you first started. You got to have a side income to put in the bank. That's where you get ahead."

It was night when I left. His wife put a handful of jelly beans and Hershey kisses in a bag for me to eat on the road. The snow had already accumulated on my windshield but thankfully the blizzard warning had been dropped. As I drove I had plenty of time to go over the day in my head.

The big thing I'd learned today was that Mr. Hayden seemed to know a lot more about farming than many of the white farmers around him. I wasn't sure if I was overstating it or not, but the more I thought about it, there did seem to be a life-skills gap based on experience. When comparing former slaves with former owners, the former owners simply didn't have the same set of basic agricultural hands-on daily skills. As wealthy immigrants, many men had never worked the land in the New World and were at a disadvantage because of that.

White women had similar problems after the war. I'd interviewed a descendant of a slave owner who said her adult mother had to be taught how to cook and clean because she had never done it for herself. For the first time, it occurred to me that, post-slavery, perhaps white men had a similar weakness. They couldn't manage their own farms.

There was a lot about the Haydens I didn't know yet, but wanted to find out. With the master story still floating around, I at least wanted to know about Gus. Because it was an unusual name, I assumed that it wouldn't be too hard to find in court records. I set out to learn more about the white Haydens. Who were they? Where had they come from? Where were they today?

Back in Kentucky, I drove to Lebanon, once a wealthy, aristocratic, Catholic farming town in Marion County. Settled in 1789, Marion

County was also the home of the whiskey-producing Maker's Mark Distillery, which is a National Historic Landmark. I stopped at a gas station to look at the Yellow Pages and counted more than five hundred Haydens. Most named John, William, or Matthew.

I went to the courthouse to search archival records for Gus, but when I got to the courthouse, I was told by the receptionist that all of the documents before 1867 had been burned in a fire set by local Confederates who hated the county clerk. She suggested a long shot. The library up the hill behind the post office housed a genealogy room. In it I could find books of personal records compiled by families who had roots in Lebanon, sometimes covering as many as nine centuries.

After a nap in the parking lot, I checked my e-mail on the library computer, then walked to the genealogy room. The door was locked. I stood in line at the front desk to speak to the librarian, who then called a blonde volunteer from the Marion County Historical Society who was wearing a light purple knit skirt suit over to help me.

"Yes, we do in fact have a book on the Haydens. Right this way."

The genealogy room, a glass-enclosed, dimly lit space about the size of an elementary school classroom, had reading tables and bookcases stacked to the ceiling. "Unfortunately, nothing here can be checked out. You have to look up information in the room."

"Where do I go to make photocopies?"

"You can't. The books can't leave the room."

She walked over to the wall and pulled out a maroon hardcover book titled *Hayden/Rapier and Allied Families, Colonial Maryland, Kentucky, USA*. It was a whopping 516 pages. I flipped to the index and scrolled to the G's while reciting the alphabet in my head. I couldn't find the name Gus. But the book was rich with details and history of the family dating back to Holland in the twelfth century. I wrote down the name and address of the publisher, closed the book, and went back to the computer to Google MLD Genealogy in Houston, Texas. I learned that the initials stood for Sister Mary Louise Donnelly, and her phone number was listed.

I didn't call her immediately because I wanted to come up with a game plan on how to ask if her family owned slaves. I eventually let that idea go and just came right out and asked.

"Hello, Sister Donnelly. I was in Lebanon, Kentucky, recently and came across your genealogy book on the Haydens."

"Yes, it is there in the public library."

"I am doing research on a descendant of a Hayden slave whose owner was named Gus Hayden. I didn't find a reference to him in your book. Does that name sound familiar?

"No, it doesn't, but that doesn't mean anything. I am descended from Francis Hayden, who came over to Maryland from England. His son was William, and William's son was George. George's son was Basil Hayden Jr., who settled in Holy Cross, Kentucky."

That wasn't hard, I thought to myself. She didn't flinch when I mentioned that I was only focusing on the slave-owning side of her family. So I put it all out on the table.

"I found two brothers from Lebanon whose parents were Hayden slaves. There's a rumor in the family that the slave owner Gus fathered children with the ex-slaves after the war." Did the story at all sound familiar I asked Sister Donnelly. "I didn't see any reference to the Haydens owning slaves in your book."

She said she had never heard of that but that she wouldn't be surprised if it were true.

"But one of my ambitions was to meet one of the slaves. There wasn't all that much in our records about them."

I continued to ask questions because she was very receptive. Were the Haydens wealthy farmers? Did they have money?

"They were wealthy farmers. I found the will of my great-great-great grandfather Hayden. He said he wanted his slaves to go to good Catholic masters. What a dichotomy; I almost died. That was hard."

The Haydens had money when they arrived as new immigrants. When Kentucky was first settled, people like the Haydens brought white indentured servants with them from the Old World. And when that stopped, Sister Donnelly said, "they had to have someone to work the cotton fields and that's when they started to bring in slaves."

"It was really a class system, which came from England. Some of the Irish were servants also. A person could have their transportation to this country paid for if he or she would be a servant for so many years. And then it depended on what their occupation was. When the indenture system went out of vogue, that was when slavery got strong."

I was excited to have found Sister Donnelly, and so glad that she was comfortable talking about all of her family's history. I milked it for as much as I could. I took the opportunity to ask her the bold question about why she thought her family had owned slaves. It was a release of sorts.

I'd been curious about the question much of my life. Why did an individual buy and sell another human being? What was the personal reason? The justification of slavery dates back to a time before Christ. It has been argued by Aristotle in *The Politics* that some people are born to be masters and others are born "by nature" to be slaves. I've always wondered jokingly if real plantation owners would quote Aristotle's theory if asked why they owned slaves. I had wanted to pose the question to Sister Donnelly since she first picked up the phone.

Her answer had nothing to do with history. It was a surprisingly simple conversation. Her family was lazy, she said. "They were what you would call gentleman farmers."

"What does that mean?"

"White people who didn't want to do much of the actual work."

Before we hung up, I agreed to send her a copy of the Crawford article on Charlie Hayden and a $50 check for a copy of her book. A few days later, the package arrived in the mail along with a three-page typed letter, folded in half inside the front flap. She said she found the story about Charlie enlightening and was thrilled to hear he had a street named after him. "I've been in Danville many times and I wish I had met him," she wrote.

Apparently, after we had spoken, she went through a folder of some of her unpublished records on the Haydens and found that the Gus I was looking for was actually named Augustus, son of Joseph Hayden and Sallie Haskins, who emigrated from St. Mary's County, Maryland, to what later became Marion County, Kentucky, in 1782. In her letter she wrote that Augustus died in 1888 and on his death certificate the family wrote the name Gus.

I had one more Hayden family member to meet in Lebanon. Winnie Robinson was a first cousin to Ezra and Charlie. A distant relative had heard through the grapevine that I had met with Charlie and didn't want me to leave the state without talking to her aunt. Mrs. Robinson's father was Austin's older brother Charlie, after whom the Charlie in Danville was named. Both Austin and the senior Charlie were owned by Gus. Mrs. Robinson was the youngest girl of the fourteen children and the last of Charlie's children still living.

"You need to get the full story of the Haydens," said Ruby Hyde, who put me in contact with her aunt. She was very vague during our initial conversation in the lobby of a Holiday Inn in Louisville. "She'll tell it like it is."

Mrs. Robinson, eighty-seven, lived in a low-rent, single-story public housing complex across from a senior citizen home. The apartment units were separated by a cool, brightly lit, cement hallway. A short, skinny woman who looked no more than sixty, opened the door wearing a blue polyester skirt suit and brown house slippers. She seemed happy to have a visitor and was a talker. She was also very nice and offered to bake some chocolate chip cookies next time I was in town and came to see her. While I still felt as if I was breaking an unwritten family code of silence, I let my curiosity get the best of me. I decided to ask the Gus question once and let it go if she didn't answer.

"Was Gus the father of some of the black Haydens? I heard that maybe—"

She jumped in to finish the sentence.

"Gus is the father of all the children on that side. He started the generation," she said referring to Austin's line.

"Charlie?"

"Yep."

"Willie?"

"Yep."

"Ezra?"

"Gus was his father."

She went on to include her side of the family.

"See some of my sisters was black because my daddy was black, but there were others who were light."

Playing devil's advocate, I pointed out that if her mother was light, which she was, then the same parents might have children with varying complexions. She had a come back ready for me. "There's a white lady that lives right behind me down the hall. She's a Hayden and she comes down here all the time and we talk about the Haydens. We always say that we probably are family. She talks about her Hayden family, how they were good but don't stir them up. Same thing with my Hayden family—they were good but don't stir them up because they had hot tempers."

I immediately asked for the apartment number. I told Mrs. Robinson I'd be right back and made a beeline down the corridor. No one answered. I called several times from Mrs. Robinson's apartment and left messages, but nothing. After about an hour of waiting for her neighbor, whose name was still on the tip of her tongue, to return, no luck. That's okay, I thought to myself. I knew enough.

6

Kentucky

"I Found Ray Charles"

I changed my flight at the last minute to stay in Kentucky an extra week. A couple of days after I got back from Lebanon, I received an e-mail out of the blue about a 101-year-old woman living in Mayfield, less than five hours from where I was staying. Both of her parents had been slaves. In the e-mail, her neighbor Ray wrote, "She lives by herself, is very independent, and clear as a bell." I was excited to have a new interview on my list after an exhausting wild-goose chase across the state that had left me with nothing to show for it.

The day before, I'd driven three hours to Henderson to talk to a reverend whose name I found in the booklet on Kentucky centenarians I'd brought with me, only to Scotch tape a note inside his screen door because no one was home. Showing up in person was the only way to get in contact with him because he didn't own a phone and the street address was all I had to go on.

On the three-hour trip back, I stopped at Baskin-Robbins to treat myself to Pralines 'n Cream with extra rainbow sprinkles to celebrate making it there and back without any problems. Falling asleep at the wheel had become a big concern as I stayed up later and later to transcribe tapes and got up early to hit the road. Ice cream triggered happy memories for me. When we were little Mom treated us to it once a week after school on the way to ballet and tap-dance lessons. Wearing pink leotards and pink tights, Kwanza (Sheria wasn't born yet), her friend Beth Lasher, and I would run inside and run out with our ice cream cones dripping down the side of our hands, licking and laughing in the backseat of our station wagon until we got to the dance studio, when my mood always changed for the worse.

Kwanza and Beth—who was white, though I didn't realize it then—were the same age, so they were in the same dance class. I was by myself in a different age group—a black girl in a room full of white girls who didn't want to stand next to me. I'd smile when they looked in my direction in the wall mirror as we did our pliés; I wanted them to see I was a nice person. But it never worked. They continued to ignore me, giggled and pointed at me during breaks when the dance instructor turned her back to change the music. I was confused as to why girls who didn't know me seemed not to like me. After watching a film on the civil rights movement in school one day, I wondered if their attitude towards me had something to do with whites not liking blacks.

It was Black History Month. My first grade teacher, Mrs. Ober, played the short documentary before lunch. Being the only black person in the room, I thought it would be fun to watch a movie about black people. Surely I would get extra attention from the teacher and other students during the Q&A session as the one with the most experience on the subject.

Boy, did I get a huge wake-up call. First, the civil rights documentary didn't make any sense. Blacks had to sit in the back of the bus because they were black? I got more confused when the narrator talked about how blacks weren't allowed to go to the same schools as whites, drink out of the same fountain, or vote.

What was going on? Why were adults doing such mean things? Clips of dogs attacking children? No, that couldn't be. Police hitting women with baseball bats?

While the scenes burned to memory a story of white against black, I started to feel uncomfortable sitting Indian style in the dark next to my best friend, Billy. If my parents were on one side then that meant her parents were on the other, right? Did Billy's parents do those things in the movie? Frustrated and confused, I stopped watching; I was almost in tears and it was only a movie.

As I backed out of the Baskin-Robbins parking lot, I wondered when the parents of the people I was speaking to told their children about slavery. What age was old enough to know your history? I thought first grade was too young, and it was too soon for me to think I couldn't chase Matt and John at recess because I was black and they were white; I was still trying to figure out why they ran in the first place.

I made it to Mayfield in no time. The old and new sections of town were divided by railroad tracks. A sprawl of McDonald's, Lowe's, and a Wal-Mart that stretched on for three lights overlooked a vacant downtown filled with empty redbrick storefronts with FOR LEASE signs posted in the display windows.

As I drove south on Mott, a one-way street with more stop signs than cars, I looked for Calvary Presbyterian Church. The neighbor who sent me the e-mail on Mrs. Wilson mentioned it as a landmark at the intersection of 4th Street and Mott. I found the church and rattled over another set of railroad tracks into the black section of town.

What earlier had been an abandoned street now held three children on bicycles watched by adults sitting on lawn chairs in a front yard. I asked a man with newly parted cornrows where Mrs. Wilson lived. He pointed to a light-green house with white shutters at the end of the street, where a landscaper was busy working. The man, who had just finished cutting the grass and was starting on the hedges with garden clippers, stood out because he was the only white guy around.

I parked on the street across from the driveway. A tall woman with short brownish-red hair opened the screen door and waited for me to cross the lawn. We hugged. She introduced herself as Mrs. Wilson's daughter Alice, a teacher from New Jersey, who happened to be visiting her mother that week.

Behind her, an elderly woman was slowly making her way toward the door. For balance she held the back of a recliner, grabbed a corner of the kitchen table, then reached for her daughter's arm, which was already stretched out in her direction. Mrs. Wilson's smile grew wider the closer she got to the door. In the final steps, her smile turned into the kind my mom gave when I came home from college for the holidays and she was standing in the door waiting for me to get out of the car. We hugged too.

"Sana, this is my mom," Alice said. Mrs. Wilson was a tiny woman with a clear, baby-smooth complexion with very few wrinkles and large dark brown eyes. She wore a bouffant gray wig and had on bright red lipstick.

Alice went into the kitchen to make a pitcher of iced tea as I curled my right arm for Mrs. Wilson to hold on to. Together, we walked back to her recliner in the living room. She still hadn't said anything, yet she couldn't keep her eyes off me. After she sat down, I left Mrs. Wilson grinning in my direction to reach into my bag to grab the tape recorder. To break the silence, I made small talk about how happy I was to be there. Finally she spoke.

"You drove here by yourself? No one came with you?"

I reached to take the glass of tea from her daughter. "Just me and my map."

"You just get up and go," she said, looking straight at me. "They say that what you have, if you don't use it, you lose it. And Sana, you ain't gonna lose nothing. You're like me." It was the nicest thing anyone had said to me in months. "You're speaking to one of the oldest women you can talk to with good sense. My mind is as sharp as the day I was born. If it wasn't for my legs, I'd be dancing, but I can still tap my toes."

I complimented her on how great she looked, and she wanted me to know that at 101 she still had all her hair. "Down my back if I let it out." She used the wig because it was too much work to comb, brush, and braid her hair every day. "Got it from my mother. She was Indian."

Alice walked back into the kitchen, leaving us alone in the living room, where a built-in glass china cabinet was overshadowed by surrounding bookshelves bearing two complete sets of *Encyclopaedia*

Britannica on one side and a *World Book Encyclopedia* set on the oppo-site wall. I recognized the third set without my glasses because Dad bought the same brown set with gold-dipped pages for our family room.

I was shocked. The fact that I didn't know her mother was Native American led me to confess how little background research I'd done. So, beginning with an easy starter question—What do you remember about your mother?—we began talking.

Born around 1845, mother Fannie was Cherokee Indian. Her owner was James "Hampton" Watts, a stocky Virginian, from Halifax County. In mid-1850, thirty-six-year-old Hampton left Old Domin-ion for Western Kentucky because the U.S. government was giving away land in the newly settled Indian territory.

Along with his first wife, Hampton built a new home around Bal-timore in Graves County. Thanks to public land grants given to settlers who agreed to cultivate the land, he owned so much virgin terrain that the family bragged he couldn't cover his land in one day on horseback. After clearing farmland, Hampton did so well for himself in summer crops that his brother William wrote a letter from Halifax County on November 15, 1850, agreeing to join him after the winter. In the letter William said he couldn't travel "this faul" because "my Negro woman had increased her family in a time that it would not be [good] to carry her on the road." He had a family of twelve, including himself and his wife, five children and the slave "fellow woman and child."

William's letter said that times were hard in Virginia for farmers in 1850. "We had Drouth here this summer from the first of June to the first of September," William wrote. "The wheat bug were very numerous they destroyed the Crops of Wheat in some places." Prices for everything went up: sugar, tobacco, oats, wheat, corn "per Barl" and slaves. "Negroes is higher than you ever saw them in your life... Negro boys and girls is selling from $800 to $1000. Men from $1000 to $1200."

Mrs. Wilson said Baltimore was the place to go to buy and sell your slave. Auctions were held every third Monday. "My mother said they'd stand you on the stage naked and feel your breast and abs, look up your butt hole." Fannie was never sold at auction, but when she was seven, Hampton assigned her to his oldest son John Robert, nicknamed "Bruzz." He was only two-years-old at the time. In all Hampton had seven children by four wives and enough slaves to give each child one of his or her own.

Every few minutes, Alice stuck her head into the room to ask her mom if she needed anything. Listening intensely with my chest leaning on a light stand in between us, I took short breaks, sitting back in the chair to give my spine a rest. I'd noticed over the past couple of months that I was having problems hearing and needed to watch Mrs. Wilson's lips move to see the sounds she was making in order to catch every word.

Like her answer to the question, Where was your dad from? At first I didn't think I heard her right.

"My daddy was real dark and came from Africa."

"On some level we all did," I responded in jest, brushing aside an answer that I thought was more of a general comment that slaves came from Africa. I repeated the question and she gave the same answer—even after I hinted that it didn't make sense. While neither the family nor I could find outside confirmation that her father was from Africa, there was also the fact that he was born around 1840, four decades after Congress banned the slave trade in 1808. I thought she remembered wrong.

But what I didn't know then was that the 250 year old slave trade continued off the books as late as 1860. The government turned a blind eye to ships that landed here by what ship captains called "accidents," citing excuses like bad weather conditions, or ship repairs or restocking of supplies. In fact, fifty thousand slaves were illegally smuggled into the United States from 1808 to 1860. It could have been possible Mrs. Wilson's father was one of them; I thought there was something sad in never knowing the answer.

Mrs. Wilson's father, Wesley Hopkins, was first owned by a man in Virginia, who also later settled in Kentucky. Wesley was then sold in Baltimore to W. W. Hopkins and his wife Lucy, a farming family living in a small nearby town called Wingo. "My father said there was a colored man who stayed down there and when girls got old enough to have babies, they would send them to him until they got pregnant. Then they would sell the child."

I was surprised Wesley told his daughter about something so morally infuriating. Dads are usually silent, protective types who speak up when, say, asked for money. In my experience they typically shy away from discussing real life with daughters. I said what I was thinking, and Mrs. Wilson immediately corrected me. Her father didn't tell her about owners breeding slaves. She overheard it.

As a curious young girl, Mrs. Wilson used to eavesdrop on conversations her dad had with his friends—that's how she knew much of what she did about slavery. "I used to hear my parents talk about it with other adults, but not with us."

That was not the first time someone said their parents didn't openly discuss slavery with them. Early in my research, I got a similar report from a family of three in D.C.—one son and two daughters— whose father had fought in the 45th Union Infantry Regiment. The fading, ninety-plus-year-old siblings recalled watching their father through a screen door, sitting on a rocking chair on the porch, talking to his cousins about slavery.

When I asked if he talked with them about it, the answer was no.

I didn't press them to expound because I thought I knew why what it was: shame. It was a fairly common psychological reaction as recorded by a number of researchers who studied groups such as survivors of torture in Chile under the Pinochet regime and those imprisoned in Nazi camps, for example. A former house slave in her nineties interviewed in North Carolina in 1937 was quoted as saying, "My folks don't want me to talk about slavery, they's shamed niggers ever was slaves."

But now I wondered if there was more to this than shame or embarrassment. It seemed as if parents were comfortable talking about slavery with other adults, just not with their own children. Interested in getting to the bottom of it, I shared my puzzlement with Mrs. Wilson.

Alice had reentered the room by this time and stepped in to respond. "Mother is missing a lot of information. Abusive things that had to do with being sold." While Alice explained, Mrs. Wilson nodded in support. "Those facts her parents didn't tell her."

"Why not?" I asked.

"Because it would mean that we were defeated before we start. If you tell a child that the people they see on the street, those people used to own me and did this and that, who wouldn't be angry?"

At first I thought maybe Wesley and Fannie were progressive parents. Then again, all they wanted to do was to make life easier for their children. Supportive parents do that. Why should they have been different because they were slaves? They made a conscious decision not to discuss what they suffered themselves during slavery because they didn't want Mrs. Wilson to grow up bitter. Right or wrong, the goal was to put the best interests of their child first. Their hearts were in the right place. No parent wants to see a child go through life filled with anger and hate.

As Mrs. Wilson and Alice discussed what to have for dinner, I flashed back to a memory of a time soon after I got out of college when my parents chauffeured me around on a Saturday in racially segregated Fort Lee, New Jersey, to find an apartment. Tired, Mom and I sat in the car while Dad walked into a real estate office to ask a question, only to have a broker tell him the office was closed, even though the hours of operation on the door said it was open for another two hours. Dad stayed until another broker helped him, then came back to the car and told us what happened. Mom was about to say out loud what I already knew was going on when Dad looked at her and shook his head no. She didn't say it.

"I thought parents didn't tell their kids about slavery because they were ashamed or embarrassed," I finally said to Mrs. Wilson.

"If they told me everything they had gone through, I wouldn't have wanted to do it."

"Do what?"

"Work for white people. Be around them. Send my girls to school with them."

Alice commented. "They wanted mom to create her own view of the world in her own surroundings....The people she liked, the people she didn't like. My mother did that with us. If her parents told her and her brothers and sisters everything about slavery, it would have been harder for them. They knew that."

Mrs. Wilson wasn't told the details of the bad things that happened to her parents as slaves, and she didn't know the good either. Long after her father died, a local historian named Lon Carter Barton was the first to tell her that her father fought in the Civil War. Wesley was one of approximately 40,000 black soldiers from the border states who enlisted in the Union Army after Abraham Lincoln's Emancipation Proclamation went into effect on January 1, 1863, inviting blacks to join Northern troops. Wesley walked off the Hopkins plantation to enlist in the Eighth Regiment, Company C, stationed in Paducah, Kentucky, about thirty-five miles away. He was twenty-four when he was mustered in the summer of 1864

Wesley returned to Kentucky to marry Fannie in May of 1868. Mrs. Wilson didn't know exactly how her parents had met, but she remembered her mom telling her that they'd met before the war in Baltimore. They had thirteen children on a farm south of Mayfield. Mrs. Wilson was the last of the bunch, born in 1900 when her mother was fifty.

When I asked her about growing up in the South, she told me about the terror she felt facing former slave owners desperate to hold on to their past. "They didn't like it when colored people got freed so they still had third Monday to terrorize us," said Mrs. Wilson, referring to the time in the month slaves were auctioned. "Whites would come around and shoot at houses."

One night when Mrs. Wilson was ten, a lynch mob of "Night Riders" surrounded her home, calling for her father to come outside. "I'll never forget," Mrs. Wilson said. Her mother fell on her knees and started praying. Wesley got his gun. "My father said, 'I'm not coming out, but you all could come in.' They got the message and left." Another time, her brothers went to a night concert and got caught coming home late on a third Monday. "They made my brothers dance until they fell out. They came home with holes on the bottom of their shoes."

When she was twelve, her father died after catching pneumonia from walking two miles in the winter to visit his niece. He was eighty-two. That same year, in 1912, Mrs. Wilson started to work outside the home doing housework with her mom because the family, which consisted of just the two of them by then, needed money. When Mrs. Wilson wasn't cooking in white people's homes, she suckered and wormed tobacco on the days a neighbor was too sick to work in the fields. In addition to school, she got private tutoring lessons from a teacher who rented a room in the house.

In 1928 Mrs. Wilson married and eventually had four children before she and her husband separated in 1965. "You see all of those books?" She pointed to the rows of bookshelves that gave the living room a library feel. "I bought music encyclopedias and plain encyclopedias. A white teacher said I was beating them with school." The music books alone cost $100. That was a lot of money considering Mrs. Wilson was making $5.00 an hour for much of her career as a "filth cleaner." Those were her words. She washed clothes, cleaned spit up as a nanny, and took care of patients with urinary incontinence as a night nurse. "Sometimes I'd get up out of bed and go over to wash dishes late after a party and get $10 an hour. I found Ray Charles those days."

"What does that mean?" I asked.

"You hit something good."

There was an innocent frankness and honesty about Mrs. Wilson that made listening fun. She spoke openly about herself in a way that made me alternately comfortable and at times surprisingly awkward, especially when she referred to herself as a nigger. I didn't expect to be sensitive to this since rappers and comedians use this racial slur more than anyone else. But this was the first time I'd heard it from someone old enough to have been called one by whites—who certainly weren't using it to be friendly.

Ms. Wilson kept calling herself a "white person's nigger." She said it once, then a second, third, and fourth time. I ignored it at first, hoping it would go away. But she kept bringing it back up.

"Why do you call yourself that?" I finally asked.

"Because that's what colored folks called me and my kids growing up."

"Why would they call you that?"

"They said I was cleaning doo-doo for pickles children." Translation: She was a nanny for white parents. "But I couldn't have done better if I had a college degree."

I couldn't go on without asking her what a pickle was.

"They'd call white folks pickle just like they called me a nigger." I asked her what she'd do when blacks called her that.

"First, I cried," she admitted. Tired of blacks picking on her, she actually thought of quitting her cleaning jobs. But she didn't. Amidst the around-the-clock runny noses and dirty diapers, she took full advantage of the job and her bosses. "I had what they needed and they had what I needed."

"What did you need from them?"

"Money. I needed it to educate my children. I told them I would give them a damn good chance."

And she did. She sent all four children to college with the help of scholarships. She bragged for the next few minutes that her children, "wore the nicest clothes I could buy. They didn't want for nothing." A newspaper reporter asked her once where all her energy came from. She told her, "I slept fast. Got up early and went to bed late."

Because we were spending so much time talking about her children, I took the opportunity to ask about successful parenting and raising good kids. Why did she think freed slaves, who started their lives with nothing, and children of freed slaves, who had little more than that, were able to raise college-bound kids? And how do they compare to today's poor who have a hard time keeping children in school and out of jail?

This was a persistent question for me. For a long time the answer given by black leaders and poverty experts has been that you can't expect low-income, uneducated, disadvantaged parents to be able to inspire their children to do better. I question now if that assumption was true. I don't think Mrs. Wilson believed it. She believed what was holding a lot of children back was not that disadvantaged parents couldn't improve the lives of their children, but that most didn't want to.

"Some have no fighting heart. If their children do equal that's okay. They don't strive for those children to do better." Years later, I was reminded of her comment during a conversation with a volunteer at a charter school in Harlem. An eighth-grade student was accepted to a New England boarding school to start freshman year on full scholarship, but his mother told him to turn it down. Surprised by the decision, the school board asked why she didn't want her son to go to one of the most prestigious high schools in the country. The mom responded, "Because he'll think he is better than us."

It was getting late. I decided not to stay for dinner but instead to spend the last hour of daylight finding a hotel. After throwing my notebook and tape recorder into my bag, I held Mrs. Wilson's hand as we walked to the den to tell her daughter I was headed out. Alice, it turned out, was standing near the kitchen table talking to her cousin Ava, down from St. Louis for a visit. She must have just walked in the door because she still had her keys in her hand, jacket on, and pocketbook on her shoulder. Dressed in jeans and a dark blue T-shirt, Ava reminded me of skinny Natalie Cole when she was on the *Thankful* album cover. Trying to remember the words on the eight-track Kwanza and I used to sing to on the way to Grandma's house, I briefly introduced myself, and continued toward the door'. ". . . '*Cause love is soft. Love is sweet. Love is just a little baby.*"

The two of them must have been talking about my visit because Ava wanted to know what was the most important thing I'd learned from Mrs. Wilson before I left. I told her about the new theory as to why most blacks don't know the details of their family's slave history and the idea that parents didn't tell their children about their experience as slaves because they didn't want them to grow up consumed with hate.

"Why were those significant to you?" she asked.

"It made them oblivious to the hate around them. Since they didn't know about the depth of the tension between whites and blacks, it, in a way didn't exist."

"Yes, that's how she raised us, too," said Alice, "We had no clue." Alice and Ava suddenly started laughing, obviously at some private joke. I only caught a couple of words: high school and integration. I joined the laughter, not really knowing what was funny. Then I pulled out my tape recorder and asked them to explain.

In the summer of the 1954 Supreme Court ruling on desegregation, they had read a newspaper story on the decision. They'd just graduated from eighth grade and started to tease each other that they were going to the white high school in the fall for freshman year. They didn't read anything into the ruling other than that the law said they could go to the white school. Some friends backed out, but for others it had become a dare.

"There must have been about ten or twelve of us. We walked into the high school that September and the secretary went ballistic. From that point on," Ava said, "all hell broke loose."

The principal met with the Mayfield board of education and city council to complain. But there was nothing they, nor he, could do. He had to let them attend school or risk breaking the law.

Sitting in her recliner, Mrs. Wilson tilted her head up to look at her daughter standing behind the chair, smiling but not saying a word.

"We all were like dumb donuts—that's how oblivious and unafraid we were," Alice said, as she told the story of walking to the first day of class with her baby sister, Dorothy. As they got closer to the school, they saw state troopers had blocked off the street. "I said, 'Dorothy, what's up with all these police cars?' She said, 'I don't know. I wonder what's going on.'"

On the front lawn across the street from the building, white students and parents hollered in demonstration. They yelled whatever they could think of: "nigger," "go home," "big slut."

"Did you want to turn around and go home?" I asked.

"No. We left the protesters standing outside and went to first-period class."

What they didn't know at the time was that their parents and friends were close by in cars, ready in case it was necessary to get them out of there fast.

I turned to Mrs. Wilson. "You weren't scared for your daughters?"

"They wanted to do it."

"We didn't even know what we were doing," Alice jumped in.

That first year wasn't easy. Students and teachers called the new students stupid; said they smelled; yelled that the only thing blacks were good at was making babies. "They couldn't understand that I could make an A while they made an F. We knew we had the ability, but they didn't know. They didn't know that we could do better. Not as well, but better," said Alice.

Mayfield was one of the first public high schools in Kentucky to officially desegregate in the fall of 1954. Soon after, in order to desegregate the entire city, the school district changed all the housing zones for schools statewide to be integrated automatically, Alice recalled. Up until that point the state had taken a "wait and see" approach to the Supreme Court decision. "People say, 'How could this happen in this little town within two years of the Supreme Court ruling?' They are just flabbergasted when I tell them what we did." Alice said. "We just didn't know how much whites hated us and didn't want us there."

"If you knew, would you have still done it?"

"I'm not sure. I definitely would have thought twice."

Mrs. Wilson had her own moment in the spotlight in 1984 when the local newspaper, The Mayfield Messenger, ran a feature profile of her life, in which she mentioned that her mother had been a slave for a man named Watts in Baltimore. At the time she didn't know his first name. After the story ran, Mrs. Wilson got a call from a Messenger subscriber, Gertrude Grey, from Wingo. Mrs. Grey recognized the last name as that of her great-grandfather, who was the only wealthy Watts in Baltimore and who had owned a lot of slaves.

Mrs. Grey invited Mrs. Wilson over for a visit and she accepted. They talked most of the afternoon.

"It didn't make you uncomfortable going to visit her?" I asked.

"No. Should it have?"

When they got together, Mrs. Wilson realized they actually had met before, when they were both kids.

"After slavery ended, her grandmother didn't know how to keep house. She'd had slaves doing it for her family all her life. Watts hired my mom to teach her to do that stuff, wash clothes and cook meals. I used to go with my mom to their house. We were about the same age."

After that first time, they continued to visit each other off and on. "We saw each other a lot more when my legs were better and I could drive. She used to call here every Christmas and send me a card." They'd talk about the Watts family history, comparing notes. Sometimes, Mrs. Wilson said, she'd remember things Mrs. Grey had never heard before. But for the most part Mrs. Grey knew more about the Watts history—places, names, dates.

I was curious to meet Mrs. Grey as well. The next day, I went to the local library and tracked down her phone number in Wingo. We spoke briefly on the phone, and she said I could drop by the following afternoon.

She lived about fifteen miles southwest of Mrs. Wilson, so I dropped by Mrs. Wilson's on the way there to say "hi." When I told her I was going to visit Mrs. Grey, she told me she was going too. Actually, she told me she'd get her coat.

"I'm not sure if I can take you, Mrs. Wilson."

"Why? I'm old enough. I can still make my own decisions."

It wasn't that I didn't want to take her along. I didn't know if her daughter, who had gone back to New Jersey, wanted her to get in the car with me. I planned on being gone for several hours and all I could think of was my grandmother and how protective I am of her around strangers. But I couldn't say no.

"How about this? I need to get gas. When I get back, I'll call your daughter at work and see what she says."

"I don't need her permission," she reminded me.

"I know, but it would make me feel better if she knew where you were headed and said it was okay."

I was gone for an hour, thinking that she might have lost interest by then. But when I opened the screen door, she had changed into a crisp blue oxford with a stiffly starched collar. She'd put on different pants, tan Dockers, and had on red lipstick and gold clip-on earrings. She'd changed out of her slippers into her shoes, found her walking cane, and already had a jacket on. She was ready to go.

"My daughter is waiting for you to call her. I told her I was going with you."

She'd written the phone number on a pad near the phone, and before I could say anything, Alice laughed. "Well, if she wants to go and it's okay with you."

"It would be nice to have company actually."

"I don't know how much you will be able to get out of Mrs. Grey. She's been sick," Alice warned.

I hung up the phone after agreeing to have her mom call when we got back.

"I told you. I can go wherever I want. She can't tell me where to go. Do you know where you are going?"

When we arrived, I knocked on Mrs. Grey's door a couple times and peeped through the front window. I was looking for a doorbell when she answered.

I told her that I had a surprise in the car and went to help Mrs. Wilson walk across the grass. She'd already grabbed her cane from the backseat and was headed to the front steps. But Mrs. Grey didn't recognize her when she got there. It was odd. I introduced Mrs. Wilson at the door and still no reaction. No more than a stranger's welcome.

We went inside. I asked Mrs. Grey if she could tell me about her family and the people who owned Fannie, Mrs. Wilson's mom.

"Who?"

"Fannie. This is Fannie's daughter, Mrs. Jennie Wilson." I pointed to Mrs. Wilson, who was sitting across from me on Mrs. Grey's right in a lounge chair, holding her cane between her legs.

"You know, Mrs. Wilson. She came over to your house and you two talked about how her mother used to cook and clean for your grandmother."

"My grandmother Mullins, she was a Watts. Her daddy was Hampton Watts. I think we need some hearing aids. Let me get them. I usually don't have them on unless I have company because I don't talk to myself."

Mrs. Grey hunched out of the recliner and walked to the kitchen. I looked over at Mrs. Wilson and she was shaking her head and grinning, making a small circle in the air around her ear with one hand.

"She's gotten old," Mrs. Wilson said. "I'll be 102 in January and I'm in better shape. She doesn't remember a thing."

Mrs. Grey walked back into the room and didn't look in Mrs. Wilson's direction, only at me.

"Okay, Mrs. Grey, let's start from the top. Your grandmother's brother, Bruzz Watts, used to own her mother."

"Who was your mother?" She turned to Mrs. Wilson.

"Fannie. She was a Native American Indian. I used to come down here all the time. It came out in the papers that my mother was a slave under Watts. I used to come down here quite often when you was younger and sometimes you would give me vegetables."

"Well, Granny Mullins's daddy was Hampton Watts. He married two, no three times and he kept marrying younger women and they took all his money. He was a pauper when he died and he had been well-to-do. He owned slaves and he moved from Baltimore to Dublin County."

"Well, he owned my mother cause she said they brought her here."

We sat as Mrs. Grey tried to put the pieces together herself as we went along.

"Who was your mother?"

"Fannie."

"There was a woman who lived over near Calvary Presbyterian Church, and Grandpa had to get her once a week to teach Granny how to cook and keep the house. Granny Mullins had slaves do that for her. She'd say that she never even made the bed she slept on. She always had that proud thing about her where she was brought up not to do nothing."

"This is after they freed the slaves, right?" I started to help her along.

"Yes. Now that was Granny Mullins' daddy, and she didn't know how to do nothing when she married cause he had a bunch of slaves. So she got Grandpa Mullins to get this freed slave to come and teach Granny how to cook, and how to wash and iron. Papa never forgot her."

Mrs. Grey stopped midsentence and started on another thought. "When I was a child, we would go to Mayfield in a wagon in the fall and in the spring. My dad would always stop when we got up there around Calvary. We would stop at a colored woman's house and take her something to eat. It might be fruit, cheese and crackers, or something else."

Mrs. Wilson and I looked at each other and nodded as if we knew not to say anything else, just let Mrs. Grey ride out her thought process because she was coming around to figuring out whom Mrs. Wilson was.

"He would buy her something when he was in Mayfield and he would stop there and give it to her. I asked Mama when I got older, I said, 'Mama, who was the colored woman Papa would always stop by and bring her fruit?' And she said, 'Well hun, that woman raised your Granny Mullins.' I can still see them little colored children peeping around the back of the house when we came by. Of course we were afraid of the colored and I guess they were afraid of us."

"What was the name of the colored woman you used to drop by to see?" I was trying to trick her into saying the same name Mrs. Wilson and I had been saying for the past twenty minutes.

"They called her Fannie."

Gotcha, I thought to myself.

"That was my mother," Mrs. Wilson shouted and sat up in her chair.

"Pardon."

"Fannie was my mother."

Mrs. Wilson looked at me and nodded. She was getting tired. We'd been going back and forth for almost two hours. As we got up to leave, Mrs. Grey asked us to come back for lunch the next day. I politely asked for a rain check and thanked her for her hospitality.

I walked out of the house with a lot more information than I knew going in. Though it was draining to pull information out of Mrs. Grey, it was worth it to hear history from the other side. After we got into the car, Mrs. Wilson said, "I think she's lost her mind and I am older than she is."

The interview with Mrs. Wilson inspired me to track down another Mayfield local, the historian, Mr. Barton. Mrs. Wilson mentioned his name so many times that at first I thought he was a member of the family. He was the one who went to D.C. to research Mrs. Wilson's father's Civil War history as a personal project. He filled out the paperwork for her children to receive veteran family scholarships to college. He did this, he did that. Mrs. Wilson just raved about him so that I wanted to meet to exchange research notes.

Mr. Barton, a retired history professor from the University of Kentucky, lived in the new section of town in a white Dutch colonial two-story with a Confederate machete in the entrance hallway—an artifact he inherited from his great-uncle, who found it. He was soft-spoken and lived alone except for a housekeeper who was the same woman his parents hired to babysit him as a child.

We sat in his living room as I told him about my travels, and he told me of the importance of primary resources to get a story straight. He wanted to hear about my searches so far and how I found subjects.

After an hour of him asking me very specific questions about things like the order of my upcoming interviews, which I didn't know, it was his turn to talk about his research. To my surprise he revealed that when he was a college student at Murray State in the 1940s, he had interviewed the last living slave in Graves County for a class project. In a county that once had three thousand slaves, Barry Blythe, known around Graves County as Uncle Burly, was the last one alive. As Mr. Barton started to tell the story of his interview with Uncle Burly, he got off the couch and sat on the floor in front of me with his legs crossed. To be part of his experience, I leaned in, my knees at the height of his chest. "I made eight trips to talk to him because he was in good physical condition. His mind was excellent. Uncle Burly was close to 100 then and willing to tell all." This should be good, I thought.

Uncle Burly told Mr. Barton that he was separated from his mother and father when he was eight years old. His whole family had been together up to that point. When it was broken up, he went to Callaway County to the home of Zachariah Blythe at Linn Grove, who was quite a political figure at the time. That was where he spent most of his slave days until he was freed at fifteen. "Anyway, Zachariah Blythe turns out to be Bill Clinton's great-great uncle. Bill Clinton's birth name was William Jefferson Blythe and his father was a descendant of Zachariah Blythe's brother, Andrew Anthony."

I knew from the progressive pace of his voice he was leading me somewhere but didn't see that one coming. Like the car crash in the season-six *Alias* finale, this Clinton kicker came from out of the blue. But that was all he could remember from the interview—that Uncle

Burly was connected to President Clinton. He had lost the transcripts some years ago and was unsuccessful in finding the actual paper.

Admittedly, I was disappointed. What happened to Uncle Burly as a slave was a question he couldn't answer. Then it occurred to me why I wanted to hear more. Maybe I had a warped curiosity, like staring at a highway accident and then driving off thanking God it wasn't you. I wanted to hear the bad and the ugly that happened to him to understand, for lack of a better word, the level of slavery he had experienced. What kind of person was I? Did I really need to hear how many times Uncle Burly was whipped in order to believe slavery was cruel and barbaric? Or that he was starved? Or maimed?

That night, dialing the toll-free number Dad set up so we wouldn't have to pay long distance to call home, I spoke to my parents. Mom likes us to call her on Sunday night so we can tell her nothing has changed from the last time we spoke. Dad got on the phone to ask if I could help with the drive to Pittsburgh the next week to drop Sheria off at college.

Before he got sick, he drove solo to all of the Butler girl college moves, refusing to let anyone else take the wheel even for fourteen-hour drives, with stops only for gas, bathroom breaks, and food.

Secretly proud that Dad asked me, and ignoring his rationale that I was the only daughter with a flexible schedule, I said, "yes," without hesitation. I hung up the phone and went to bed that night resolved that I didn't really need proof of the horrors of slavery. If nothing else happened to Uncle Burly, he was auctioned away from his mother and father. For me that would have been torture enough.

7

Kentucky

PIT STOPS

There must be something in the water in Kentucky. The list of people to interview there just kept growing.

I reached over to the passenger seat to pick up the *National Geographic* road atlas of all fifty states purchased at the last gas station fill-up. Opened to the Kentucky page, the map showed the way to Cerulean as Route 24 east. I drove past Benton, Grand Rivers, Eddyville, and Princeton with almost no traffic. Rain clouds in the morning cleared midway through the trip to a brilliant blue sky around Land Between the Lakes.

Cerulean was a small town, population 1,100, and the home of 106-year-old Leslie Dixon. Her name appeared on page 15 of the handy-dandy Kentucky centenarian booklet along with her picture and the phone number to her daughter's house where she lived. The book also included seven other possible interview candidates whom I tried to contact with no success.

Mrs. Dixon's daughter Larue gave directions as best she could without knowing her street address off the top of her head because she said no one went by house numbers in her town. Mailing a letter to Cerulean was as easy as writing only the person's name on the envelope. The local post office would know where to deliver it.

After a left onto Route 128, I was told to look for the town sign. "What do I do after that?" I asked.

"When you see someone, ask for my husband James—everyone knows him."

Pulling off to the side of the dirt road in front of a one-lane bridge that crossed a creek, I studied the map. The city limit should be nearby. But there was nothing around—not even another car to ask for help. I continued driving straight. Eventually, the road opened to a Field of Dreams, rolling cornfields and farmland as far as the eye could see. I came across a patch of cleared land on the right, where a lone red house with a white porch swing had a blue Chevy in the driveway. Larue had said she lived in a red house. But she didn't say anything about being surrounded by cornstalks. I parked behind the Chevy and got out to knock on the front door. No one answered. I knocked again. Again, no answer.

I decided this must be the wrong red house because Larue should've been expecting me. I quickly got back into my rental car and pulled off, waving—just in case someone was scared by a stranger at the door and was peeking out the window through the blinds. A half a mile down the corn patch, at a fork in the road, I came upon a white sign with the town name in black uppercase letters. I could no longer go straight unless I wanted to drive into the woods. Should I turn right or left? I did eeny, meeny, miny, moe then turned right.

At another stop sign I saw a man with a Jheri curl riding a lawn mower. I stuck my head out the window to ask for directions to the James's. Sure enough, he knew the name. "He lives up the road in a red house on the hill."

Larue greeted me at the door, and we walked to the back bedroom where Mrs. Dixon was sitting up on the bed dressed in a white silk blouse and grey rayon skirt that covered both her knees. She had lost her legs below the knees in 1997 due to complications of diabetes. Mrs. Dixon kindly offered to share her space on the bed, but Larue gave me a chair, which I pulled up close to the edge.

Mrs. Dixon had picked up the phone when I called last week before driving to see Mrs. Wilson in Mayfield. She told me that her grandfather Henry Wood and mother Louse (pronounced "Louise") had been slaves on the same McKinney plantation in Cave Spring. She then handed the phone to her daughter, who'd been asking "Who was calling?" from the kitchen.

Mrs. Dixon's most recent memory of her grandfather during slavery was when the war was over; he started to pack their belongings for him and his daughter to leave. "Mama always said she saw old missus crying the day they were free. She asked her, What was she crying for? And the missus told her, 'Your Pa is free. We want him to stay on but he said, no, he's going on for himself now.'"

It never failed. No matter how many times I heard a story of the day a slave was told he was free, I got chills. But this was the first time I learned about the day being emotional for the owner's family. I wanted to know more about the McKinneys. I rewound the conversation to get some basic information on her family history. Information that would be helpful when I visited the courthouse archives tomorrow to do research.

"Do you remember the first name of the owner?"

"No, I don't. I never did get that. My grandfather said the first master Woods that owned him was awful cruel to him. He auctioned him off for money and the McKinneys were the highest bidder."

"Did your grandmother live on the same plantation?"

"My grandfather said she passed in slavery from working so hard. He said they had her out there building rail fences like a man. As soon as she took care of her children, they had her back out there cutting trees down and sawing them with the menfolk."

When I asked about her life in Cave Spring, I couldn't get much out of her besides that everyone in the family worked hard all of their lives. When the well in the back of the house ran dry, a young Mrs. Dixon walked "a long ways" with two buckets to the spring in the caves to get water. In the summer she picked blackberries for money to buy buckskin shoes for the winter. "I was thinking about that the other day—all them berries I picked. We sold them for 10 cents a gallon. To think now they are getting $7.00. I've come through a whole lot. I'm telling you, Lord."

But mainly we talked about washing and ironing. "We had a hard way to make a living—made little or nothing." By the age of nine, she and her mother (Mrs. Dixon's father died when she was eighteen months old) cleaned clothes six days a week for whites in the area. For each person the pile would be as high as from the floor to the top of a chair. "Sometimes I wake up now and can hardly roll these fingers, as much washing and ironing I did." And when she said the word ironing, her voice dragged heavy. The solid cast-iron irons, heated directly on the top of a stove, needed a cloth wrapped around the handle because when used it was almost as hot as the flat surface. She said she used a seven-pounder for the shirts and a five-pounder for the collars. "Those irons y'all got now are the saddest."

I didn't know what else to ask. I stopped grasping when I heard myself ask the name of the people she used to iron for to keep the conversation going. She didn't remember. Pointing to a black iron in the corner, she laughed and said, "You kids today wouldn't use that now, would you?" She told me to pick it up. My arm dropped to the floor.

"Likely not, Mrs. Dixon." The iron felt like it weighed more than ten pounds because I made a point not to touch those dumbbells in the gym unless I wanted to sweat.

I had my work cut out for me the next day at the Trigg County courthouse. I didn't have ages or dates of birth for either her grandfather or mother; neither did I know the first name of the McKinney owner.

I stayed one night in Dawson Springs at Rita Ridley's House Bed & Breakfast, a Victorian home ordered from a Sears and Roebuck catalog in 1907. The owner picked the color and design of the first and second floors right from a page. When the house arrived by rail car in 30,000 pieces, it was assembled like Legos.

Rita Ridley's was the least expensive B&B I could find without crossing into Indiana. Most of the night was spent in Rita's room downstairs. I sat in a chair across from her bed in my sweatpants pajamas, talking about life in New York; she described her children and grands pictured on the wall and the moment she knew her husband was the one—a question I love to ask married couples. When I got up to call it a night, she asked what I wanted for breakfast in the morning; then, to my surprise, said she enjoyed my stay so much it was on her.

The courthouse archives were easy to find the next day, but information wasn't. Records were kept in a dark, cool, brick cellar at the bottom of a narrow winding black iron staircase. It didn't look like anyone had been down here to organize or tidy up in decades. Dusty ledgers stacked on top of each other were out of order. Record books of wills and deeds were thrown back on shelves any which way—up right, leaning sideways, or flat.

An employee of the courthouse walked down after I arrived to ask if I needed anything. That was when I learned I could be in the wrong building. Parts of Cave Spring at one point had been called at least five different names that are now spread out in different counties.

"Do you know in which county the person was a slave?"

"No."

"Do you know the name of the owner?

"Just the last—McKinney."

She didn't recognize the name. "Well, good luck," she said, and went back upstairs.

I picked up an 1865 index ledger to look up the last name McKinney to get an idea of how many lived in Trigg County's Cave Spring. There was a page full of McKinneys. If I had more time to sort through them all I would have stayed, but at the looks of things I needed at least a month. I left the basement thinking somewhere amidst the chaos and cobwebs, a family history was lost in the abyss.

I called the next day to tell Larue about the archives drama and that I would try to make it back if I had time. I never did.

Visits like this used to frustrate me when I couldn't find collaborating evidence of a parent being born before 1865. I also used to feel like I wasted time if an interview didn't reveal something profound. Letting go of that was easy because the pressure was turning me into a story Nazi. Once I stopped judging their stories, I had more fun. No strings attached was my new mantra.

It came better late than never; in time for an afternoon with ninety-one year old Jennie Stafford in Louisville. Her daughter Helen, whom she lived with, called to tell me about her mother's father, Union soldier Henry Finn of the 115th Regiment Colored Infantry. He was twenty-two when he ran off a plantation in Franklin in Simpson County to enlist twenty-four miles away at Bowling Green on September 22, 1864.

Mrs. Stafford was a bony woman with small limbs, square jaw, shiny grey hair with white strands, and an Indian-red complexion— inherited from her father. "I wanted to look like my mother. She was a beautiful brown; my daddy, his father was a full-blooded Indian and I didn't like that look."

We talked about how her father came home from the war with a certificate to practice dentistry. He set up a practice in Franklin, pulling teeth. In the rural South that's what happened when children had cavities. There was no such thing as fillings, though they did exist elsewhere at the time. Both my parents know a little about that painful history. They wear partials to eat because they have no teeth in the back of their mouths—but you didn't hear that from me. With a cavity-free mouth all her life, Mrs. Stafford only recently lost her teeth after a heart attack. "I sure do miss them."

We had an audience in the living room for the afternoon. Her daughter sat near the front door and Mrs. Stafford's grandson listened on the carpet near the stairs. Encouraging Mrs. Stafford to talk faster, both of them started to ask questions.

"Did your daddy ever say anything about how he had to live?"

"Was he ever beaten?" the grandson followed up.

"He could bake the best pancakes you ever tasted."

"What did he do, Granny? Did he work in the fields? Did he work with horses?"

"He used to get whippings with switches and straps. Oh Lord, he had a hard way to go. It's no wonder he had stripes all over him."

Then Mrs. Stafford said something I never forgot. She said her father never hit her.

"He could remember that pain. I think that's why I never got a whipping."

The comment stayed with me because my dad used to tell the same story. That his grandfather, who remembered his own father beaten as a slave, would not hit or let anyone hit his children. Not ever. "When we got in trouble with Grandma, we knew to run to him. Sometimes we'd stay glued to his side the entire day," Dad joked. "We knew as long as we were with Papa, Grandma wouldn't use her switch."

For the longest time, all I ever knew was that black parents didn't just hit, but beat their children. As a joke, comedians spread the same notion around—as if the need to beat is so strong there is nothing to do about it but laugh. It is such a well-known trademark even white comedians joke about it. HBO's Bill Maher, during an episode of *Real Time*, laughed that parents proudly tell their teenagers, "I'll beat the black out of you," as a way to keep them in line.

The justification for the beatings gained pseudo-credibility in the legal world in 2004 when a Portland, Oregon, defense attorney cited post-traumatic slave syndrome in defense of his client charged with the beating death of his two-year-old son. The defense claimed that because masters beat their slaves, this conditioned his client to think it was okay to beat his son. The lawyer's argument actually gained pseudo-credibility from college professors who in essence said the father likely didn't know any better; the terror of beatings as punishment by a slave owner had been passed down for generations and was stronger than a parent's ability to make a decision as to when to stop hitting a child. The father was found guilty.

8

Tennessee

INTERRACIAL ADOPTION

When I got back home to Brooklyn, I had twenty-three messages on my answering machine, a handful of letters in my mailbox, and two full screens of new e-mails. Word had spread fast.

But what got me traveling again was a fax from Jerome Orton in Syracuse, New York. Mr. Orton was secretary and treasurer of the Sons of Union Veterans of the Civil War, a nonprofit organization of real sons and daughters of Union soldiers. Over the past decade Mr. Orton had used his own money to design certificates and mail them to new members, as well as to send sympathy cards to families of deceased ones.

His fax included a list of nine people whose fathers had fought against the South. As far as he knew, they were all still alive. "I did not have as much as I thought on Afro-American children of Civil War veterans," he wrote. "Some have died.... I have lost track of a lot them. It is a real shame. I knew quite a few about 10 years ago."

Still in my pajamas, I started making calls early the next morning. I worked my way down the list of names—but almost all the numbers Mr. Orton had given me were disconnected, and I could find no new ones for the people he'd listed. But finally, I got lucky. I dialed a number for Bertha Griffin, one of three daughters of the Rev. Peter Vertrees, a soldier in the Sixth Kentucky Infantry who'd been born in 1840. A woman answered.

"I'm looking for Mrs. Bertha Griffin," I said.

"She's dead, young lady. Died in January." My heart dropped, then rose as the woman added, "I'm her sister, Lillie Odom. Can I help you?"

I explained how I'd gotten her number, and a little about the project.

"You can come down if you want," she said, "but my father wasn't a slave."

How could that be? "Jerome Orton told me that your father was black and was born in 1840. Was he born free?"

"I don't know that, but he wasn't a slave."

I kept pressing until I finally learned that her father was the child of a mixed couple. This wasn't so unusual in and of itself—there were many documented accounts of white owners fathering children with slaves. What was surprising was this: Peter Vertrees was born to a white mother and black father.

Mrs. Odom agreed to see me in person, though she reminded me twice that she had nothing to contribute.

I booked a flight for the following Thursday and spent the extra few days researching the social status of mixed-race children during slavery. Most historians have focused on those who were the product of rape by slave owners where the offspring were almost always born a slave, inheriting the mother's status. But mixed-race children from white women were not slaves but sold as servants until adulthood—after which they were freed. The law, which varied the age to as old as 31 in some states, was designed to punish the mother for miscegenation. In Virginia, an unmarried white woman who gave birth to a mixed-race baby had to pay a fine within 30 days of birth or face indentured servitude for five years. This was the primary source of the increase in free black population in some states in the 17th and 18th century. When Peter was 19, one half of the mixed population lived in upper southern states around the Mason-Dixon line, including Kentucky, Virginia, and Maryland, according to the 1859 census.

I flew to Nashville and drove to a small saloon town called Watertown, about 40 minutes east, where I booked a two-week stay in a railroad hotel that once serviced passengers in the 19th century—the track was just a hundred yards from the front porch. I arrived in the afternoon, put my suitcase in the room adjacent to the newlyweds I shared a hall bath with, and went to look around the historic public square, which resembled an old Western movie set, complete with storefronts with tall brick facades.

Sitting in a gazebo across from The Pickin' Post music store and Nona Lisa's Antiques & Accessories, I called Mrs. Odom on my cell to make plans to meet tomorrow at her house in Gallatin. But when I tried to nail down a time, she said she was too busy. Friday was check day, Saturday was errands, and Sunday was church. We'd planned to meet off and on over the next two weeks, but now she could only do one day. She was only free the upcoming Monday.

The following week, I drove to her house, a blue wood-frame one-story with white lap siding and a narrow front porch. It had a solid brick foundation in the front, which gave way to carefully stacked brick support pillars in the back. Her father built the house in 1888, and it sat in a historic part of town, a few yards from an intersection that now led to a Wal-Mart.

I tapped on the door, and a big-boned woman with dyed blue highlights in her graying brown hair opened it. She gestured for me to come in then turned her back to walk back into the house. "I don't know how much you are going to get out of me," she said as I followed behind in a single file as we walked to the family room in the back. "I'm tired and my knees are bothering me."

I didn't want to intrude on her time because at this point that was what I felt like I was doing, being a nuisance. But then she plopped down onto a sofa—a maroon, brown, and off-white plaid three-seater that was exactly the same as the one in my parents' family room. I took this as a sign to sit down.

"I would love to figure out something and then I will be out of your way. Mr. Orton said your father was in the Union army," I began. "And black Union soldiers were either runaway slaves or free."

"Which side had the gray uniform?" she asked.

"Confederates," I answered.

"Then he was a Confederate."

More questions popped into my head. Did he enlist alongside his owner? Did he have an owner? Was he freed and then asked to join the Confederacy? Did he join on his own? Mrs. Odom, glued to *The Price Is Right*, started to explain her father's complex family arrangements without even looking at me. "Back in that day, a white woman who was not married and who had a child by a colored had to give the baby up to the courts when it turned five," Mrs. Odom told me. "Now that was the law."

"So he didn't grow up with his parents?"

"No." My pedestrian question seemed to annoy Mrs. Odom, as if I was supposed to know the answer already. So I listened without saying a word, nodding my head when I understood a particular detail, putting on a scrunched look of confusion to encourage additional information when I didn't.

This is what I learned: The law required Peter's white mother, Mary "Polly" Elizabeth Skaggs to hand over her son to the courts when he turned five. The court would then send her son to be an indentured servant to anyone in town. The mom didn't want that to happen. She made a special arrangement with the clerk of Edmondson County Court to allow her son to be an indentured servant for the family of the boy's father's father—who was white. The grandfather would rear his grandson as one of the family and "provide the necessities of life," the clerk wrote in the court document. Peter's grandfather, Jacob Vertrees, was a wealthy white plantation owner with slaves. Peter's father, Booker Hardy, was Jacob's illegitimate son, likely a product of a relationship Jacob had with a slave on a relative's nearby Hardy plantation.

Because of the law Polly knew she wasn't going to be able to raise her son herself, but the petition offered the next best thing. "My father was not to be sold, not to be enslaved at all. That is why she carried him to his grandfather," Mrs. Odom said. "He would not have been treated as one of the family if she had not done that."

A rich, white plantation owner took in his illegitimate mixed grandson to be part of his family? Seemed odd.

After slavery ended, Mrs. Odom continued, "My father would go to see them every so often and he would sit at the dining-room table just like one of the family. When my father died, before coming to see my mother, his two uncles stopped at the undertaker's and paid for my father's burial. He was part of the family. He sure was."

I was having a hard time believing her. But why? If I could take people at their word, believing the bad things Southern whites did during and after slavery, why did I question the good? Maybe it was because whenever I talked to people whose families owned slaves, the conversation inevitably included a "but we treated them like family" line, as if to assuage the legacy of guilt and shame, and make it clear that this plantation was not like all the others written about in history books. But Mrs. Odom carried such a strong conviction that her father was a genuine member of the Vertrees family that I assumed it was based on conversations she had with him. She was eleven when her father died. I never got a chance to ask her because to my surprise she had something better to go on.

Mrs. Odom got up from the sofa and limped to the kitchen counter. Picking through a pile of clipped coupons from the Sunday paper and old *TV Guides*, she pulled out a thick black-and-white composition book.

"Would this help?" she asked laying it on the coffee table, frayed loose pages dangling from the side. "It's my father's autobiography."

My eyes widened. She said something after that but I didn't hear what it was because I was focused. I opened the book to the first page, where her father wrote an introduction, dedicating the book to empowering those who could learn a thing or two from his life: "I am sending these volumes out in the world not in a boasting way, but with the hope that some poor souls who may be discouraged in life may be inspired by reading this and resolve to find a way or make a way through this world."

He was torn with what to title the book and wrote on the top of the first page, "Autobiography of Peter Vertrees or The Story of My Life and Work."

"Can I make a copy of this?" I asked Mrs. Odom.

"No," she said.

"I just want to run up the street and have a copy made—I'll be right back."

"You can't take that with you. That's the original. It's the only thing I have left of my father. You are going to have to read it here."

I grabbed my pen and asked for a blank piece of paper to start writing things down word for word. My longhand was borderline illegible because I was writing fast in order to jot everything down. The first chapter was titled, "My Childhood." The first lines I copied from the Peter's journal read: "I was born in Edmondson Co. Kentucky near Green River several years before the Civil War. The date I have never known, the place I cannot remember and my father I never saw."

I was scribbling wildly, with Mrs. Odom watching closely to see how I was going to keep up the momentum for 70 pages. "My mother got on a gray horse and put me on behind her and rode several miles through thick woods until she came to the home of Mr. Jacob and Mrs. Kitty Vertrees. We went in and Mother made her arrangements for me to stay though I did not know this until afterwards. Mother took me in her lap and I fell asleep; when I awoke Mother was gone, and I have never seen her from that day to this."

That was way too long for me to write down in its entirety. I abbreviated the sentences to be, "Peter remembered the day his mom dropped him off. Never saw his mother again." This wasn't going to work. I was missing the meat of Peter's words. I needed a copy. I asked if I could leave cash for her granddaughter to make me a copy when she got a chance and stick it in the mail. Mrs. Odom then came up with an alternative solution for me to get a copy right away because she couldn't guarantee her granddaughter would do it.

"I know Kenneth Thomson has a copy," she said as if I knew his name. This prompted a question on what was his connection to her family. She identified him as a distant cousin on her father's side.

"Do you have a number for your cousin?"

She got her address book from the kitchen counter and sat back down. "It's 615—"

"What area code is that?"

"Tennessee—along the Tennessee/Kentucky border."

"Along the . . . ?" My voice cracked. I'd just come back from Kentucky. I thought he was right up the street for a quick swing by later this afternoon. I jotted the number down with the intention of calling when I got back to Watertown.

Mrs. Odom's granddaughter was coming soon to take her to a 4 p.m. doctor's appointment. She was scheduled for knee replacement surgery the next week, followed by an indefinite rehab period that would prevent future meetings. As we said good-bye at the door, Mrs. Odom apologized for not being more help. No need, I said, wishing her a successful and speedy recovery before joking about how I had dislocated my left knee coming down from a rebound during a high school basketball game, trying to look cute for a boyfriend in the stands and had to do rehab for eight weeks. "The doctor said I was lucky the knee popped back in because of my big thighs."

In the car I couldn't help but think that our exchange in the doorway was the easiest part of the afternoon's conversations. Maybe because I was leaving she was relieved, and there was less need for formality.

But I felt like I left empty handed. The only questions I'd had time for centered on quick family facts. Who? What? When? Why? We hadn't gotten to any of the touchy-feely personal questions. What did it mean to have a father who wasn't a slave during a period when almost every black person was? And how did that relationship translate into her family's identity in a country which has shaped its view of the black community, like it or not, around slavery and its effects? Did the Vertrees' feel as if they were better than other blacks? And what was life like for an interracial "family" on a plantation? Maybe such questions would be answered by the journal.

No longer disappointed that I couldn't see Mrs. Odom again, I called Mr. Thomson. We set a time to get together at his home, less than an hour away, up Route 25.

I arrived the next day to find a two-story Italienate with chipped white paint, surrounded by overgrown shrubs and overhanging tree branches. The lawn had just been mowed, and there was construction in progress in the backyard where he hired contractors to build a one room house for his 90-plus-year-old cousin to live.

Mr. Thomson's son answered the door and invited me in. Waiting near the doorway for Mr. Thomson, I looked around a wide dining room and noticed that he was an art collector. Antiques mainly; large family portraits, lithographs and paintings of family race horses covered the walls. Antebellum cherry-made furniture including a sideboard sugar chest and banquet table completed the room. I couldn't really see into other parts of the house because all the lights were off and the curtains pulled, to keep sunlight out that would damage the collections.

Mr. Thomson walked up behind me from what looked like a secret trap door under a staircase. Startled, I jumped when I heard his voice. "As you can tell, I am a collector," he joked, with a sheepish grin. In his early 70s, with a head full of thick gray hair and a pouch around the middle, Mr. Thomson had a strong Southern accent and an old soul, born two centuries too late.

On the phone I'd told Mr. Thomson I was mainly interested in the manuscript, which I think I hurt his feelings. As a war buff and hobby genealogist, who'd spent most of his life researching the Vertrees family tree, Mr. Thomson was the one with all of the history memorized in his head. Dating as far back as early 18th century, he had quite a story to tell.

He started in more modern times, with the three sisters whose names I recognized. They were all listed on the fax several months ago when I tried calling not knowing two of them were dead. Elverlina had been the director of the family gospel choir and a schoolteacher until she was 88. "She had more energy than anyone in that family," he said. Bertha, the sister who'd died earlier that year, married a Methodist Minister who owned lots of property and had an office behind Mrs. Odom's house. "The only thing you couldn't talk to Bertha about was age," he said. "When I told her age at the funeral, Lillie got up and said, 'She's gonna rise up and ask you to go outside.'"

And Mrs. Odom? Mr. Thomson confirmed an impression I'd gotten from talking with her, that she always seemed to carry a subtle sense of superiority.

The topic had to come up sooner or later. There was no way I could talk about a black family with white blood without bringing up the sensitive topic of racial hierarchy and its partner in crime, skin color. The traditional thought being that light-skinned blacks still have more social, educational, and economic advantages than dark-skinned blacks, solely because of their more Caucasian appearance. I knew that the topic, which dates back to slavery and is the oldest conflict among blacks in this country, was eventually going to rear its head. But hearing it aired by a white Southerner was a tiny bit awkward.

But I decided to trust his thoughts because his nerdy side did a lot to ease my discomfort. He spent his afternoons watching the *Antiques Roadshow* on PBS and when a dealer appraisal is wrong, he calls the show to point out the error in the estimate so to run a correction. "I've called several times. But I haven't heard back from the producers."

We talked about Peter writing in his journal that he'd never met his father or any black relative—which sounded strange.

"Did he ever pass?" I asked.

"As far as I know, he wanted to be black. He didn't want to be white," Mr. Thomson said. Then where did the "better than" notion come from if the father wasn't spreading the color stereotype that looking white and having European features was better than looking black with African features? What made the family feel privileged? Mr. Thomson answered it was because of their last name.

Having the family name Vertrees opened doors in Kentucky where the family was well-known and respected for producing successful lawyers and at least one judge. Though their father was illegitimate, they were acknowledged by this wealthy, connected, political family that, despite what I thought could be true or not, told white neighbors to leave Peter and his family alone. That was the reason they got better treatment; because whites in town knew who they were kin too.

Peter wrote about this big brother protection from his uncles in the journal. "[They] were all near grown when I was bound to their parents. They did not mistreat me and did not allow anyone else to do so."

Now both Mrs. Odom and Mr. Thomson were saying the same thing: that Peter was one of the family. Even Jacob's wife who knew Peter was an offspring from an affair with another woman was on board with it. How did that work?

"There was an old saying when I was growing up in the South that whites like individual blacks but not the race. In the North they love the entire race, supposedly," Mr. Thomson said.

He pointed to a comment in the journal about how Peter's grand-mother, a devout Christian, took Peter with her to church where all of her white friends and neighbors would be: "I would sit by her side during service and listen to the preacher," Peter had written.

"Didn't the family also own slaves?"

"Not only did they own slaves, they were racists too. His first cousin was racist, and one of his uncles, John J., caused some trouble. He was a racist too but he helped teach Peter how to read."

The relationship created a strange paradox. His grandfather owned slaves but gave Peter an informal education and the money made working odd jobs as a teenager he was allowed to keep as an allowance. Traditional history asserts that this preferential treatment wasn't always given to mulattos fathered by slave owners; they tended to ignore their existence.

As irrational as it sounds, Mr. Thomson pointed out that it wasn't impossible to love an individual and hate the community he came from. An example in recent years was of South Carolina Senator Strom Thurmond and his illegitimate daughter with his housekeeper. He preached fiery hate and "segregation now and forever," for much of his life while at the same time discreetly visiting and paying college tuition for his black daughter to go to school.

Peter lived his life in between two worlds, straddling a white community that suggested he segregate himself from other blacks or as family friends told him "stay away from them," and in a black community were he had to put in double duty to gain acceptance.

But Peter did have his elitist moments. And if he hadn't, I would've been skeptical about the sincerity of his thoughts and memories. The first time it came out in his journal was after he left the Vertrees house and was driving a horse and wagon for a man in Gallatin. His technique was to hold the reins in one hand and his spelling book in the other to practice his reading. When a group of blacks saw him ride by they poked fun at him. "I have seen my own people on the streets of Gallatin laugh and make fun of me. I would look at them and say to myself, 'I will be above you some day.'"

Much as I was disturbed by his reaction, I also noticed that he was an equal opportunity elitist. Whites weren't immune from his judgment. In 1862, when he was serving as a cook and bodyguard for an uncle in the Confederacy, in his downtime he learned to "attend balls and drink and curse and gamble." He stopped all those things the next year, when Jesus Christ called him to ministry. Peter then wanted the other people in his company to denounce their lives as sinners. "My first attempt was made at an outdoor service for white people," he wrote. "When the service closed the people went away and thought nothing of me." Ironically, this inspired Peter to decide he would never give up until he helped others find "the blessed Christ—The friend of sinners."

With more knowledge and greater understanding of the period than Mrs. Odom had, Mr. Thomson was almost as interesting as what I had originally come for. I'd been in his house for hours when I was supposed to pick up the journal and leave. He was a hardcore researcher, with much of his research published in Blue & Gray magazine, where his son had landed a new job as associate editor in Columbus, Ohio, which was where he was headed when I walked in the door.

He has researched Peter's family tree as far back as 1716 during the reign of Louis XIV. When Protestants were being persecuted, two

Vertrees brothers, Jacob and John, who belonged to a noble family, fled France to Holland and from there set sail for America. When they arrived, they changed their last name, Van Tress, to Vertrees and settled in the territory that was being claimed by both Pennsylvania and Virginia, years before the Revolutionary War.

John later joined the Revolution and became a captain, Kenneth told me, one of the 175 Virginia volunteers who joined George Rogers Clark in the Northwest Territory. The Indians called them "long knives."

There is no record of the later life of Jacob, but his son, Isaac, was a private in the Pennsylvania Line during the Revolutionary War and was discharged in 1779 at Fort Pitt. Shortly after that, Isaac came to Kentucky with his family, which consisted of his wife Elizabeth and his two sons, William and Jacob. In 1800 he deeded his land on the forks of Otter Creek near Vine Grove together with his home to his son Jacob. It was his grandson, also named Jacob, who had an affair with a slave and fathered a son, Booker. And it was fifteen-year-old Polly who had the affair with Booker, which produced Peter.

Mr. Thomson confirmed that when Mrs. Odom's father was five years old, his mother had a legal document recorded at the Edmonson County Courthouse that indentured her son to Booker's biological father. "The grandfather was to provide the clothing and everything for his welfare until he was grown, which he did. I don't know when he changed his name, but I think in the Census records it was Skaggs. When he got grown, he changed it to Vertrees."

I asked why his father Booker didn't ask for him.

"Because he didn't have any rights in those days in the courts."

Mr. Thomson had traced pretty much every branch of the family tree — even tracing Mrs. Odom and her siblings to their great-great-great uncle Patrick Henry.

"Ms. Odom is related to the patriot Patrick Henry? 'Give me liberty or give me death' Patrick Henry?" I questioned.

The short answer was yes: they shared the same great-grandparents. The long answer contained name after name, and I'd just about given up trying to connect the dots when my ears perked up: the Vertreeses were also distant kin to President James Madison, "by way of one of Patrick's sisters, Susana Henry Madison, who married Gen. Thomas Madison, the first cousin of President Madison," said Mr. Thomson.

By the time I left Mr. Thomson's house at sunset, about three hours later, I had a clearer picture of Mrs. Odom's family tree, but I had O'D on genealogy. The autobiography was a smoother read with telling snapshots of the war from behind the scenes.

For much of it, it was just an interesting read. For example, in the winter of 1861–1862, Peter and his doctor uncle spent much of their time visiting sick soldiers in their infantry whose illness was listed in the medical records as "nostalgia," or in layman's terms homesickness. As we walked to the door, I ran back into the living room to grab the copy of the journal I had left on the coffee stand. I was brain exhausted.

We stood outside for a few minutes before I departed and chatted about his construction project, which turned out to be a one-room house he was building for his cousin to live in. I told him it was very thoughtful of him to make a home for her to live next door. "I would bring her into my house, but she can't climb stairs and the spare bedroom is upstairs. This way she won't have to."

That night I read through Peter's autobiography before going to sleep. Each chapter was about four to five pages long. On numerous occasions he referenced his white family, using "Dr.," "Mr.," or "Judge." The two exceptions were in the first chapter, when he described the last memory of his mother and his adopted mom. There were holes in the story that didn't strike me until I reached the end, such as the fact that he never mentioned the other slaves on the plantation, though surely he saw them. And it wasn't until later in his adult life that he started to mention interactions with other "coloreds like himself."

After Peter's biological mom left him during the night at the Vertrees house, he recounted that Kitty became his mother. She seemed

to feel affection for him, and she taught him to be truthful and cour-
teous, as Peter described it. "When I cried for my real mother, Mrs.
Vertrees did everything she could to make me feel better, giving me
sugared biscuits and other dainties relishing to a child appetite. Many
cold winter nights has she gotten up from her bed and come to mine
and felt of my feet and would tuck the cover about me so snugly until
it was almost a matter of impossibility for me to get cold."

The references to his being hired out come early in the manuscript, as if it was something that happened within a year or two of
his arrival. The writings about working outside the house indicated
that he kept every penny he earned. "When I was older, I was hired
out to different persons for wages. I was the proudest youngster in
the state of Kentucky when I made my first dollar."

His foster mother sent him to various places, distant relatives'
and friends' houses. But he was never sent back to work somewhere
he was mistreated. He wrote of working at a saloon, where he had to
serve three suppers a night, and when he fell ill one evening and went
to sleep, "the proprietor kicked me and cursed me. I ran away and
went back home. Mrs. Vertrees did not approve of the way he treated
me, so she did not send me back."

Halfway into the book, I couldn't believe how well Peter really
did seem to fit into the family. Granted, there were a few issues that
stood out: like his family leaving him home alone to look after the
house when they went on vacation. During those times, he would run
wild: "The family would hardly get out of sight before the 'boy' in me
would manifest itself . . . I remember one time frying eggs and filling
them full of sugar and could not eat them. I wasted a great deal in that
way; but would have everything in place when the family returned.
They least suspected that my 'boyish' pranks had reigned supreme
during their absence."

In October 1861, when Peter was 21, in the early months of the
Civil War, he received a letter from an uncle who'd enrolled in the
Sixth Kentucky Infantry Regiment in Glasgow, Kentucky. John Luther,

a well-respected physician, wanted Peter to join him as a cook and bodyguard. When his uncle was later promoted to head surgeon, Peter became an assistant surgeon. In the winter of 1861–1862, Peter and his uncle spent much of their time visiting sick soldiers in their infantry whose illness was listed in the medical records as "nostalgia," or in layman's terms, homesickness.

Peter never brought up the issue of slavery either in this chapter or anywhere in the book. But he seemed to have fond memories of his four years as a Confederate. He never saw combat but witnessed a snowball fight the morning of March 22, 1864, in Dalton, Georgia, when soldiers awoke to an unusual snowfall, "deep enough to cover shoe tops and wet enough to pack." The noise attracted the attention of nearby troops from Tennessee: "The men were drawn up in opposing lines and it was typical of real warfare to see the men on one side advance and the other retreat. They kept this up for about a half hour and quit, neither side claiming victory."

A month before the end of the war, Dr. Luther was released from duty and Peter was allowed to leave too. He moved to Tennessee to live with his other uncle, Judge James Cunningham in Gallatin. The judge paid for Peter's college education at Roger Williams University in Nashville. This chapter revealed more about Peter's position in the family and touched on the idea that maybe it wasn't truly considered as much as a family as those who were white and never served as a servant. The thoughts stemmed from an incident Peter wrote about while at Uncle James's home. He had to shine shoes for his sons—Peter's much younger cousins—to wear on Sunday for church. The sons were supposed to get the shoes ready for Peter to shine on Saturday night but this one particular time they didn't and gave them to him on Sunday morning to shine. Peter refused because Sunday was Sabbath and as a result got in trouble after the boys told on him. "Naturally the children reported this to their mother and she called me in question. I told her why I refused. She became angry with me and reported the matter to Judge who was still in bed. He got up and hurriedly dressed himself and came out to see what the trouble was about."

The journal continues on with the story that his uncle told him "if you can't do what is needed to be done about the house you will have to get you another home." I'm reading this and thinking to myself, what kind of family is this? After the uncle finished scolding, Peter said he didn't respond and spent the night in the black community and went back Monday morning to settle the dispute. Peter told his uncle that he didn't feel comfortable working on the Sabbath because that was how James's mother raised him. "Your mother taught me to keep the Sabbath Day holy." After the uncle heard that, he let Peter off the hook and essentially apologized but told him it was okay to take Sunday off but he needed to return in time for work Monday morning.

Before that entry there were no obvious signs that Peter was treated like a servant in the family —and I'd looked for them, believe me. Can someone of an opposite race be fully accepted into a family of another race? I don't know. But Peter's story was the closest I'd gotten to the idea that it was possible.

But I did find it interesting that after that entry, Peter seemed to write more on his work in the black community as if he was spending more time there. He organized his first congregation in 1874 and described in the journal that not every white person was his friend. One night, while members were assembled in church, a message came that the "Klu-Kluxs" were coming to break up the service. Peter ordered the lights off and told the women to lie down flat on the floor and the men go outside to do what they could to protect them. He wrote that one "real old" lady instead of lying down on the floor, ran to a window to see if she could see them coming. "She knocked the stick from under the window and it fell across her neck. She screamed out, 'Oh my God they got me!' I rushed to her and lifted the window and she fell back in the house, glad to lie down and obey orders."

The men stood around the Church on guard with guns to use for defense. The "Klu-Kluxs" heard that members were prepared to protect themselves and they did not to go to the church. When everyone came back inside, Peter did a head count. One member, an old gentleman named Uncle Duke, was missing and showed up out of nowhere when he heard the news. Peter remembered that, "After the excitement abated, Uncle Duke came up with a half rail on his shoulder asking, 'Where are they? Where are they? All I want is to see one of them.' He had run off and hidden himself until he knew the danger was all over."

Before going to sleep I thought about my day with Mr. Thomson and again reflected on how comfortable I was with him talking about slavery, skin color, and race. Sensitive topics that most people "didn't want to get into."

Why was Mr. Thomson different? I think it was as simple as the fact that he came from a mixed-race family. Given his loving family connection to his cousins, his ease with me was just that. Not that I think people need to have close interactions with races outside of their own, but when they do, you can tell the difference.

And who knows how Peter's uncles later interacted with blacks down the line but I do think having him as member of the family had to have changed their perspective on race at the time.

How do I know? I can only point to something that happened in 1896 when the Supreme Court made the notorious decision to approve the principle of Separate but Equal. The Plessy v. Ferguson case passed by a vote of 7 to 1. The one lonely, gutsy dissenter was Justice John Marshall Harlan who was raised in Kentucky with a half brother who was black.

9

Mississippi

DEAF IN ONE EAR

I took the next morning off as I considered my new time problem: I had too much of it. I wasn't scheduled to leave Tennessee for another week.

After wracking my brain for ways to stay productive, I remembered a fax from the Mississippi Department of Aging was crammed in my laptop bag. On it was a list of names of the oldest residents in the state. I scanned the two pages for the oldest of the oldest: Bessie Hollins, 112, of Jackson won the prize. I dialed her number.

When a man picked up, I asked for Mrs. Hollins.

"That's my wife. She's dead," he said.

Under the same phone number on the next page was another name—B. B. Hollins, 106. I talked fast so he wouldn't hang up.

"Is this Mister B. B. Hollins?"

"You're speaking to him."

I started to give him my spiel.

"Hold on, let me put my daughter on the phone," he said. I quickly tried to get in the qualifier question but was too late. Mr. Hollins had already taken the receiver away from his ear.

"Yes, yes, they were slaves," his daughter, Beverly, told me, after I explained my mission. "He grew up on the same plantation his parents worked on. Come on down. My father would love to talk to you."

I asked if she knew the birthdates of her grandparents. She didn't. But the program from her grandmother's funeral service was around the house somewhere. Like all funeral programs, the first page had a picture of the deceased and underneath was the date of birth and date of death. She put me on hold to go look for it.

"Okay, here it is. It looks as if Grandmother Hollins was born in 1867."

We spent the next five minutes estimating the age of her grand-father; I surmised that there was a great chance her grandfather was born before 1865 because older men tended to marry much younger women. Until now that was all I saw.

Beverly chimed in. "That sounds about right."

I too felt pretty confident that the math would be right. All I wanted was for Mr. Hollins's father to be two years older than his wife. That wasn't too much of an age gap. Most of the people I'd found so far had wives who were as much as twenty years younger.

Just to make sure, I asked Beverly to put her father back on the phone so I could ask him directly. "He won't be able to hear you. The phone buzzes in his ear because of his hearing aid."

We agreed that I'd drive down the next morning for a couple days. I'd visit the courthouse while I was there to figure out the dates.

Before she hung up the phone I asked if she lived with her father. She didn't.

"Your father lives by himself?" I asked.

"Oh no, he got remarried and everything. Still lives at home but, walks around with a cane. The only thing wrong is he has diabetes. I take him to the hospital once a week for dialysis."

"Remarried? Seriously?"

We laughed.

"Yes, he found himself a younger woman."

After Beverly gave me the street address and we said goodbye, I felt a rush of panic. I'd said yes to driving to Mississippi from Tennessee. Was I crazy?

I ran to the public library in the main square to log on to the Internet to see how long that drive was. I introduced myself to the librarian, Marie, who already knew who I was because she had seen me coming in and out of the Watertown B&B. Any other time, I would have made a mental note that people in town were watching me. But I neither had the time nor the energy to care.

Marie let me sign onto a computer with her password. I typed in the address into MapQuest. Spotting scrap paper and a pencil near the keyboard, I wrote a to-do list: Find a place to stay near Jackson; bring CDs; print local directions to Mr. Hollins's.

MapQuest finished downloading. I looked at the screen. What? 430 miles? 9 hours, 15 minutes? Are you kidding me? I hadn't spent that much time in a car since the summers when Dad drove to North Carolina and Mom padded the back of the station wagon with Benji sleeping bags for me and Kwanza to sleep on.

To mark the first leg of the long road trip, I asked the innkeeper, Sharon, to cook a big breakfast: grits, eggs, and biscuits from scratch, with a bowl of fresh peaches. I told her about my sudden change of plans and I guess she heard the stress in my voice because as I got up from the table, she handed me homemade strawberry bread wrapped in aluminum foil to take with me. Her husband Bob got up early to say good-bye as I packed the car. "Just remember: odd-numbered interstates go north and south; even numbers go east and west."

En route, I stopped for gas and french fries. When I got sleepy, I pumped a CD and sang at the top of my lungs. After dealing with highway construction, accidents, and rush hour traffic, I finally made it to the banks of the Mississippi River in Vicksburg, the last exit on I-20 West before the Louisiana state line. It took 11 hours.

I had made a reservation in Vicksburg, where a room was less expensive than in Jackson, at an inn called The Corners. When I arrived the innkeeper, Betty, greeted me at the front door to hand me a key. She upgraded my room free of charge from a double bed in the attic to a first floor queen facing the back verandah and flower garden. I was the only guest and had the house to myself. Two couples who'd already checked out were sitting in rocking chairs on the front porch drinking tea under the state Confederate battle flag. As soon as they left, I took their spots on the porch, overlooking the Mississippi and Yazoo Rivers.

After Betty cooked breakfast the next morning, she joined me in the dining room to ask about my travels. She admitted she was curious to know what business I had in Jackson because she rarely booked a room for a single woman on her own—especially not a black woman.

I hesitated to tell her. Though she seemed nice, I didn't know how she would react if I mentioned slavery. A lot of Southerners have strong opinions on the subject, particularly those flying Confederate flags in their front yard. I didn't want to get into a heated discussion. I took the middle ground and told her I was traveling the country looking for people whose parents were born before 1865.

"You are talking about slaves, then?" she said.

I smiled. Maybe she wasn't one of them.

"Yes."

"You should find a lot of them around here."

"You think?"

"They must be really old. The black guy working in the garden around the house, you know, his great-grandfather was a slave on this plantation."

I expressed my surprise that the inn was a former plantation, and Betty insisted on taking me on a quick tour of the grounds, pointing out holes in rocks made from cannon balls, shot from submarines on the Yazoo.

After walking the grounds with Betty, I glanced at my watch. It was getting late and Mr. Hollins was expecting me. I told Betty I'd love to visit more but had to make an appointment.

Mr. Hollins lived off an overly developed commercial hub of chain restaurants, car dealerships, and strip malls on a dilapidated side street untouched by investment dollars. Even the road was discriminated against with pot holes and weeds sprouting from cracks in the tar. His house, which looked like it could have been painted white at one point, was gray with black stripes along the boards where the wood was rotting.

I walked up the front steps to knock on the door, but no one was home. I went back to the car and sat alongside the road. Ten minutes later, a car pulled up to the driveway. Mr. Hollins got out and walked in the house with his wife trailing behind him. I got out and started walking toward the car; Beverly met me halfway on the lawn. "We're just getting back from the hospital. I forgot to mention that today was his dialysis day," she said.

We went inside and sat down in a small family room almost knee to knee on couches. Mr. Hollins wasted no time poking fun of my Yankee drawl and joking that he wasn't going to answer any questions unless I paid for his time. "Only if you accept Visa," was my witty comeback.

Warming up, I lobbed him a few quick questions to get the facts out of the way and his answers came back as fast as if we were playing flash cards. He remembered the name of the plantation his father worked on: Georgia Green, a peanut plantation in Natchez. He remembered the name of the plantation owners: Lomax Hollins and Mary Elizabeth Hollins, second-generation Dutch immigrants by way of Tennessee. Mr. Hollins even remembered why his father Germain Pixie stayed for another decade as a sharecropper: "He had nowhere else to go."

The tape was about to run out but before I changed it, I asked when his father was born. "How much older was your father than your mother?"

"He wasn't older. He was younger," Mr. Hollins said.

"He wasn't born before 1865?"

"No. He was born in 1875 on the farm. My grandparents were slaves on Georgia Green."

My jaw dropped. I didn't say anything, just stared at the floor for what must have seemed like a long time because Mr. Hollins asked if I was okay. I'd gone through all this and he wasn't a son of a former slave but a grandson. I thought about continuing the conversation but

I needed to rest if I was going to drive back to Tennessee tomorrow. After thirty minutes of casual chitchat with the tape recorder off, Beverly walked me to my car.

I left Mississippi with mixed emotions. On the one hand, I obviously was disappointed. On the other hand, I knew in the back of my mind there was a slight chance the trip wasn't going to work out— but I took the chance and went anyway.

10

Alabama

LESSONS FROM THE GRAVE

School was out for the summer at Alabama A&M University (AAMU) in Mobile and the campus was empty, which made slowing down but not stopping at pedestrian crosswalks easier to get away with. Straight off a plane with luggage in the trunk and up against time, I needed to find the State Black Archives Research Center before it closed at 5pm. I had ten minutes.

In a hurry and stressed, the New Yorker in me came out. Beeping the horn at people to get their attention. Skipping polite banter when someone walked up to the car, merely shoving a piece of paper with scribbled directions out the window in their face, saying, "I'm looking for this building." Finally, an older woman set me straight. I had the wrong building name; I was asking directions to a building that didn't exist. The center was inside a new building to the right of the post office, she explained before putting in a little dig, "You must be from up North." I apologized for being in a rude rush and wished her a good day as I pulled away.

The door to the center was still open. On the table, spread out and waiting for me were copies of original service papers of First Duty Sergeant Jackson, who had been a soldier in the 110th U.S. Colored Infantry. He was the father of the woman I'd flown to Alabama to meet. The center had the century-old papers on display: the assignment and discharge notices, a copy of the Morning Report of Captured Negroes from the National Archives, and a pension application.

The curator heard about my search from a friend of a friend and had called to tell me about the collection and the daughter of Jackson who made the donation after her nieces said they didn't want to have the Civil War documents handed down to them.

I'd made plans to meet 103-year old Sammie Mason tomorrow, which made today the only time I had available to swing by to make photocopies of everything. As I was putting coins in the copier, the curator walked in and asked if I needed anything. "Mrs. Mason is a wonderful woman," he said. "These papers meant the world to her, as I'm sure she will tell you. She and her nieces graduated from this university, so we were lucky she trusted the center with her family's history."

I had hesitated at first to make the trip to Mobile because my dad's health wasn't getting better. I'd changed my research approach over the past few months to allow me to be home to see him as much as possible. I'd organize as much as I could ahead of time in order to make the trips shorter—just a week or a couple days away rather than a month. I wanted to be close to home in case he had to go into the hospital again. His cancer was back. He'd told Mom not to tell us so we wouldn't worry.

But I knew. The second I got in the car I could smell the cancer growing. Like body odor it seeped from his pores, a stale, sour smell that I wanted to scream and yell at. Tell it to go away and leave us alone.

"How was the bus ride up?" he asked as he started the engine. I went home for the weekend before leaving for Alabama.

"Fine," I answered as I turned away to buckle my seat belt, and look out the window.

"Run into any traffic?"

"Nope."

I'd started to go home for a couple days each week. Dad and Mom would stay upstairs in their room most of the time watching sermons on The Word Network or old black and white westerns on American Movie Classics. Dad liked it upstairs because the bathroom there was closer to his chair. But for this visit we gathered downstairs in the family room on Friday night to watch videos that Dad converted to DVD. For almost two hours we watched the family open Christmas presents under a fake tree in 1973, right after I was born. We lived in a two-bedroom apartment in the projects in Norwich, Connecticut, across the street from my grandparents.

I remember a lot about when I was young. Mom, for instance, used to put a kid's table in the middle of the kitchen on Saturdays so Kwanza and I could play restaurant. We'd order the day's specials from a handwritten menu featuring peanut butter and jelly sandwiches with chicken soup. I remember Kwanza and I grabbing on to Dad's ankles so he couldn't walk away and laughing because he was strong enough to drag us with him. I remember picking grapes with Dad from the vine he'd planted and trained to grow on wooden posts in the backyard near the shed. What we didn't eat, I'd put in a glass jug in the basement to make wine, but got sticky mold instead.

The trips had become an escape to get my mind off worrying about Dad so much. It was Mrs. Mason that reminded me about picking grapes with my father. She told me how she'd watched her father plant grapevines and nut trees in her own yard. It was one of only two memories she had of him. The other was of her sitting on his lap as he showed her older sister how to thread a needle and knot the string.

We were sitting in her living room on a cloudy afternoon the last week of June. A retired teacher with glasses too big for her face, short-cropped gray hair, and good posture, Mrs. Mason sat upright in a black polka-dotted dress with black stockings. She was having a bad day because her feet and ankles were swollen more than usual. She'd spent the morning with her health aide collecting all of the programs and articles that mentioned her AAMU donation. She didn't know I had stopped by the university yesterday to get some of those very documents.

While her words made me think briefly of my dad, her relationship with her own father was more complicated than mine. Her father had died when she was four. From early on she considered the Army papers a surrogate for him. She was quick to tell me that the papers her father left behind helped her to grow up and inspired her over the years. I thought she was exaggerating about her father's role in her life and how much the Civil War documents meant to her. After all, her father was dead. How much influence could these papers really have?

A lot. The paperwork turned her father into her hero and gave her a role model. "I cherished his papers as if they were him," she said. Jackson was a slave on a plantation near Elkmont in northern Alabama along the Tennessee border. Leaving behind his first wife, in the winter of 1863, at the age of 31, he ran away to join the Union's 110th U.S. Colored Infantry along with two other slaves—one said to be his brother. They walked 40 miles to Huntsville to register to join the fight. "My father took a great big chance, leaving from over there and hustling through those briars and bushes, knowing that if they got caught they would be shot or beat to death," said Mrs. Mason. "That's what has been on my mind all these years and whenever I get down I think about it."

Mrs. Mason and I began talking about the papers she'd given to the AAMU. The research center held an official dedication ceremony in 2001 when it accepted the Civil War documents. There was a greeting from the university president and remarks from a local military historian. Mrs. Mason spoke too. Giving up the collection, Mrs. Mason told the audience that day during her speech, was like giving up a piece of herself:

> It grieves me to part with these papers, almost as much as if I were losing a loved one in death…When other girls had rough times, they turned to their fathers. I couldn't turn to my father, but I'd think of him trudging to Huntsville…wanting to do the right thing. When I think of that I can't stop— I have to pick up and go on.

Mrs. Mason had asked her mother to show her the papers when she was young, even before she could read what they said. She spent years in her room creating an image in her mind of who her father was, pieced together from stories her mother told her and what she had in front of her. After she was done, her father had became someone she was proud of; someone she could brag about to her friends. "It was important that he wanted to be free. . . he was a man who wanted to take care of his family and the only way he thought he could do that was to leave [slavery]."

The fact that her father was part of this nation's history was important to Mrs. Mason. I didn't really understand before how important it is that our parents mean something positive—just as parents want to show off their children, we want to show off our parents. Mrs. Mason thought that if people saw her father as a strong man, then they might ultimately see the same strength in her. Or maybe, more importantly, she'd see it in herself.

I asked if we could look at the papers together because it sounded like I had missed something the day before. Before this afternoon, I'd just seen a stack of old files.

There was his original "assignment notice," dated the day before New Year's Eve in 1863 when he arrived at a Union army outpost at Pulaski, Tennessee after he joined in Huntsville. That fall, Union scouts were paid $16 a month and $100 a head to recruit slaves to leave the plantations to join what would become one of the nation's first black fighting regiments. The Union Army had occupied Northern Alabama at the time, including northern Limestone County where Jackson was a slave. By Christmas Eve, the 110th U.S. Colored Infantry had 960 new recruits. A few days later, Jackson stood in line for his uniform. He was recorded to be five-foot-six with a "yellow complexion."

Her father stood out as an independent thinker and leader. Catching the eye and ears of a white general, he was promoted to corporal just thirteen days after enlisting. Then a month later came another promotion to sergeant with a salary of $6.00 a month. The sergeant title was listed on his discharge papers three years later. Part of his duty was to write daily reports to hand to superior officers. From that Mrs. Mason made the conclusion that her father had also risked his life to educate himself, mastering reading and writing as a slave. At the time the state of Alabama prohibited such education, punishable with 33 lashes for the first offense and then to be sold for the second.

That summer, the regiment was assigned garrison duties in the middle of Tennessee and along the border of Alabama. On a September morning in Athens, Alabama, Jackson was captured by Confederates when his company was overrun while guarding Fort Henderson. The victor, Confederate General Nathan Bedford Forrest, a former slave trader, was a vicious racist already under Congressional investigation for the mass slaughter of 450 black troops shot while surrendering.

Suffering from three gunshot wounds in his left thigh, left shoulder, and right hip, Jackson marched with other prisoners 60 miles to Cherokee where they were loaded onto a railroad cattle car headed south. Under the orders of General Forrest, captured white soldiers would be shipped to Mississippi or the banks of the Alabama River while all black soldiers, whom he refused to recognize as prisoners of war, were forced back into slavery in a Confederate labor camp in Mobile. If it was up to him, General Forrest said he would've rather sent them back to their masters and let them deal with the runaways.

Mrs. Mason had her father's capture papers, dated September 24, 1864, and in a shoebox, she had kept the history of what his troop went through after being captured. "He said he was always hungry on that train," said Mrs. Mason, remembering the story passed down from her mother. "My daddy said the only thing they had to eat was the corn they picked out of the cattle manure in those cars."

Upon arrival, Jackson, who still had a bullet in his shoulder, was likely one of the 122 listed as sick in the hospital or quarters. About 806 black soldiers were put to work on the camp in Mobile, using makeshift tools to dig trenches deep enough for a soldier to stand in and shoot. He also loaded and unloaded cargo, and did carpentry and blacksmith work. Once again, Jackson was facing an uphill road to freedom. Another soldier from the 110th described their new lives in an affidavit, "If we lagged or faltered or misunderstood an order we were whipped and abused. Some of our own men were detailed to whip the others."

Finally, on May 1, 1865, a month after Lee surrendered, Jackson was freed.

I asked what the sum of the capture papers told her about her father.

"He wasn't scared. He was determined." She acknowledged that the goals she described for herself were based on the bar her father would have set for her. "I heard so much about my father from my mother telling me what he would have expected of me. I made myself remember what my dad would have expected and I tried to live it out."

Take education, for example. The value of an education was another attribute that Mrs. Mason credited to her father. She had to master every subject. She had to get A's and wouldn't settle for less. "I had to sit up nights and my mother would fuss. She'd say, 'I think you're going to kill yourself,' but I'd say 'I got to know this answer.'"

Though her mom always encouraged Mrs. Mason to stay in school, she said it was her father who motivated her to go to college. Since she obviously had never talked to him about it, I asked her why she thought he would have wanted her to go.

"He had something up here," she said pointing at her head, "that made me know he would have died trying to get us into college. I was determined to know that he was pleased in his grave." Mrs. Mason went to school, and even taught school in a building that was erected on the site where her father had been shot and captured during the war. She said this connection made her feel close to him.

Clearly, Mrs. Mason had put immense pressure on herself to be a good daughter and live up to her father's standards. It made me wonder: Am I that hard on myself? If so, why? Not that I was an angel growing up, because I was far from it. I got into my fair share of trouble when I was younger, but except for a couple mishaps here and there, I too felt this need to make my parents happy with me. I studied my behind off in school. And when I got A's on my report card, the first thing I always thought of was running home to show my parents and hearing them say, "Nice job, Sana."

But my parents were alive. Mrs. Mason was seeking approval from someone who was not. At first, I thought that was strange. Making life decisions from pieces of paper seemed like an odd thing to do. But those memories spoke to Mrs. Mason, and she recognized that she needed her father's memory to guide her along in life.

We went on to discuss what life was like for her father after the war. He returned to Elkmont and married the widow of one of the slaves he ran away with, who'd been killed. His own wife had remarried. He changed his last name to Dawson, after the daughter of his previous owner, who was most likely the one who taught Jackson to read and write. Mrs. Mason said that, "When they ran away, they decided that they would take her name the rest of their lives because she was nice to them."

"Did you ever meet Mrs. Dawson?" I asked.

"I never met her. But I met offspring from her family"

"Did they know who you were?"

"They were nice to us. They had a drugstore in Elkmont. In the years when food was rationed—you wouldn't know anything about that, you had to sign a book to get bacon, syrup, and stuff like that. The drugstore would buy enough so we could get some without a ration. And they wouldn't let Mama stand in line."

"Why did they do that?" I asked. It seemed an unusual action for whites at the time.

"They hadn't forgotten that my family had something to do with where they were then."

After his second wife died, Jackson married Mrs. Mason's mom in the 1880s. He was 40 years older than her mother and had one surviving daughter when they met. Together with that stepsister, an older sister, and Mrs. Mason they made three. Her father wanted boys, but when he got three girls, he made up for it by giving them all boy names: Maddy Jack, Johnny May, and Sammie Webster.

Mrs. Mason and her sister were born in the house their father bought after returning home from the war. I asked Mrs. Mason if her father was a sharecropper, as many former slaves were. Under constant pain from his war injuries, Jackson was never able to work the fields again and drew a government pension. That's good, I said— sharecropping was a hard life with little pay. She agreed but added that sharecropping parents focused on saving pennies to send children to school. "You'd be surprised to know whose fathers were sharecroppers who went to school and became doctors."

Mrs. Mason loved to compare herself to her father. She found the most obscure connections easy to make. "He was a man who didn't say, 'yes' to everything. He had his own ideas." She considered herself just as stubborn. Everyone knew that once she made up her mind, it was almost impossible to get her to change it. "They tell me there's no way you're going to make Sammie D. go your way. If she doesn't see it that way, she just doesn't see it that way."

Neither she nor her father liked confrontations to get their points across: they'd pick their battles. "That way, when you do give your opinion, people really sit up and pay attention. I've been told by more than one person that if something came up in church that my dad didn't approve of, he'd just get his hat and his walking stick and go home. He wouldn't be there arguing it. And I find myself the same way."

Some parents seem to have an influence on their children that can last their entire lives. Mrs. Mason welcomed it. I laughed when I thought about the extent to which that control continued to operate with me. Even with stupid stuff like opening a car door.

Long before child safety locks were a feature of cars, my dad came up with his own version. He told me not to touch the lock buttons because it would mess up the car's electrical wiring. If I wanted to get out, to let him know and he would push the unlock button. Fast forward to me at the age of twenty-seven sitting in an SUV waiting for my boyfriend to unlock the door. Let's just say that after I told him why I didn't want to do it myself, I lost a lot of cool points.

Mrs. Mason was over 100 and still the fear of disappointing her father controlled the way she carried herself, and explained her reserve and composure. How does a parent get us to feel indebted to them? When you consider the fact that they have spent years, if not decades, caring for us, feeding and clothing us, watching out for us, keeping us safe and healthy, paying for things, smoothing the way for us, worrying about our minds and hearts, etc., etc. I came up with one word: Guilt.

Guilt felt mostly unconsciously, I think. That was what Mrs. Mason and I shared, the thing that drove us to get good grades, not break the rules, and do all the good stuff parents want out of their kids. Mrs. Mason felt an obligation not to tarnish the memory of her father, whom she highly respected for risking his life. I felt an emotional responsibility to make sure my parents had something good to say about me to their friends. Pride is also in there somewhere, wanting our parents to be proud of us too. Mrs. Mason invented a father to live up to—a demanding parent that drove her to become her best self. As for me, I never knew that much of what I did growing up made my parents proud. Dad never really overemphasized the good. When I brought home all A's in eighth grade one year, I remember asking either for a cash reward or to go out to dinner. Dad said no to both. "Why should I pay you for something you are supposed to do in the first place?" He was a tough one. But I still wanted that prize as a token of my hard work. So I would always ask myself: What can I do in order to get Dad to give me my gold star?

So while everyone else was partying and getting drunk in college, I felt an irrational responsibility to study. Yuck. I definitely would have skipped more classes if he hadn't pulled me aside as he was leaving my dorm room freshman year to say, "This is the last time in your life someone is going to pay for you to learn. Take advantage of it." The underlining of that remark: Years of sacrifice from us, your parents, to save to pay your tuition in cash so you wouldn't have to take out student loans. You better do good. I made Dean's List that year.

At first I thought children are motivated by guilt, but after talking to Mrs. Mason, I decided there was more to it. We use our parents to motivate us to be the best versions of ourselves. We tell ourselves they'll be angry or disappointed if we fail to get the gold star. But I think at some point it becomes more for us than for them. And when a parent dies—as they all do, I was starting to see for myself—striving to live up to our memory of their expectations is maybe the best way to keep them alive.

11

California

THE RENTAL MARKET

In May of 2003, I was headed to Las Vegas. Mel, a good friend from college, was turning 30 and all the girls who were still friends from school were going to party. She was the last of the New York gang to be inducted into the "What am I doing with my life?" club. Everyone had good jobs. Most of us had finished graduate school. We were trying to figure out what was next. She was a mutual funds manager, who had spent the bulk of her time since graduation in Fort Greene, Brooklyn, hanging out with us East Coast girls before moving west. She lived in a sweet apartment in Orange County with enough space for me to stay for a week before driving north to Vegas.

This also meant that I could make plans to meet William Lincoln Dunlap. He'd been looking for me to visit for the past five months, and had even called once to see if I was still going to make it out there. But my credit card didn't have room to cover hotel, airfare, and rental car. Now, because I could stay with the birthday girl while I was out there, I had a little more wiggle room in the budget.

I found Mr. Dunlap after hearing that he and more than 100 friends got together to celebrate his 100th birthday in an active living and retirement community in Mira Loma, off of the 60 freeway. His mother, Eliza, was a baby when slavery ended, but to be honest I was more captivated by Mr. Dunlap's grandfather, former Mississippi State Senator George Washington Albright. Despite having decided that I wasn't going to focus on grandchildren—in part because they weren't as much of an anomaly—I'd never met anyone whose family member was part of the glory days of Reconstruction. I couldn't pass this up.

I had only learned of the large numbers of black political leaders in the postwar South a few years ago, during my time with Mr. Wright. Never having read about people like Albright in history class, I considered listening to Mr. Dunlap talk about his grandfather as make-up for lost time. What does it take to go from slave to state senator?

Born in 1846 on the John Albright plantation in Holly Springs, Mississippi, Albright lived with his mother, while his father belonged to a different owner. At the age of 11, he saw his father auctioned, sold, and shipped to a man in Texas. Around the same time, Albright learned to read and write. Risking the penalty of 39 lashes on a naked back and having his thumb cut off above the second joint, Albright was taught by the owner's children in the plantation kitchen while his mother cooked and looked on. According to Mr. Dunlap, his grandfather was one of the first slaves in the area to speak anything other than English, learning both Spanish and Portuguese.

"When freedom came to the Africans in Mississippi, my grandfather was the first one to rush in and take advantage," said Mr. Dunlap, a kind, unassuming man, wise without the look of age, who described his grandfather as not just farsighted but very. "Today, many people say to hell with that, because they still live under the idea that they are downcasts and don't have the freedom as the whites. His idea was to show them that they could do anything that whites could do." In 1874, a twenty-eight-year-old Albright ran for state senator and won, serving one term, from 1874-1879.

At 102, Mr. Dunlap lived by himself in a two-bedroom apartment where he had been since 1987 when his wife of more than 50 years died. Leading up to Country Club Lane, where he lived, was a billboard with bright oranges advertising a nearby grove less than six miles off the ramp where you could pick oranges off the tree. Eager to load my trunk with bushels and fresh squeezed gallons, I drove about 10 miles to the left off the exit, then turned around and drove a few miles in the other direction. I saw nothing but urban sprawl, homes, and fast food drive thrus. When I finally arrived at Mr. Dunlap's, I was late and thirsty.

"I don't think many of those small farms exist around here anymore. There has been so much development in the past few years," Mr. Dunlap said. He and a neighbor, Albert, who came by every day to see if he needed anything from the store and to make sure the pharmacy was up-to-date on his prescriptions, were on the porch. Albert left us there watching golf carts drive by as he headed off with a pill bottle that needed refilling. The sun started to peek through the clouds, and I closed my eyes to feel the cool breeze on my arms and legs. We decided to stay outside to talk over glasses of cold lemonade. I'd left the tape recorder in my bag because there wasn't a place to set it in on our rocking chairs. But then Mr. Dunlap mentioned his grandfather's first job as a teenager. "Wait, wait, go back to that," I said as I dug through my bag for the recorder.

Barely fifteen years old, Albright risked his life to travel to plantations in Mississippi to tell slaves about the Emancipation Proclamation. The plantation owners were keeping news of it from them. The same thing was happening across the South. According to Albright, a newly formed clandestine organization of slaves took it upon themselves to spread the word on their own, calling themselves Lincoln's Legal Loyal League. Mr. Dunlap knew the details from a newspaper interview his grandfather did when he visited Mr. Dunlap and his wife in Queens.

"[I] got together small meetings in the cabins to tell slaves the great news. Some of these slaves in turn would find their way to still other plantations and so the story spread," reported Albright in the article, which was written in 1937. "We had to work in dead secrecy; we had knocks and signs and passwords."

"When I knew Granddad he was always fighting for the black man," Mr. Dunlap said. "At first I had no idea that grandfather was more than just a grandfather, you know?"

Golf carts started to drive by more frequently, though from the view from the porch, I still did not see a soul on the green. Most were being nosy, looking our way as they passed. It was funny to watch a distracted driver veer outside his lane while stretching his neck to get a good look at Mr. Dunlap's granddaughter, or so I was rumored to be. Mr. Dunlap loved the attention, and all but stood up to wave to his neighbors. I played along, too.

In between onlookers, I brought up my fascination with the Reconstruction era, heavily reported by 19th and early 20th century white historians and journalists to be a failure—charging that black lawmakers mismanaged state and federal funds, wasted money, exercised poor judgment. Even I kind of believed that elected officials didn't know what they were doing then, which was why whites had to regain control of the government to restore order. I never knew the truth was the exact opposite. Granted the information was out there for me to find out for myself much sooner. But if I didn't know what I knew was wrong, why would I question what I thought was the truth?

Albright and his colleagues did a lot of good things for the state. "I like the idea that he left a trail that lasts today," said Mr. Dunlap. During his first year in office, Albright introduced the first temperance bill which became law. He voted to allocate money to build free schools in a state that didn't have any before the war, he eliminated the state debt, and before the end of the year, created a surplus. Former slaves and poor whites teamed up on the same side, rewriting laws that only allowed those who owned property to vote or hold office. Before the new legislation, only plantation owners could run for office. "No wonder the rich folks hate the memory of those legislatures to this very day," Albright had remarked. I asked Mr. Dunlap if he knew whether the undue criticism of his grandfather's time in office bothered him.

It didn't. "He knew not to listen to what people were saying."

But how was he able to ignore them all?

"He knew who he was and who he wanted to be. He was always living with his own mind," replied Mr. Dunlap.

The article in which Albright was quoted talking about Reconstruction echoed the same sentiment. "People even today try to discredit our rule." At the peak of political power, black officials claimed 55 of the 115 seats in the house, 9 of 37 seats in the senate, and speaker of the house. His close friend Rep. Hiram Revels, was elected to fill the Congressional seat of former Confederate President Jefferson Davis. "That was enough to make all of the dead slave owners turn over in their graves."

The mere decision by Albright and others to run for office during Reconstruction displayed patriotic courage and sheer determination. The desire to participate in the process of building a new government was stronger than the threat of getting killed. The systematic extermination of political leaders was as common in Mississippi as it was through the rest of the South. The state already held the record for lynching more blacks than any other. Murder plots were carried out with fine-tuned precision. Under orders from former Confederates, the Klan worked from a hit list of the most influential in the state. And it included Albright. Thanks to an anonymous note left at his home one day, warning Albright to sleep away from home, Mr. Dunlap's grandfather escaped such a fate in 1875. Some of his friends weren't as lucky, including Charles Caldwell, described even by former plantation owners as one of the most courageous and talented black leaders.

Why didn't freemen soften their leadership voices to save their lives? Cut back on playing an active political role to take more of a back seat? Why did they keep fighting back? I asked Mr. Dunlap.

The fight in his grandfather wasn't something he could turn off and on. He was born with it. "It was in their blood to be that way," said Mr. Dunlap, adding that his grandfather also motivated people with a deep, magnetic voice and "didn't take no for nothing." When he wanted something done it had to be done right away. "He'd say 'jump' and you jumped."

Mr. Dunlap's response to the question of leadership seemed too easy. I pressured him to explain what he meant by "it was in their blood." He didn't have an immediate answer. He kept starting one sentence after another, leaving the previous one unfinished. On the third try he answered, "They were just living their lives. He said that you needed to hold your head up and live like America is supposed to be: united."

The air was getting dry. The morning clouds had disappeared, leaving the afternoon sun beaming. The growing heat didn't bother Mr. Dunlap, who moved west in 1968 because his wife, whom he picked up at a subway station in Manhattan, wanted to be closer to her sister. I couldn't take it. My inner thighs began to sweat and stick. The underside of my right knee, crossed over the left, was dripping perspiration down the side of my calf. I asked if we could go inside. Grabbing our glasses of melted ice, I went into the kitchen, placing them in the sink. He stopped in the living room to grab an old weather-worn cardboard box underneath an empty fish tank filled with rocks—home to Tom, the snapper turtle. I asked Mr. Dunlap what he was looking for.

It was a photo album. "I want to show you something." He sorted through its thick black pages. Glued and taped to the pages were aged yellowish-brown newspaper clippings. Most of them didn't have dates but I could tell they were old by their content. A blurry ad listed a book for 25 cents. "Guilty on Check Charge" was a short blurb on a man in Queens who was sentenced to 30 days for giving his landlord a $26 bad check. A national fishermen's club called "Hook, Line and Sinker," was being formed because men were having a hard time finding someone to listen to their stories. Dues were two fish stories a year.

He only had one photo in the album: a black and white catalog image of two sterling silver candlesticks he said he designed for Tiffany's while working for a silverware company in New London, Connecticut after World War II. Mr. Dunlap had been a machinist at Revere Silversmiths but needed to join a separate union for designers when he came up with the idea of the candlesticks. The way he told it, a few didn't want to work with a black man until the daughter of the owner stepped in. "The boss lady told the men either they worked with me or they got new jobs," remembered Mr. Dunlap.

We sat shoulder to shoulder in the middle of the couch, the album on his lap. Spreading out on the end cushions made the sofa tilt unevenly because of a broken left leg propped up by a piece of plywood. Looking for something in particular, he was flipping too fast for me to see the entire clip collection. I asked him to stop when I saw an article that caught my attention: "Brain Study Challenges 'Bourgeois' Theory" was all I could read from my angle.

"Where did you see that?" He flipped back.

I put my thumb in between the pages to mark the spot. Brittle and discolored from the glue, the delicate, undated cutout, from The New York Times, was about a study of human brains done outside of the U.S. that debunked the theory that differences in brain size divides humans into higher and lower races. Refuting what the researcher called "bourgeois" scientists who frequently contended that those of African descent exhibited "apelike ridges in their brains," the study of more than 500 human brains proved that the same features "are to be found in the brains of many distinguished scientists and of many persons of European stock."

The article was short but it spoke volumes. I never knew there was an academic study that disproved the brain size theory, but I certainly knew there were studies that said it existed. You can't be black in America and not know that there is a large body of work devoted to proving that there is always something wrong with black people: They are less inclined to work as hard as whites; more likely to eat the wrong foods; less likely to brush their teeth; less inclined to exercise; their children are less likely to sleep properly.

Reports, studies, and research, presumably by whites, that claim whites can do anything blacks can do but better are very rarely refuted. The 1994 bestseller The Bell Curve, by Richard J. Herrnstein and Charles Murray on IQ and race, argued race meritocracy, essentially saying black people by birth are less intelligent than white people. When the book came out, I remember being disappointed by contrarian rebuttal to the book's theory. Withering criticism by an academic amounted to no more than him saying "it's not nice to call blacks inferior." No one rushed to showcase scientific evidence to the contrary, maybe because there isn't much out there. I'd imagine that it is a lot more difficult for a black political scientist to obtain a research grant from an organization of white intellectuals with the hypothesis of black IQ superiority.

Either way, Mr. Dunlap stopped keeping score. "I don't worry myself over stuff like that. I have my own idea when reading the paper and I make up my mind what I am going to believe."

A knock on the door revealed Albert with a prescription bag from the pharmacy. When Mr. Dunlap got up to go into the kitchen to discuss the medication, he set open the door to a wire bird cage next to Tom. A white bird that was no bigger than my hand from pinky to palm flew out. First it hovered around the ceiling over its cage, then flew into the guest bedroom, following the sun's rays along the front windows to the porch. After that, it zipped across the living room to the kitchen and back before making its way to the headrest of the brown faux-velvet easy chair near the door.

Today's conversation reminded me of the last time I was on the West Coast, to interview Mr. Wright. The notion of moving past slavery had arisen then, too. I thought about Mr. Dunlap's comment that his grandfather just wanted to live his life, pondering the fact that people today say blacks have not moved on from slavery, when in the years after slavery it was actually whites who didn't, experiencing what I've come to refer to as post-traumatic master syndrome. I think the answer lay in an understanding among slaves and freemen that what happened to them during slavery was not their fault. Many were able to quickly move on, leaving those who created the "peculiar institution" to redefine life without it.

Over time, both sides have approached getting along, aka race relations, very differently. Today's race relations conversations have both blacks and whites at the round table coming up with solutions. As the years have gone by, blacks have been tricked into taking responsibility for why they are discriminated against, as if it were caused by something they did and could somehow help to correct. If I speak proper English, go to the right schools, dress appropriately, and smile more so people won't be scared of me in a dark alley, things will get better. I think it is safe to say if blacks could end discrimination against them, they would. But at the congenial race round table, minorities are rarely the ones doing the discriminating, so you can't help but wonder why they are there at all.

Enough already. My thoughts were exhausting. After Albert left and Mr. Dunlap sat back down, I made plans to come back tomorrow. He suggested late afternoon because he had a morning appointment. I stood up to open the door and quickly closed it. I'd lost track of the bird. Mr. Dunlap saw me looking around for him. "He won't fly out. He's in the back somewhere."

On the ride back, I listened to the radio to drown out thinking. Race relations have been on my mind since the White House panel on race ended several years ago, with no conclusive solutions. All the while, studies on discrimination pop up everywhere, on such subjects as health care, applying for a loan, buying a house, renting a car, and checking into a nursing home. The list is endless.

My naive stab at understanding why individuals—not groups—discriminate began with a one-person panel discussion with the woman I stayed with the first time I was in the Golden State. I'd met Elizabeth at her daughter's 30th birthday party in New York years ago. She was a chief neurosurgeon at a hospital out here. I immediately liked her when I overheard her tell the story of why she was almost kicked out of her all-girls' college in Georgia after asking a black guy to a sorority party. She lived in a red ranch house with a Zen garden in front, complete with a wooden bridge and tiny rock waterfall. She was the kind of person who would tell you when you looked fat in a dress. I loved that about her. As I've come to realize with age and ugly photos, people like her are few and far between.

Like me, she was an open-minded thinker and always had interesting thoughts to share.

I knew that Elizabeth was retired now, so I called her from the car to ask her to breakfast tomorrow. I felt like company. There was something sad about finding Mr. Dunlap, a feeling I hadn't felt after leaving other people's homes. What had happened to the black community? The question sounds very cliché, but that was essentially what I wanted to know.

I had invited her out ot eat becuase I felt like company. The conversation with Elizabeth started getting good when she introduced a term I'd never heard before. I asked her some question about race and she answered with, "Have you heard of the term psychology of the oppressed?"

When I said no, she continued. "It talks about how the oppressed have a hard time seeing themselves as anything but." For example, blacks still have not been able to, as she put it, get over the fact that they were slaves and that is what holds them back. According to the theory, they don't try to succeed because subconsciously they always expect to be oppressed and look for that oppression.

I couldn't argue with her because academics say the same thing. But instead of calling it psychology of the oppressed, they say post-traumatic-slave syndrome. I've also heard some call it the victim mentality.

Then I asked her something I'd been meaning to ask a white person for years. "There are people who just don't like blacks, right?"

"True."

True? I knew she was going to agree. But hearing her say it kind of hurt my feelings. No one wants to hear confirmation that people who don't know you don't like you.

"Why do you think that is?"

"I don't know."

I replied that not knowing makes things difficult because people can't tell which individuals—a boss? A real estate broker? A salesperson?—don't like them. "Why hasn't someone tried to understand why? I think if we tried to figure out where it comes from, it would improve race relations."

Without hesitation or a politically correct answer, she said, "We don't have to. We are the majority."

Written down, her response sounds harsher than it was at the time. At least she was honest.

When I got to Mr. Dunlap's I discovered his appointment had been to look into rental rates for a studio apartment for me to move into.

"I thought this was a residential home for seniors, Mr. Dunlap."

"Oh no, this is open to everyone. When I first moved here it was just me and my wife and four other couples. Now we have over 100 people, all different ages. You should think about it. We have a pool, and the golf course you can see from here. And I built a woodwork shop over near the office. The restaurant here has good food, too— you would like it."

"I do like good food."

"We should go there before you leave. And you said you like oranges— we can find you a place where you can pick oranges."

"I'll have to pass right now, Mr. Dunlap, thank you. I like New York."

"I do too. I used to live in Jamaica, Queens. I had just finished making payments on my house and was getting ready to retire when my wife said she wanted to move out here."

The change of scenery this morning helped me forget the mood I'd been in when I left late yesterday. There was something sad about being with Mr. Dunlap, a feeling I hadn't felt after leaving other people's home. At times, I wanted to scream when I listened to Mr. Dunlap talk about his grandfather—find something to hold on to and shake the disappointment out. But that would be unfair. The images of a stronger earlier generation had not been erased from memory easily, but beaten, tortured, and shot down through no fault of our own. It took some time, but it worked. I asked Mr. Dunlap if it was possible to reverse things. "Maybe," he responded. He didn't sound convincing. As far as he could see, the upcoming generations showed little promise. "The kids today are far different. Expect the next generation to destroy itself." Ouch.

Television played a big part in this opinion. He was disturbed by the fact that children are bombarded daily with images of violence and sex. Televisions need to be turned off, he believed. I would guess he would say the same about violent video games, had he known of them. The past generations that showed such promise "didn't have the knowledge to do evil like they do today. A child 8 years old now knows more about everything than I did when I was 20." That was a problem, according to Mr. Dunlap—kids feeling as if they can be treated like adults and trusted to make adult decisions because they do adult things. "We always respected older people, had to be polite, and all those things that bring you up, not down. We knew our place."

I kept asking questions. What did he think parents were doing wrong today? "They don't think about the future. They say 'We don't have to decide now what our child is going to be.'"

"How do you think your grandfather would raise kids today?"

"He would teach them to always respect the age you're living in."

"What does that mean?"

"A child should be able to be a child. But a parent should know what is best for that child. Kids today can't decide who to follow. But they have to follow their parents neither of whom were properly raised."

A few more sentences and a glass of ice water later, he headed down a path I felt we were eventually going to take. The problem was the parents. And Mr. Dunlap wasn't talking about all parents; he was talking about poor parents.

Children of disadvantaged parents are more likely to not break out of their socioeconomic class. Social scientists tiptoe around the issue when they say someone or something is holding them back. But not Mr. Dunlap. "With all of the education they have, they're not grabbing it. They're not taking hold of it—they're burning it up."

In the past, I would have played devil's advocate, insisting that the problem was not the parents, but money and resources. Low-income parents can't afford the nurturing advantages the middle class can: money for books, time to coach little league, skipping work to go to a museum—I would have argued that poor inner-city parents are doing the best they can with the limited resources available.

Albert knocked on the screen door. Asking if he could check Mr. Dunlap's medicine cabinet, Albert disappeared into the back for 10 minutes, clanging and thumping around drawers. He came out of the bathroom with a list of what Mr. Dunlap needed, and they discussed it in the kitchen.

I sat waiting, thinking, that as judgmental as it may sound, disadvantaged parents raise their children, let's just say, differently from what I've seen in the middle class. I'd watched their approach in silence for eight years living in Brooklyn and Harlem. Only when Mr. Dunlap brought up the subject, I thought to register the images collectively. The stuff I'd hear out my window on the street, how parents talked to their children. What they'd say. I used to look out the window to see who was saying them because I couldn't picture a parent actually talking to a child that way. "Stupid, don't you fucking listen?" "Get your ass over here." "I am going to bust your head open next time." "You ain't getting a damn thing." Or "What do you want?" a subway classic, asked by a mom immersed in her Walkman as a child pulls on her shirt for attention.

And I don't believe it is the breakdown of the family that is breeding dismissive and hostile parents, because there are a lot of great, single parents out there. I agree with Mr. Dunlap's assessment of the problem. Some people have children but don't really want them, and as a result don't really care how they talk to them. "Parents today don't want to be bothered with raising kids. They don't have the patience to teach them anything. They just want them to know."

But there had to be more to the argument that that. Because people who really don't want children work hard not to get pregnant or elect to have an abortion. Something else was going on. I flash backed to my first year in Brooklyn when I heard a man out my bedroom window on a cell phone with what sounded like his ex-girlfriend and the mother of his son. They were fighting about his dating another woman. I was straining my ears to get it all. He told her that they were no longer a couple and he could date whomever he wanted. They went back and forth, and suddenly he said, "You want to hurt my son? You crazy bitch. If you are serious I am going to hang up the phone and call 911 to have the police come get you. Don't you touch him. I'll take him." Apparently, the mom had threatened to harm their son if they couldn't be a family.

As disturbing as it sounds, I think some parents want the full time husband or boyfriend and a child but not the child by itself. When they end up with the latter, one parent, usually the mom, feels stuck and bitter. This is why, in my opinion, some single parents can raise successful, well-adjusted children who make positive contributions to the world around them and others fall short.

A child who doesn't feel wanted will hold onto that rejection for his entire life. I know because that was what my brother did. Yes, I have a brother.

My dad was in graduate school in D.C. when Jeff was born. Jeff's mother was an ex-girlfriend from high school who had married an Army man but neglected to mention that fact to Dad when he went home to Connecticut for summer break in 1961. When Jeff was born his mom didn't want him and came right out and said it. She gave him to the state to raise because she didn't want her husband to know about him when he got home from the Vietnam War. And she didn't want Dad to have him either, because everyone in their hometown would know she was the mother. Her husband, who eventually learned the truth and pulled a gun on Dad, had a short temper. Dad calmed the husband down and talked him into giving the gun to him.

It took Dad years to get Jeff out from court's custody and foster care. He had to prove he was the father to a baby who was born to a mother who was married. When Jeff finally came to live with Dad and Mom, I wasn't even born yet. Older brother Jeff was all I knew. My son Jeff, was all Mom knew. I knew nothing of the past until I was in high school and Jeff had gone to Germany and didn't come home for decades. He did drugs. Was in and out of jail. In and out of counseling. On and off probation. Pushing 50, he has never reconciled his early years. What he knew ate at him and eventually destroyed him. Which was why I cringed when I heard the cell phone conversation that day. The son on the other end faced an uphill battle if his mom continued to advertise that she no longer wanted him.

This wasn't a good subject for Mr. Dunlap and I to discuss, because I fed on Mr. Dunlap's comments and his comments validated my stories. We both decided to get out and get some fresh air. But it was too hot to walk it off so we went for a drive.

"I haven't been around the neighborhood in a while," he said as he got into the passenger seat.

"There's not much out here besides homes and gas stations," I joked.

We drove to where Mr. Dunlap remembered seeing an orange grove and got on the highway to the next exit, where he thought there was another one. We drove around cow pastures looking for a third one. We stopped at Burger King for some fries before heading back to his house so he could take his afternoon meds.

After he'd done that, we changed the subject back to his grandfather. Or rather I did. I couldn't get enough of learning about Albright's life and wanted to hear what he did after Reconstruction and about his mom Eliza.

Albright was a farmer in Emporia, Kansas, and an oilman in Los Angeles before becoming proprietor of The Brown Palace Hotel, a 41-room hotel near Denver, Colorado, where his daughter Eliza was in charge of hiring and managing the housekeeping staff in the late 19th century. This was the first time Mr. Dunlap mentioned his mom,

Eliza, whom he described as a gentle, polite woman with a natural soprano voice. She raised Mr. Dunlap in Denver, where she thought it was easier for him to avoid overt racism.

"I was raised fairly well, with a broad mind," said Mr. Dunlap.

"There was no segregation?" I asked, forgetting that he had said earlier that black people were rare in Colorado.

"Not that I didn't feel it, but I didn't really know about it."

Mainly he felt it on train rides from Colorado to California, where they visited Albright. Mr. Dunlap, his mom and his baby sister, Grace, were often the only blacks in coach. Restless, his baby sister liked to run up and down the aisles. "The white people didn't want to touch her. They'd pull their arms in. My mother caught hold of her and said 'don't do that." Mr. Dunlap said he didn't understand then why his sister had to sit down. "She was just a baby and she looked clean and good all the time. My mother had her in a pretty little dress, pressed and starched."

The Brown Palace Hotel, where Mr. Dunlap's mom worked, had a colorful background. It was purchased by one-time carpenter Winfield Scott Stratton, who traveled by foot with his dog all over the Colorado mountains, looking for gold and found it in 1891. After a day's mining, he went to the hotel wearing boots and dirty clothes and asked for a room to take a bath. They sent him away because he was too dirty. The next day he purchased the hotel with gold and walked into the lobby with the deed and fired everybody.

Mr. Dunlap showed me a photo of Stratton his mother had saved and continued the story. Stratton had discovered one of the richest gold mines in U.S. history and became one of the country's first millionaires when he sold it a few years later. "I was just a young kid when I asked my mother why Mr. Stratton didn't get married. And she said that it was because he had black blood in him and didn't want to start any trouble."

"Oh, he was passing as white. If he had kids they'd come out...."

Mr. Dunlap answered before I could finish the sentence. "Yeah, come out looking black. That was a no-no in those days."

To keep drunk and unruly miners in check, Eliza doubled as Stratton's security guard. "I remember very well Mom showing me how she was an expert shot. She could hit a dime with a revolver," Mr. Dunlap remembered. "And I used to wonder, 'how you do that?' She said, 'When I was working for Stratton, I carried a revolver in my apron because the miners would come into the house and they'd get drunk and want to see Stratton. I didn't tell them they couldn't see him—all I had to was pull out my gun and Boom! everybody cleared out.'"

Stratton wasn't the only one looking to strike it rich in the late 19th century. Albright himself struck gold close to the turn of the century. Oil was pretty big in Los Angeles around the time he moved out to the West Coast. The first discovery occurred around 1865. By 1897 there were 500 oil derricks operating in LA. The big oil mogul worked for Standard Oil of California, which was owned by the Rockefeller family.

Albright bought five plots of land 50 by 150 feet each about four miles west of downtown Los Angeles, and started digging for oil and hit pay dirt. He carried oil in barrels by horse and wagon to the refinery to sell. Though no one in the family knew how many barrels he was filling a day, it must have been a lot, because the wealthy people in town started talking.

"The Rockefellers had been looking for more oil and they couldn't get my granddad to sell. They couldn't understand this Negro, the only one around, being too stubborn to go with them. They didn't want to kill him, so they decided to cut him off. They bought all the acreage around him and he couldn't get his oil out. He finally had to give in."

"Where did your grandfather learn how to pump oil?"

"I don't know. He was smart. He found out how to do that. My granddad had a way of knowing what was good."

"How did your grandfather learn so much? Did he go to school before he was elected?"

"He got smart by traveling with the right people. During his term as a senator, he ran into all kinds. When he heard or saw something, he didn't forget about it. That's how he got his education, from mingling and listening."

Socializing in the right circles. Knowing what you wanted and who you wanted to be. I asked if those were key to his grandfather's confidence to do anything he set his mind to.

"That's right. That's the way. You don't go from grammar school to graduation from Yale. You gotta pass through all the stages in between. And he had the intuition to figure out which way to go."

Write down goals and work towards the big picture—that was the same advice Mr. Wright gave. Sounds simple enough, except for one thing that isn't as easy to find on a to-do list: a motivating force. Albright and Wright both had an inner fire, which weathered them through troubled times, not allowing them to give up until they achieved success.

It kept Albright going to work in Jackson to serve his country as an elected official despite death threats. It woke Mr. Wright up every day to go to class at a law school that would have preferred he drop out. It encouraged Mr. Hayden to go into business for himself when neighboring farmers made a pact not to hire him. Being fired up is a deterrent to what I've come to call "No" people—the people who are out there to tell you "No" every step of the way. It may be couched in other phrases like "you can't do that," "you aren't good enough," "maybe next time," or "you're not qualified." "No" people don't want to give others a shot. And they are very successful at what they do because most people aren't fired up enough to ignore them. Determined and dedicated, Albright knew they existed and ignored them all.

Mr. Dunlap and I talked about how parents don't make them like that anymore. He continued, "You don't have a lot of leaders in anybody's race today. Everybody's stealing away and fighting for the almighty dollar."

When I returned home, I started to read up on Albright and ran into a research problem. As I suspected, he was well known among historians in Reconstruction circles, mentioned in a number of books and journals. But most of the information was footnoted to the one 1937 newspaper interview. It made it difficult to track down additional information on something Albright mentioned in that clip that I found absolutely fascinating.

I wanted to learn more about the network of slaves who snuck onto plantations to make sure other slaves knew of the Emancipation Proclamation. Albright said Frederick Douglass, Harriet Beecher Stowe, and other abolitionists scheduled a meeting with President Lincoln to discuss creating the Lincoln's Legal Loyal League, or sometimes called Loyal League or Legal League or the 4 L's. There were only a few sentences here and there in different history books. Still, the information seemed to always come from the same source. Granted the group operated in secret. But still, wasn't there anyone else who wrote or talked about it years later?

I had a hard time believing the answer was no. As a last resort, I called the Abraham Lincoln Presidential Library and Museum in Springfield, Illinois. The curator of the Lincoln Collection had never heard of the League. He nicely challenged whether it ever existed. If it did he sincerely doubted the people Albright mentioned ever met with President Lincoln. The library gets inquiries about what he called "long-lost stuff" all the time. I wrote him an e-mail citing the sources where the League is mentioned and how I originally heard of it. "It was very common from about 1890 onward for older people to recollect meetings involving Lincoln that never occurred," he wrote back. In other words, the 91-year-old former Mississippi state senator was too old to remember correctly. "The outright lies of people in the 1890s astound me, and after that, well, one gives latitude to older people whose memories invent their past for them."

In the same e-mail, he called references to the Loyal League "historical re-creation." There was no way something so organized and cunning run by slaves could have existed without a lot of people knowing about it. "An informal operation can be named, but its actuating power cannot be accepted on the basis of a memory or a hunch," the curator said. But, as an afterthought, he admitted there could be information out there he didn't know about. In the last line of the e-mail, he wrote, "Please prove me wrong! This would indeed be an interesting discovery."

I accepted the challenge. Of course, a historian at a presidential library knew more than I did about comings and goings at the White House. However, I had something else going for me. I was hard-headed, as my parents marked me as a seventh-grader when I told my school bus driver I was going to get off at a stop I wanted, and did. (I got an after-school detention for that.) But then it was a bad thing. Now it was a good thing. I'd spent years listening to old people accurately remember dates, times, places, and events. I couldn't easily believe Albright made up the Loyal League, especially since memories of youth are usually the clearest in seniors.

After some digging, I found what I was looking for, right under my nose in unclassified documents at the Central Intelligence Agency. The CIA acknowledged that not only did the Loyal League exist, but membership included slaves who doubled as spies for the Union Army. They weren't allowed as of yet to fight as soldiers because Lincoln had yet to give his Emancipation Proclamation speech. But their presence across the South was invaluable to the North. Perhaps as early as the start of the Civil War in 1861, slaves had banded together to track and leak Rebel movements, get their hands on battle plans, and record meetings of Confederate officers who tended to dismiss their presence in the room when discussing tactical ops. Loyal League members or not, slaves were considered to be enemy number one by General Lee. In a letter in May 1863, he wrote: "The chief source of information to the enemy is through our Negroes."

Unfortunately, I was never able to confirm the White House meeting that Albright mentioned between President Lincoln and the abolitionists with 100 percent certainty. The closest I got was a book written in 1883 by a government employee named Allan Pinkerton. He detailed the spy system of the U.S. Army during the Civil War, using official papers prepared for President Lincoln. Some of the documents had never been made public.

In his book, *The Spy of the Rebellion*, Pinkerton, the Chief of the U.S. Secret Service during the Civil War, talks about how a "trusty" Loyal League messenger had direct access to him and his office. It is a safe bet to assume a slave wouldn't be able to arrange that kind of contact without an okay from the top. The CIA admits that many of the documents connected to slaves spying during the Civil War were destroyed. That left the question of who to trust and what to believe up to me, bearing in mind the theory, "absence of evidence is not evidence of absence."

12

North Carolina

DRIVING WHILE BLACK

The plan was to make Mr. William Dunlap my last interview. I'd been on the road off and on for six years now. New leads had become few and far between. There wasn't enough work left to warrant a full-time commitment, and family members of people I'd spoken to back when I started were calling to tell me of their deaths. Almost everyone I'd interviewed, and kept alive in my notebooks, had died. It was time to move on.

A couple of months after I got home, I started to clean up my office. I threw away old files to make room for printouts of new job listings in television; I was going to go back to my old job. A red folder was stuck in the back of a file drawer with a crinkled white paper sticking out from the top. Instead of tossing it in the trash, I opened it. Inside was a lone newspaper clipping of an article celebrating the birthday of 90-year-old Herman Hood, whose father, Rev. John, was born on a plantation in 1853 in Lancaster, South Carolina. I'd forgotten this lead was back there.

I left the file on top of my desk for the rest of the afternoon, thinking about what to do. I had no money left. I wanted a steady paycheck with health benefits to pay for non-generic prescription drugs. I was tired of racking up credit card debt to travel and deferring payments on my graduate student loan. Still, it was a good lead. I told myself, I'll follow up on it one weekend after I settle into a new job.

I kept clearing room for a place to put my job-search stuff. But I felt uneasy all day. A voice in the back of my head hounded me to make the call. Make the call! I finally sat down and picked up the phone to call Mr. Hood in Gastonia, North Carolina. His number was listed.

Speaking to his daughter, Juanita, I made plans to visit in a couple of days. After I hung up, I dialed the credit card company to request a limit extension so I could pay to stay for a week. All the while, there was this sense of relief. I'd decided to go because I was afraid I'd miss out on something if I didn't.

The road to Gastonia was paved in outlet malls. The billboards started popping up outside of Chapel Hill on I-40 West. There was a string of exits advertising discounted kitchen utensils, antiques, books, and lingerie. I had no time to stop, but I pulled into the slow lane behind a dump truck to check out the factory outlet names from the highway. Traffic was moving too fast to pick up anything except the hard-to-miss big red JR's Cigarette Outlet Store and off-exit directions to Biscuitville. Near Greensboro I grabbed breakfast at a McDonald's drive-thru. I spread strawberry jam on the sausage biscuit in the parking lot, then held it in one hand while steering with the other. I was on time, and wanted to keep it that way.

According to the article I'd dug out of my drawer, Mr. Hood had been living in Los Angeles by himself for 38 years. He'd been working for a real estate company that had sent him all over the country to build houses after earthquakes, tornadoes, and floods. He said he'd helped build more than 2,000 homes in his lifetime. In early November, Juanita asked her dad to come home to celebrate his 90th birthday with a party and spend Thanksgiving with his children and grands. Though no one knew it then, he was already dying of cancer. By the time they discovered it, the doctors thought he had had colon cancer for a long time but it was only when he made it to his daughter's house that he began to feel sick.

"My baby brother picked him up at the airport and when my father got off the plane, he said he was hungry so they stopped at the Waffle House," remembered Juanita about the day he arrived. "When he got to my house he said his stomach was hurting. The doctors ran tests in the emergency room and said he had prostate cancer. It had spread into his bones, all over his body." The doctors told Juanita her father might live three weeks or as long as six months, max.

That sticky humid Monday morning, a few days before the July 4th weekend, was seven days short of six months.

Juanita was her father's caregiver. She moved him into her house the day he checked out of the hospital to live upstairs in a guest bedroom above the garage. "Naturally, I was going to take him home and take care of him myself." His wife, Mozelle Byrd, Juanita's mother, had died in the same room last year.

When I arrived, the hospice nurse was upstairs giving Mr. Hood a wash-up and getting him dressed for the day. I waited downstairs in the living room with Juanita, still trying to figure out why I had felt so drawn to meet Mr. Hood.

"Is this your father?" I was pointing to a wallet-size picture of a man with brown freckles and cropped, silver hair, wearing a starched wide-collar white shirt and sea-blue polyester suit jacket.

"A long time ago," answered Juanita, a tall woman with a long head and neck and model-defined cheekbones.

The nurse came downstairs to let Juanita know her father was ready. We went up. After being in and out of homes for all these years, this was it—my last conversation. Understanding more about history on the road than I ever did in a classroom, I followed Juanita to Mr. Hood's room wondering, What am I going to learn today? I already had a new perspective on a broad range of issues from Reconstruction and skin color to affirmative action and the Civil War, subjects I never gave much thought to outside of an academic setting. Now I have a deeper understanding of how black history has shaped our identity, often in the wrong direction. I never would have known these things if I hadn't spent the past years finding them out.

Mr. Hood, lying in bed with Sesame Street pillowcases and sheets tucked under his shoulder, turned his head to the door. "Remember the lady I was telling you about?" Juanita asked her father as she walked into the room. I stood in the doorway. Usually I am not uncomfortable walking into a person's bedroom but this was the closest to death I'd come. I felt awkward. Knowing he was likely going to die in this room made me more respectful of his space. Juanita waved me in and moved to the side so her father could see who I was. Still I waited for Mr. Hood to say it was okay.

"Come in and sit down," invited Mr. Hood. His voice was soft and fading. Without moving his head, his eyes pointed to a chair against the wall in between the mirrored dresser near the door. When I grabbed it his eyes trailed to the side of the bed where I pulled the chair in front of Big Bird and Cookie Monster.

He looked tired. When he stopped guiding me his eyes drooped half shut. His jaw sagged like a sad clown when he wasn't talking. From the neck down, he was skin and bones. You could see that his legs under the sheet were contorted into slightly raised sideways Vs instead of straight.

By the time I reached the bed, Mr. Hood had taken his arm from underneath the sheet and placed it on top with his palm face down. I dropped the pocketbook off my shoulder and curled my hand around his fingers. "Happy to meet you, Mr. Hood."

Juanita, who'd been washing breakfast dishes when I arrived, went downstairs to finish cleaning up the kitchen. She said she was going to bring a glass of water for him when she returned. Mr. Hood nodded. We both watched her back as she walked out. Don't leave, I wanted to cry out. I wanted her to stay and keep an eye on her father to make sure he was feeling okay. He was so frail.

I stood there frozen; I was at a loss for words. He was looking at me and I was looking at him. I asked if he wanted the water now because if he did I could bring him some. He said he would wait for Juanita. There was a calmness and peace in the room that I've heard surrounds people when they are dying. When I stopped trying to think of something to say I became content to just to sit there in it.

Skipping the formal introduction about why I was there, I blurted out a comment that was a continuation of a conversation Juanita and I had been having downstairs on the couch.

"I was talking to your daughter, Mr. Hood, and she said there were fifteen of you guys. They sure don't make big families like that anymore."

"No, they don't do that no more." I was about to say something else when he kept going. "Five boys and 10 girls." I again thought he'd finished his thought because his voice tapered off. But he kept going. "I was always crazy about my sisters."

He talked in slow motion, but I didn't mind. Watching the energy it took for him to get out what he wanted to say made me want to hear it more. "They were thinking I was a girl, I wanted to be around them all the time. They'd be talking and after a while they would say, 'Boy, you get out of here—you don't have no business in here.' And I'd say, 'I didn't hear what you all were talking about anyway.'" He sounded happy remembering. For a couple words he turned to face me but mostly he stared wide-eyed at the air in front of him as if he could see faces in the empty space above his head.

To house the family, Mr. Hood's father bought an 80-acre farm south of Gastonia in Sandy Plains. While working in a cotton mill, he heard the land was for sale. "This white man wanted to retire because all of his family died and he didn't want to take care of the place no more," remembered Mr. Hood. His father went to talk to the man and bought the land for $10 an acre. On it, he built a one-floor, 11-room house with two bathrooms, where all the boys shared a room with two beds and the girls each had their own.

Juanita came back upstairs with a cup of ice water and a straw. She bent the straw toward Mr. Hood's mouth and held the cup as he sipped.

The last fifteen minutes in the room by myself with Mr. Hood were challenging. He kept falling in and out of sleep every few minutes, pausing sometimes after a word to catch his breath. From time to time he would hiccup, and the sheets over his chest would jerk up and down. When he did that, I'd try to stop the interview because I felt I was draining him. But he would say to keep going.

She overheard us talking about growing up in "the old house," as Mr. Hood called it, and chimed in. "My grandfather and grandmother were very, very close with their children to try and make them do right. To give them a home that they could call their own."

Whatever they did seemed to have worked. I asked them both about the closeness of the family unit then and now and what has changed. Juanita credited the fact that her grandparents were serious about religion, raising the family in the church. And Mr. Hood agreed he didn't see much of that anymore. With a mom who was a Sunday school teacher and a dad who was a preacher, Mr. Hood and his brothers and sisters were not just required to go to church every Sunday; their father had them participate in the service, scheduling one child a week to recite a speech about God in front of the congregation. They'd say prayers in the morning when they woke up and at night before bed, memorized Bible verses including the family's favorite, Psalm 23, the Lord's Prayer, and listened to their parents discuss scriptures. "My mother and father did that too," said Juanita about evenings spent at home with her brothers and parents.

For his part, Mr. Hood credited having nothing to do and nowhere to go as the reasons why his family stayed close. "In the country back then, all we had was each other." At night, everyone was home in pajamas and nightgowns after sunset. There was no television or phones for distraction. "There wasn't too much going on. We sat there most of the time. My sisters would play the piano, to keep us happy around the house." After dinner his mother came up with bedtime activities in the living room, like having them practice pronouncing words or showing her the days of the week on a calendar.

The Hood parents even fought fate to keep the family together. After a nod to Juanita that he wanted another sip of water, Mr. Hood told the story of how his mother defied the odds to save Juanita's life when she was born. The doctor didn't think she was going to make it through the night because she was a preemie, weighing just one pound, four ounces. "My wife was crying," remembered Mr. Hood. "She couldn't do anything, so my mother took Juanita from the doctor, slid her down into her apron pocket, and went into the kitchen." His mom got a steak from the icebox, put it in a jar, and boiled it on top of the stove to get the blood from the meat. "That's what she fed her to build her up. She had to use a medicine dropper and she wouldn't take no more than 3 or 4 drops at a time." His mother kept Juanita until she gained weight. When she was busy during the day, she'd put her granddaughter in her apron pocket or in a shoebox on the kitchen table.

Juanita was always the favorite in the family because she was the only girl. Mr. Hood's father was crazy about her too. He'd say, "That's my sugar, I want to keep her." When her brothers would play flight and argue, "Daddy would always tell them, 'Why don't they be sweet like Juanita?' After he said that all his friends started calling her Sug."

"What does Sug mean?"

"It's short for Sugar. He'd say, 'she was the Sugar of the Crop because she was the sweetest of the whole family.'"

Mr. Hood's parents wanted to be parents even after raising 15 children of their own, and when their children were having children, they couldn't get enough. They even volunteered to take Mr. Hood's four away from him and his wife to raise them. "My parents wanted to keep my children for themselves. I don't know whether they thought we weren't capable of raising kids or what. But they just wanted to take care of them."

We'd been talking well into the afternoon without a mention of the word slavery. And I didn't notice. Because I didn't think he was going to be able to hold a conversation for this long I had him steer it in the direction he wanted. Hearing him talk was beautiful—there was a joy in his face I had not seen with anyone. When I described Mr. Hood to friends later after I left, I used to say that you could tell he was loved. That his parents loved him when he was growing up. It was the very first thing that came to mind.

Eventually, near the end of the afternoon, I brought up the topic of slavery. Rev. John was nine when slavery ended. He was born on a plantation he only remembered as owned by the Crocketts, then sold to a Hood plantation in Lancaster, South Carolina, to an owner he only knew as the boss man. Rev. John had seven brothers—including a twin—and one sister. "Each had to go under a different name." Mr. Hood said. I asked what he meant by that.

"When my father was seven they were all sold, each to different owners. I couldn't understand why his twin had a different last name. I asked him one day, 'Why don't all of your brothers have the same last name?' He said, 'Well son let me explain it to you. We were sold.'" The Hoods bought Mr. Hood's father. The Funderburkes got his twin. The Crocketts kept a brother. The Clintons bought another brother. One was a Hamm. Another was a Hargrove. Mr. Hood couldn't remember who purchased the seventh brother. "My auntie, they never knew who bought her."

"Did they all stay in South Carolina after the auction?"

"Some stayed in the area. Others left the state. One went to North Carolina."

"Were they able to stay in contact? Did they see each other again?"

As soon as the war ended, the first thing the brothers did as freemen was look for one another. While the brothers never found their sister, using word of mouth and walking to as many as six plantations, one by one they tracked each other down. The last one to be reunited with his brothers was Rev. John. His owner wouldn't let him leave the Hood plantation. The boss man told the freed slaves that if any of them tried to leave he'd hunt them down and kill them.

Mr. Hood's uncles came up with a plan to help his father escape. He talked about how they smuggled him out in a mattress. They had to slice the mattress open and put him inside and sew the seam back up, put it on a wagon. Rev. John never went back to South Carolina after that because he always thought the Hoods would be looking for him.

Juanita brought up a plate of sliced carrots and cucumbers, cheese and Nabisco Ritz crackers for me. I inched the chair away from the bed, and turned my head to Juanita to ask in a whisper if it was okay to eat in the room. Mr. Hood wasn't eating, at least nothing to put any weight on. I didn't want to eat in front of him if he was hungry. "I am all right," he said—he heard every word.

After explaining to Mr. Hood that the experience of slavery has been viewed by social scientists as the root cause of the breakdown of the family structure in the black community, I asked what made his uncles and father exceptions to the rule by risking their lives to bring the family back together. He didn't know how to answer the question because he'd never heard that analysis before, which I found interesting. It made me wonder where that theory came from. When I started to look into marriage and family life during the 100 years following the end of slavery, I found that 80 percent of black households were headed by married, two parent families.

Despite all they had been through, freed slaves allowed themselves to be vulnerable, to love, and be loved. Mr. Hood's father had crosses up and down his back from when the boss man whipped him. "He'd beat him if there was anything wrong around the house...he had to hide their horses from the Yankees and if he didn't do it like they wanted, they'd put him over a barrel and strap him on and beat him."

I asked about the anger his father surely had to have had towards life—what did he do to keep it from consuming him?

"He was upset over all the stuff that went on. But he had to just go on, do what he had to do. He went on a while and then he met my mother and they married."

I decided to call it a day. As I left, Juanita put together a packet to take with me: a family photo, a photo of Mr. Hood's brothers and sisters at the home-going ceremony of their father, and a journal from her mother's grandfather, Swaney Hazel, that she'd kept for years but never showed anyone. In his journal he talked about how his wife and children were sold after his owner learned that Mr. Hazel was teaching the other slaves how to read. He spent his entire free life trying to track them down and was only successful in finding one daughter.

It went on to say, "I was an old man when I got word that one of my daughters was living a couple towns over and that she had been looking for me and that she had had her own family. I got up early in the morning to ride up there and spent the whole day with them all."

The journal ends shortly after that because Mr. Hazel died later that night when he returned home.

I closed the diary with happy tears. All of his life, all he wanted to know was that his children were okay. To have so many people and things working against him for him not to be a father didn't take away his fight to want to be one.

The tears stopped for Mr. Hazel and continued as I thought of my dad. Mom, too, but Dad had been on my mind a lot lately because he was dying. I'd like to think that if something happened to us, if we got separated as a family, he too would spend his life searching for us. Maybe it was a selfish thought, but I still wanted to be loved like that.

Stopping off at Office Max down the street from their house, I made copies of everything. On second glance, the photo of Mr. and Mrs. Hood, Juanita and her brothers, with its crisp white background, looked staged, with everyone deep in thought looking down at open books. But what the family photo lacked in flair it made up for with subtle emotion, such as Juanita almost sitting in her father's lap, with his arm around her waist and hers around his shoulder, both leaning in to each other.

I couldn't remember the last time I sat in my dad's lap. He was never the touchy-feely type. Never really hugged us or at least initiated the hugs. His thing was to pat you hard on the back—that was when you knew you did good. At the finish line after a track meet or college graduation, he'd walk fast to be the first to come over and only after he was done did other family members start coming up to say congratulations.

Dad was one of those Southern quiet types—uncomfortable around a lot of emotion. I only saw him cry once and he didn't tell us often that he loved us; but that was okay because we always knew. When we'd say it to him, he would just nod and smile, and pat us on the back harder. And when he did say the words, they were the lightning bolt that turned me into Wonder Woman and I could fly.

The last time lightning struck was in his hospital room after yet another surgery. On the way to New York City, I stopped in for no more than 15 minutes to sit with him and tell him the rest of the gang would be down in the afternoon. He again couldn't talk because of the trache tube. As I was walking to the door he reached for my hand. I thought he was reaching for my watch to see what time it was, so I pulled my hand back and told him the time. He shook his head and held out his hand again and I held out mine. He grabbed it, then touched his heart. I smiled. "Love you too, Dad. Hurry up and get out of here, okay?"

Every day that week, I went back to see Mr. Hood. He looked better every day, more alive. That second day, he was propped up higher on pillows, waiting for me to walk in. He started to talk faster and we laughed more. Eventually Juanita left us alone, only sticking her head in the room from time to time to see if we needed anything.

When I told Mr. Hood people would be reading about his life, he perked up. He liked that. "Others coming on now would read about me?" he asked to confirm that he heard it right. He pushed the sheets back and thought hard about what he wanted to say next. I could tell the wheels were turning by his wide-eyed gaze. But to say what? We had already covered a lot: the traditional criticism by the older generation of the younger. "Kids today don't know what they want. Don't know where they're going in life." He'd offered his insight on success on the job: Pick a career you love and make it who you are not what you do. "I was a working boy. Wouldn't call myself a hard worker. I just loved to work. Always wanted to work." He led a full life in accord with the Ten Commandments, but ultimately, was happy he didn't have to go through it all again. He felt life was easier when he was growing up. "I see everything as being heavier now than it was back then." He was ready to be done.

Then, this morning, out from under the covers came a young Mr. Hood—a confident and clever businessman who enjoyed long distance driving in his beloved 1950 black Cadillac. And if it had been parked in the driveway out front, he would have found a way to get into a wheelchair to take a picture to show folks. He got into a lot of trouble with that car.

At 37, he was the first black man in Gastonia to buy a Cadillac. "It was kind of expensive, but nothing I couldn't handle. When I came out with it, oh, it was the town's talk." The police stopped him almost every day the first month he had it. They never wrote him a speeding ticket or a warning or even asked to look at the registration. They pulled him over to ask if the new car was paid for. "The first time the policeman wanted to know whose car I was driving. I told him, 'I drive my own car.' He asked, 'What kind of work do you do? Do you bootleg?' "

Juanita came in then to check on us. "He's talking about his Cadillac, isn't he?" She stayed to hear the stories, though she clearly had heard them a million times.

Mr. Hood was also stopped three times in Miami and Daytona Beach when he drove his family to Florida for vacations that first year he owned the car. "They bossed me around there for a long time. They always wanted to know whose car it was I was driving. And I said, 'There are some white people I know down there.' And I told the police I chauffeured for them. I got me a white shirt and a chauffeur cap and that's how I got to drive without getting pulled over."

"Come on now, Mr. Hood. You dressed up like a driver so they wouldn't stop you?"

"That's right."

"Did they ever catch on?

"No. They just didn't want a black person to have a car like that."

As months went by, he started to notice more and more whites made an issue of him driving his own car. He tried to avoid taking the Cadillac to people's houses he worked for, hitching a ride instead in the pickup truck of a friend he'd hired as an assistant. One time, the car pool arrangement didn't work out and he had to drive his own car to a job in South Carolina. When he pulled into the driveway of the house he was working on, the wife and her friend admired the car. Then the husband came home. "He came and told me, 'I don't mean no harm, but whose car is that you're driving?' I said it was my car. I bought it. He said, 'I can't pay for a car like that,'" remembered Mr. Hood. The husband thought Mr. Hood was overcharging in order to cover the car note. To which Mr. Hood responded, "You don't have to pay for this car—I already paid for her." The husband went ahead anyways and fired Mr. Hood on the spot. "I put my tools in the car and I told them to make me out a check for what I had done. I never did let them get the best of me."

I asked what he meant by that.

"I didn't let it worry me. I would just laugh."

He laughed a lot that year. He told me another story of a man who called the Gastonia Cadillac dealership to speak to the salesperson who sold the black 1950 to Mr. Hood. "The white man wanted to know if I would be able to pay for a car like that. The dealer who sold me the car said, 'Sure. He could pay for another one if he needs it.'" The dealer called Mr. Hood later that day to tell him about the encounter. Mr. Hood remembered the phone conversation fondly without a hiccup or a cough, "He said people were calling him wanting to know how was I making my payments. He said, 'Seems like you are having a bit of trouble with people. From now on I'm going to tell them you just paid cash for what you got.'"

It wasn't just whites who had a problem with that car. "I had a little trouble with a lot of the black people too," he recalled. Apparently they would make fun of him when he drove by, doing things like taking off their jackets and laying them on the ground as if for him to walk on. This despite his willingness to take people places if they asked. He never felt the need to brag. "I didn't try to overwhelm them, you know. If someone didn't have a car I'd take them somewhere if they wanted me to," he said. After years of wear and tear, he sold the car to a funeral home in town and bought an Oldsmobile. Shaking my head, I said it was a shame that black people did him like that.

"Jealous." He had a grin on his face before his mouth opened to say the word.

A month went by and I got a surprise call from Juanita as I was walking out the door to Yale-New Haven Hospital. Mom had called minutes ago to tell me Dad had been bleeding from the mouth all morning and it wouldn't stop. He needed a blood transfusion. I told her I would meet them there.

Rushing to catch the next Metro-North train, I let the call go to voice mail until I heard Juanita's voice and picked up. We chatted for a few minutes about my time there and how much Mr. Hood had enjoyed it. I did too. When I told her I needed to call her back, she told me there was no need. She only wanted to let me know the news about her father's passing. "It was sudden," she said. "He stopped talking two days after you left and died three days later."

13

South *Africa*

RECONCILIATION HEARINGS

I was home one evening, flipping channels, when I came across a rebroadcast of Archbishop Desmond Tutu speaking at Fisk University on one of the public access stations. He was talking about the first time he met with President Nelson Mandela after South Africa's first democratic election in 1994 to set up the Truth and Reconciliation Commission (TRC), which was responsible for investigating the human rights abuses of apartheid.

I had heard about the public hearings in the news. There were three committees: one dedicated to victims, one to amnesty, and one to reparations. Testimony was being collected to record an official account of the atrocities suffered between 1960 and 1993. Credited with being one of the most influential forces in South Africa's transition to a free government, the commission had a "local" angle, because the United States had played an integral part in its creation.

Truth and reconciliations aren't new. They date back to the commission set up in 1974 by Ugandan dictator Idi Amin under pressure from human rights groups and the international community. But a few minutes into his speech, Archbishop Tutu mentioned how he and President Mandela came up with the idea for these hearings. He said, basically, that they saw how we Americans handled unifying the county after slavery. The "forget it and move on" approach clearly didn't work and had only led to even more division. One hundred years later, he pointed out, blacks could say this happened and whites could say that happened. There was no official record. "We didn't want that to happen in South Africa," he continued. "We don't want people to look back after we are all dead and gone and say these things didn't happen or they weren't that bad."

I went to bed that night curious as to how the commission was going to pull off what I thought was the most controversial aspect of the TRC, the amnesty testimony. To encourage perpetrators to confess their crimes, the government was guaranteeing freedom from prosecution, in exchange for testimony. The offer presented a cruel paradox, as one reporter put it. The commission needed people to come forward of their own free will to explain to families, tormented by years of not knowing the truth, what had happened to their loved ones. But once someone heard the details of their son's torture or their mother's disappearance, they had to live with the pain of knowing the applicant could walk away free. And some did—some without remorse or guilt, still defiantly saying they did nothing wrong.

The democratic government seemed to ask a lot of its citizens. In order for the country to be a unified South Africa, they were asked to try to forgive. Many people, including Archbishop Tutu, have suggested America could benefit from a similar approach to the historical record.

I woke up the next morning having made up my mind to go to South Africa to sit in on the amnesty hearings. I wanted to see how a country could account for the social injustice of the past to bring communities together for the sake of the future. A friend I grew up with in Connecticut, who had given up his job as a kindergarten teacher and bought a one-way ticket to Johannesburg, agreed to let me stay with him for two months.

The hearings were held throughout South Africa, in Johannesburg, Pretoria, Green Point, Durban, and Cape Town. Each hearing lasted no more than a week. Between 1996 and 2000, most sessions occupied only a day or two. An individual applied for amnesty for each crime confessed, as many as he wanted. The commission's responsibility was to gather the evidence from the applicant about a particular crime before deciding whether to grant amnesty for it.

The TRC faxed me a notice for a four-day hearing to be held near the Waterfront in Cape Town from September 25 to September 29. The three applicants involved were former operatives hired by the Civil Cooperation Bureau (CCB), a special-forces unit referred to as apartheid's death squad.

For the first day and every day after that, I was the only black American—or for that matter, I think, the only American—in the room. I heard accents from South Africa and the United Kingdom. Reporters from Spain and Italy had translator headsets on. And though there were wire service and newspaper journalists present, the press section had plenty of empty chairs. The layout of the room was always the same: a row of high-powered lawyers for the victims on one side, and lawyers for the applicants for amnesty on the other, each group facing the other. A panel of three robed judges sat in the middle of the back of the room, facing out.

The questions were detailed: Why was a Ford Laser used as getaway car? What was the reason for the preference for a silencer approximately twenty-five centimeters in length? How was payment received?

Everything was presented in a very matter-of-fact manner. The first two days focused on two men who applied for indemnity on the same four incidents, including the attempted murder of a political activist, conspiracy, and a bomb attack. On Tuesday the CCB coordinator for all of South Africa testified, basically saying he didn't know anything about the incidents in question because he was brought in at the last minute and the "projects" were already assigned and underway.

Wednesday's applicant, who gave evidence in Afrikaans and English under cross-examination, said he took the CCB job because it offered a better salary. Doubling as the owner of a front company called Lema, which shipped electronic appliances, computers, pocket calculators, and watches from South Africa to other African countries, the applicant was assigned to assassinate a political activist, who had to be killed before he testified in front of the United Nations. He eventually was pulled from the assignment. When asked under cross-examination why he was relieved of the job, he said making the front company look legit took up too much of his time. He didn't have time to kill the target.

One operative already sentenced to two life terms for separate incidents testified for three days. He was a reluctant applicant. He didn't want anything to do with the TRC, but when another applicant named him in the attempted murder of the same political activist he felt pressure to apply for amnesty. The target died of a presumed heart attack the day the hit man was to kill him. The hit man was later told that his target had been poisoned. At a certain point the line of questioning seemed to get bogged down in what the applicant, a cocaine and crack addict, thought were little details that distracted from the big picture. When asked about his decision not to wear a disguise on one mission, he responded, "Sir, these people hired me as a murderer. They hired me for my capacity to kill people, not for my capacity as an intelligence officer or a detective. They didn't want to see anything except the devilish streaks that I had in me."

The commission shut its doors after hearing from more than seven thousand applicants for amnesty, the vast majority of whom were white police officers. The big surprise was that many of the victims' family members were able to forgive. The TRC was considered a success and other countries have copied its model, including Peru, Argentina, Guatemala, Nepal, Sri Lanka, Serbia, East Timor, South Korea, Chile, Panama, and even the United States.

The first Truth and Reconciliation Commission in the United States was in Greensboro, North Carolina in July 2005. Greensboro TRC used the South African model to investigate a 1979 massacre that occurred when forty local KKK and American Nazi Party members opened fire on protestors demonstrating against working conditions in a textile mill, killing five in broad daylight, in front of four television news crews and one police officer. The six charged in the shootings were acquitted by all-white juries.

One of the bloodiest in the state's history, the Greensboro massacre was as infamous in its day as the murder of Mississippi's Medgar Evers and the church bombing that killed four young girls in Birmingham, Alabama. Today, the street in Greensboro where everything happened no longer exists—the city has rerouted traffic to avoid the area.

The investigation was initiated by survivors of the attack, residents who were children when it happened and still live in the area. They wanted answers: What was the role of the police department and the city? A police detective is rumored to have shot video of the massacre. Where is that video? The community couldn't move on until the whole truth came out.

But to move on, everyone needs to be on board, as they were on South African's TRC. That wasn't the case in Greensboro. The three-day hearing received no official support. The city council and business leaders were against it. The state didn't want it to take place so the commission had no authority to issue subpoenas or grant amnesty. The white mayor dismissed the commission in the press, calling it an "alternate way to create what never happened, and that is a major investigation." Exactly the point.

Victims and perpetrators of the atrocities that continued long after slavery was over—through the Jim Crow period and segregation—are still alive and can testify regarding criminal acts. Why shouldn't we pursue truth in the name of justice? Race relations is a national problem, but the solution may be local—our own experiment in truth and courage 140 years in the making.

14

Connecticut

"...AND GRACE WILL LEAD ME HOME"

As it turned out, 2003, the year after I interviewed Herman Hood, was Dad's last good year. A chief ear, nose, and throat surgeon at Yale-New Haven Hospital whom Dad respected said there was nothing left to be done. We believed him. He had been with Dad since 1990 through some fifteen surgeries, six rounds of chemotherapy, and three rounds of radiation. The cancer had come back too many times—there was nothing left to remove from that side of his face. Where they had cut out part of his jaw and cheekbone, his face had collapsed. They took out his teeth and a chunk of his gums. Dug a hole in the roof of his mouth, too, leaving it hollow all the way up to his nose. As much as his body had been through, the doctors were surprised he was still alive.

Dad started to wear tinted glasses because he hated to see people stare. The tumor was growing like a big ball of pus in his left eye, pushing the eye out of its socket, leaving it doubled in size and swollen shut. That was when the surgeon said no more—the tumor was stuck to blood vessels connected to the heart. If doctors tried to get anywhere near there, Dad would have a heart attack and die on the operating table. He didn't care. "Take it out," he begged the doctor still. He was in constant pain.

The only option left was chemo because radiation didn't faze the devil. Dad was reassigned to some assistant professor in the chemo unit whose residents didn't make a good first impression by prescribing a drug he didn't need, admitting when I questioned them that they had not even looked at his medical chart. It made me sick. He was dying and demoted.

Dad talked a lot that year. Before hanging up the phone one Sunday that spring, he said he had something he wanted to mail me; a tape recording of an interview he did with George Butler, his grandfather, a child of a slave. Dad called him Papa.

He made the tape in the summer of 1967 in Lugoff, South Carolina, on the porch of his aunt's house when he was 26. I never knew about the tape until that phone call. Dad never told me he had talked to his grandfather about his parents'—my great-great-grandparents' —being slaves. He had done the same thing I had started when I was 25.

It took him some time to make a copy. He didn't want to lose the original in the mail. A few weeks went by before the package came with a yellow Post-it on the tape case that read, "Papa got some of the dates wrong, but overall it was a good interview. Sorry it took me so long to send it." He signed it "John" which he did sometimes when he is extra serious.

When I first listened to the interview, I was in a car, and spent much of the time talking back to the tape deck, the same way some people talk to television screens. When Papa, who initially started yelling into the tape recorder until Dad whispered, "Not so loud, not so loud," said something interesting without fully explaining it, I followed up out loud with a question I would have asked if I'd been there. I figured Dad probably missed the opportunity and moved on to another topic. The next voice I heard on the tape was Dad asking the same exact follow up question.

Dad was a pretty good reporter for an engineer. He knew to get the basic questions out of the way early. When were your mother and father born? Did they talk about slavery?

"Do you remember the name of the guy who owned your father?" Dad asked.

"I heard him say that name many times, oh Lord, many times," said Papa, who couldn't remember. But he did remember the name of the person who owned his mother. "Old man Dave Robinson, he was a white boss man. He bought my mother from Sumter, a slave.

Paid $65 for my mother from a man named Willie Aman. And Dave Robinson brought her home to Fairfield. Brought her away from Aunt Liza and Aunt Anna." Dad didn't say a word; he didn't interrupt, he let him talk. Even when there were long pauses in between remember-ings, he kept quiet. "She went on to cry so hard in Fairfield that old man Robinson had to go back to Sumter to bring her sister Anna and sister Liza where she was at. She was crying so because she had left them behind."

Dad followed up, asking Papa how old his mother was when she was sold. He didn't know. But he did want the record to show, "She could read and print just as good as Mister anybody. I wish to the Lord I could read half as well as she did. Half. Not as well—half."

At a certain point Dad's grandpa must have kept looking at the tape to see if it was moving. He seemed fascinated by the voice-activated stop and go of the black box. "As long as you keep talk-ing it will keep recording," Dad told him. In the background was the sound of cars driving by. Papa cleared his throat as if to trig-ger the red recording light to come back on, before moving on to naming his five brothers and four sisters. Everyone was dead in his line except for one sister, Pauline. "I got no brother. No Aunt. No Uncle. No mother. No father. No grandmother. No grandfather. Just myself."

Slavery wasn't the focus of the conversation, which lasted about 45 minutes. Most of it was a list of names. Dad was trying to record the beginnings of the Butler family tree. We from later generations refer to that first branch as the Butler Dynasty. He asked his grandfa-ther to name brothers and sisters, uncles and aunts of both himself and his wife, Carrie Murphy, and tell a little bit about them. Carrie, my great-grandmother who Dad called Mama, had passed by the time the recording was made. Dad would later write everything down but he wanted to have a verbal record.

My favorite part of the tape was when Dad asked Papa how he met Mama, his wife. They were outside at a church camp meeting. He knew the minute he saw her, she was the one. "She was soup in my eye, and I was hard to satisfy."

They dated and were engaged for a year and a half before they got married. "I had asked for her. And they gave her to me." After her parents gave their blessing, the plan was to get married right away. But Papa got into an accident, broke his leg and couldn't walk for five months. So he pushed the wedding back a year. "After I got hurt, I was so ashamed I didn't ask for her no more." When he got ready to marry her again, he was supposed to ask her parents again. But he didn't this time. Instead, he said, "I stole her. Boy, that was the best stealing I've ever done in my life." I could hear the smile in his voice as he told the story of how he waited for her parents to go to church and then rode his horse and buggy to pick her up at her house and bring her over to his, where he had a pastor waiting to marry them.

Every few months after Dad gave me the tape, he'd ask if I had listened to it yet. "I'll get to it," I'd say even though I'd already heard it. Eventually, he stopped asking. I feel bad about it now, but back then, I was afraid to discuss the family history with him because I worried it meant he could let go if someone else took ownership of it. As long as he couldn't tell me what he wanted me to know, he'd have to stick around. What a joke I turned out to be, recording everyone else's family history but my own.

That same year he was trying to organize our family's history in every way he could. Even if I could refuse to admit I'd heard the tape, he was moving on with or without me. He and Mom spent the year going through old family photos: vacations, Butler family reunions, Christmases, dance recitals, slumber parties, Halloweens, college move-ins. What wasn't in the fifty-plus photo albums in the family room, most designated to one child with the name etched in gold capital letters on the cover and the age in gold on the binding, was in a dresser drawer in the living room, still in the 4x6 envelopes. He labeled each envelope in pencil, writing, say, "Sheria's 18th birthday" or "Kwanza's graduation dinner." He even sorted and labeled rogue negatives in shoeboxes from the '60s and '70s. They selected about 100 pictures and made two huge 5x4 feet framed collages to hang in the family room. In between are all of our framed diplomas from high school, college, and graduate school. The display spreads across an entire wall. We jokingly call it the Butler Wall of Fame. Much as I saw myself a preserver of history, Dad had me beat.

Also that year, he pulled each of us aside, Kwanza, Sheria, and me, and asked us to do something for him. All of us got the same speech.

"There's a plot of land in South Carolina that my great-grandfather owned. If I give it to you, you have to promise that you will never sell it," Dad said, sweeping the floor before setting the table for breakfast. Mom went to work out and left homemade applesauce and scrambled eggs on the stove.

"Sure, Dad," I responded in my pajamas. At that moment, I knew things were going to change. I had never seen him so serious without trying to be serious. I didn't know what to say, but I knew I didn't want to have this conversation.

"My grandfather thought the world of that land. His father gave it to him and he was a slave. Each of you girls have your own plot. But if I give it you, you must promise me you'll never sell it."

"I promise, Dad. Now can we eat?"

Dad smiled. I got him to smile.

He stopped talking and eating food in November 2004 when the doctors put in what became a permanent tracheotomy tube. The tumor was squeezing his larynx so tightly that he was having problems breathing. He had a permanent feeding tube put in because he couldn't swallow. The surgery to put in the trache took away his voice. We never got a chance to hear it again.

He hung on for another year, writing notes. He wrote notes to talk about the weather. To ask where was the remote. To tell Mom he needed extra pain meds. To see if we liked dinner. He would write to ask when we were going to go on our next family vacation. To let us know he needed a roll of paper towels to stop the drooling from the side of his mouth. Or, just to say "hi." After one visit home, Dad wrote a note as I was rushing out the door, looking to see my reaction as he jotted a couple of words. "Come home more often if you can." I nodded and told him I would. I took a flexible job with an understanding boss so I could do what he told me to do.

I went home so often in 2004 and 2005 that my sisters used to tease me that I had no life. Peter Pan was my new best friend. We each handled Dad's dying differently. Kwanza wrote him a note and gave it to Mom in the hospital parking lot to give to Dad when she went back upstairs to his room. She wrote on it "For Dad's Eyes Only" and sealed it. Sheria, who I jokingly say is the only normal one in the family, went home for Sunday dinner every week.

One day when I went home, Dad and I got into a heated discussion in his notebook about his feeding tube. I told him that his body needed real food and begged him to let me research this and buy a blender so I could liquefy the food to pour into the feeding tube. The doctors told him that taking a commercial feeding tube formula, Ensure, which had the consistency of a milkshake, was good enough. I didn't believe it. He hadn't gained any weight and was now losing it at a rate that didn't look right. He had no energy. He was getting weaker and weaker.

"Why would the doctor tell me something that would hurt me?" he wrote.

"They're just trying to suggest an easy solution for you, Dad. They don't know that we will take the time to make the same consistency but with real food."

We went back and forth. Him writing and then handing me the notebook. Me responding out loud. After an hour of this, I told him I'd consult the hospital nutritionist before we did anything and he agreed, smiling and putting the notebook back on the nightstand near the bed. He had tricked me. The conversation was never about food, he just wanted me to convince him I was right in the argument. He used to do that when we were kids to see how we put our thoughts together.

On Memorial Day weekend, I had a special professional blender FedExed to the house to start testing. I went upstairs to let him know but he was in bed. He had his good eye open and I thought it was to see who was at the door. I should have gone inside the room, but I didn't want to disturb him. Instead, I put a pillow in the door so it wouldn't close and Mom and I, who were downstairs, could hear him move.

I was the last person to see him alive.

Mom went up about 30 minutes later and the trache had popped out. We don't know how long he had been on the floor without oxygen, unconscious, but I remember his mouth was purple blue. He had a very faint pulse. When the ambulance came the paramedics couldn't use a defibrillator because Dad had a metal plate in his head from the radiation treatments. They had to do CPR. One guy did heart compressions and I took the air bag and squeezed air into his lungs from the hole in his throat.

When more paramedics arrived a guy took over the air bag and they put Dad in the van. Mom, crying, eyes swollen, hopped in the front seat and I told her I'd meet her at the hospital. Looking in the back of the ambulance as I ran to the garage, I saw that the people who were doing CPR had stopped and were filling out paperwork on a clipboard. They had given up. I pounded my fist on the back door window. Yelled in tears, "What the hell are you guys doing?" They started up again.

When we got to the hospital the nurse told Mom and me to wait in the grieving room, or whatever it was called. Mom held the nurse's arm. I charged towards the emergency room where the doctors were working on Dad. Mom called me back. "I want him to hear my voice. I want him to know he is not alone," I said calmly as I stuck my head into each room along the hall. A few of the ambulance people were still congregating around the nurses' station, waiting to hear how he was. I overheard one talking about the 8-minute ride from our house to the hospital. Dad barely had a pulse and his vitals were so low they considered him dead, which was why they stopped doing the CPR in the driveway. But somewhere on the way to the hospital, "he came back," the paramedic said to one of the nurses. "I've never seen anything like it." He came back.

He was unstable in a coma, and the doctor said there had likely been brain damage. Sheria had arrived and Kwanza was driving up from New York City. Mom and Sheria sat on one side of the bed and I stood on the other, holding his hand, talking out loud about nothing. Just talking out loud about stupid stuff that came to mind like that I hadn't brushed my teeth this morning. My making fun of myself, it always makes my family laugh. We all laughed and laughed. Even the nurse in the room got a chuckle out of my rambles. A good honest chuckle was the release we needed. And then after we stopped Mom said, "He moved his hand. Keep talking." I don't even remember what I said after that but a few minutes later his head started to move from side to side and his eyes started to squeeze as if he were trying to wake up. All of the bells attached to him started to go off because the movement was so strong. We got scared that he was going to rip out a tube connected to his throat or something. He had so many wires attached to his head, throat, and arms and he was in pain— that was the grimace he had on his face when he was in pain—that we asked the doctor to give him a sedative. This turned out to be the worst decision we could have made. He calmed down but never moved again.

For the next two and a half days he was never alone. We rotated shifts and took our positions in the room near the windowsill and next to his bed in the ICU. Dad's cousin he grew up with in South Carolina, Uncle Bouleware, came by. The second Dad heard his voice his heart rate and pulse accelerated. The nurse said that meant he could hear us. He knew we were all gathering, getting ready.

One time I was in the room by myself, reading him parts of the diary I kept on the road when tracking down the children of slaves. He had often asked me about the trips but I'd never given him any details. When the nurse came in to check his vitals, she told me something I had never heard in my entire life. Dad was crying. "Those are tears in his eyes," she said when I asked her to wipe the eye that was half open.

"Are you sure? I don't think so. Another nurse just came in and put gel on it so it wouldn't dry."

"No, honey, I know the difference. Those are tears."

That was the first and last time I saw my dad cry.

The night he died we were asleep in his room. Sheria was on a chair with her head on the radiator. Mom and I were on opposite sides of the bed with our heads near his hands resting on the sheets. Kwanza had gone back home to Brooklyn earlier in the evening because nothing was supposed to happen.

The room was quiet except for the beep of the respirator that was helping him breathe. Then suddenly my heart stopped as if someone had hit me from behind and knocked the wind out of me. "Stop it, Sheria," I said when I put my head back on the bed. But when she didn't say anything I turned around and saw that she hadn't moved. She was sound asleep near the window. I went back to sleep. A few seconds later it happened again. I couldn't catch my breath. For an instant, it felt as if my heart was physically being squeezed from inside my chest. When it stopped, something told me to look at the respirator. As soon as my eyes were fixed on the machine it immediately flashed from A to C, which meant Dad had stopped breathing on his own. I woke Mom up. Then I walked over to Sheria and tapped her on the shoulder. "I think this is it. I think he is going. We should say goodbye."

We took Dad home to bury him near the Butler land in Longtown, South Carolina, on a perfect, sunny day on the second Monday in

September 2005, in the church where he used to play guitar in the front pew. Where he walked for miles from Papa's house through the woods and crossed a creek every Sunday for Sunday school with his cousins and a bag full of clean church clothes that he changed into a few minutes before arriving on the front steps of Mt. Joshua United Methodist. Dad always said he wanted to come back home to retire and build a house on his land. We brought him home to rest.

The service was beautiful. Instead of the church choir singing solos, nieces, nephews, and cousins volunteered to sing Dad's favorite hymns, "Amazing Grace" and "His Eye Is on the Sparrow." The church was packed with his college roommates, a golf buddy from Connecticut, old friends who hadn't seen him since he left as a teenager for the North and heard he was coming home.

We all cried and laughed together. Kwanza and I were both in the program to speak. During the reflections part of the ceremony, his freshman roommate from Johnson C. Smith University told the story of when Grandma shipped Dad a turkey on Greyhound from Connecticut to the North Carolina campus, and they kept it on the air conditioner in their dorm room. If they'd put it in the floor refrigerator, the other hungry freshmen would have eaten it.

When I first started thinking about what I wanted to say, I went to bed with a pen and pad. I got the idea from listening to a radio interview with Stevie Wonder many years ago. The host asked him where he got the lyrics to the songs on his classic album "Songs in the Key of Life." Stevie said he didn't know. He said the words just came to him.

That was what I'd done for at least ten years now. I slept with a pen and pad, waiting for the words to come to me. I have the ink-stains to prove it on almost every sheet and comforter I own, as well as on pajamas. I would write things down in the middle of the night and wake up surprised at how good it sounded. I tried variations of this during the day, taking late morning or afternoon naps when I had writer's block, but it didn't seem to work as well.

The night before the funeral, I still had no idea what I wanted to say. I went to bed with a pen and pad, crying like a baby—I missed him so much. I don't remember my dream, but I remember waking up to scribble on a piece of paper that I read under the covers the next morning: "He gave us everything we ever wanted and more than we ever needed. But he never spoiled us."

15

A MEETING AT PIGGLY WIGGLY

Since Dad died, not a day has passed without my thinking of him. It's a heavy weight to bear—knowing the person who gave me so much and never asked for anything in return but to share what was on his mind, left this world without being able to do that. Dad wanted to tell the Butler family story; and now most of what he knew was buried with him. I don't think I'll ever forgive myself for that.

Names, dates and places I could find on my own. What I was upset about missing out on was family gossip. That stuff is impossible to replace—like the story of a husband calling his wife "soup." Thankfully Dad caught that precious description on tape. If he hadn't, I never would have known that my great-grandfather thought my great-grandmother was yummy: "She was soup in my eye and I was hard to satisfy." That quote isn't something found in a history book, nor should it be. It's bumper sticker material. Or a slogan for a family reunion t-shirt. Who else but family would see the beauty of that line and the powerful significance behind it: Papa had found the woman he wanted to love.

Last month, I unearthed several letters about him written in 1962 to Grandma from her oldest sister. Catherine had moved their father in to live with her and her husband in Lugoff, South Carolina, after their mother died. In a letter mailed on March 22, months after their mother's funeral, Catherine wrote, "Some days [Papa] thinks of Mama and he appears to be very sad and sometimes he cries. Of course I cry too." I experienced the watered-down version of their love, passed down through the generations. Grandma was raised by it; she passed it on to Dad; he gave it to us; and I will show mine. What a mighty force that love must have been to have lasted all these years.

Death found us again two years after Dad died. His mom, who lived across from us, had a heart attack at home in her sleep. Dad was her only son, and her pride and joy. She never was able to accept his death. Dad always took care of Grandma; he was a tough act to follow but we tried. We made sure she never wanted for anything. We hired an aide to cook and clean. When that person left early on Sundays, Mom walked across the field to bring Grandma a dinner plate. She scheduled and chaperoned all of her medical appointments, including a home visit to cut her toenails. I took a part-time job as an adjunct professor at the University of Hartford and came up before or after class every Monday for a semester to go grocery shopping for organic food and juice. I'd buy gingersnap cookies from Trader Joe's or baked root vegetable chips for her to snack on. As I got the grocery bags out of the trunk, she would wheel herself into the kitchen in her wheelchair to see the selection and when I gave her a napkin full of something she could put in her mouth, she'd say, "That's a good girl," and wheel back in front of the TV.

We concentrated all of our energy on keeping her happy. Her sudden death, less than a week after her 87th birthday barbecue, caught us by surprise. She was in relatively good shape; she was supposed to stay with us longer. And so here I was again. I'd repeated the same mistake. Of the 10 children in the Butler Dynasty, Grandma was the last. She too was a record keeper for the Butler family. Dad had learned things from her, too, and now I had missed getting it from both of them.

I did know some things, thanks to Grandma telling me stuff when I was young. Some of it was vague and I remember Dad saying some of it wasn't quite true. When Kwanza and I were young, Grandma told us about her grandfather, Grandpapa Robert Murphy; he was the person who owned the land Dad wanted us to have but made us promise never to sell. When we were in middle school, our parents volunteered us once a month to go over to our grandparents' house to help them pay their bills. This was years before Dad built them the second house across the field from ours; back then they lived an hour east then in Norwich, once a bustling factory town known for having more millionaires than most places in the country. Grandma cleaned their mansions and was a private health aide. She and Grandpa built a white and brick house under a tall maple tree with a creek flowing through the backyard. When she wanted to drink fresh water, she would carry a pot to the edge of her property and fill it up, throwing out the pebbles as she walked back to the house.

I didn't mind being recruited because all we did was write checks in the amounts she wanted; she would sign then make us coffee with cream and sugar, which we drank in front of the television until someone came back to pick us up. Coffee was a big deal—along with candy and soda—all the things Grandma and Grandpa introduced us to. With the extra time Grandma would tell us about the Murphys and Butlers. Because she had Dad with someone else before marrying Grandpa, Dad was given her family name.

Grandpa was a Roach. That was his family name. He was from Longtown, too; they grew up together in the same church. His family donated the land the Mt. Joshua United Methodist church is built on. I don't remember him talking much about the Roach family. He was good for playing "Gotcha," though—when we'd try to grab his mustache, he'd pretend to bite our fingers.

Looking back, I realize we actually fell into the conversation about Grandpapa Murphy. Grandma was rubbing her knees, complaining about the arthritis she swore stems from her rough-and-tumble days as a tomboy, scrunched up in an old tire rolling down hills on the farm.

"You did it that many times, Grandma?" I asked.

"We had a lot of land." And so the conversation started.

Her mother Carrie Murphy grew up in an old plantation house her father Robert owned. They called it the Big House. It was a mansion.

After she got married and became a Butler, Grandpapa Murphy built her a two-story house on his land about a mile and a half down the road. In the late 19th century, Grandpapa Murphy had no less than 300 acres.

"How did Grandpapa get all that land and come to live in a plantation house?" I asked all those years ago. And I still don't completely know the answer.

According to Grandma, her great-great-grandfather was Irish and owned a slave ship that transported Africans to South Carolina. His family was the Murphys and they were rich; they owned much of the northeastern part of the state to hear Grandma tell it. His son had an illegitimate son by a slave. When the grandson's son, Robert, who could pass for white, married a black woman, his father disapproved and disowned him. "They gave him land and told him to go live with the black people," Grandma said. "On the land, Grandpapa built a school and a church and he was the town doctor. If anyone got sick they came to see Grandpapa."

I'd probably spend a lifetime putting together the pieces and filling in the holes because it wasn't until Dad's death and then Grandma's that I tried to do for my family what I'd done for so many others: Listen.

When we went back to Longtown to bury Grandma next to Grandpa, who died the day after Christmas in 1992, in the same church cemetery where we buried Dad, I spread the word to cousins that I was gathering information. Little good that did. We all knew basically the same things with the same holes. Except for cousin Junior, whose real name was Fortune Carolina, Jr.—he knew a little more because he was Dad's oldest cousin; his mom, Catherine, was the oldest sibling of the Butler Dynasty. I made plans to visit him in Charleston where he moved for retirement.

A distant cousin on my grandfather's side, Uncle Leon, whom Dad used to walk to church with, also volunteered to make some calls when he got back home to Baltimore. "I'm not sure if the people you need to talk to are still alive. I think they may all be dead. But I'll call around to find out." I wanted to jump in and say, "I know, I know. Please don't remind me that I may be too late." But I didn't because I knew he would come through with someone. His brother still lived in Longtown and if anyone was going to find someone, it would be the two of them together.

Stumbling in black heels that sank into the ground where the dirt was soft, I tiptoed over to Dad's grave. His tombstone is six plots down from Grandpapa Murphy's born in 1840 and died in 1924. A black butterfly kept flying around my face as if to get my attention. I'd shoo it away, but it refused to leave and sat on my shoulder as I whispered to Dad: "I'll be back soon."

Uncle Leon, who wasn't really a blood Uncle but was considered as close to dad as a brother, called me months later to tell me he found someone for me to talk to. A 104-year-old woman who lived near the church was still alive and his distant cousin Lacine White agreed to meet me in the parking lot of Piggly Wiggly supermarket and take me to see her.

"You might be wasting your time, you know. People down South don't like to talk about things," Uncle Leon said.

I wasn't sure what he meant by things and asked, "Like what?"

He thought I wanted to know more about Grandma having had Dad as a single teenager, which was a big deal in the South in 1941. I hadn't thought about that, but now that he brought it up I put it on my list. I've always known that Dad wasn't planned. Nor did Grandma want to marry her boyfriend who lived across the road when she was growing up. Dad never knew his father. That I knew. He met him once as an adult, after he had graduated from college, when his father was in some kind of veterans' or nursing home. That one time Dad went to see him, "His father didn't know who he was. John never went back," Grandma told me a long time ago, when I asked why my last name was Butler instead of Roach, like hers.

"Because I was a Butler when I had your father so he was going to be a Butler," she answered.

In the summer of 2008, not long before the third anniversary of Dad's death, I took a trip to Longtown. I left from North Carolina, where the family had celebrated July 4th the weekend before, during a storm. Rain pounded the windshield coating it frothy white; I could hardly see the windshield wipers let alone the road ahead.

The weather dampened my plans to stop at the farm stands that popped up like wild dandelions on the side of the road. Yellow peaches were in season, sweet and ripe. Handwritten signs in water-proof magic marker leaned against the sides of pickup trucks parked under a white tent or on covered tables nearby while the driver waited in the front seat for the rain to stop. If I wasn't trying to stay ahead of the next downpour, I would have at least stopped at a stand near Waccama Lake where the road sign also advertised wild blueberries by the pint.

The closest exit to Longtown off I-20 is five miles south of Camden, home to Mary Boykin Chesnut who recorded travels with her husband during the Civil War in her famous journal, "Diary from Dixie." Longtown is the oldest part of Fairfield County and its early history is the least well-known; the oldest and grandest estates have been destroyed by war and Father Time. One cotton plantation house was said to have 365 windows—one for every day of the year. When Sherman's army marched through Longtown in February 1865, soldiers set it on fire. Despite its wealth, the town, which was once called Log-town for the large number of log cabins, was not mentioned on early maps prior to those created by the Confederates during the war. The heavily wooded land once supplied the fur trade for the Wateree Indians. The town is considered the easternmost settlement in Fairfield, but parts of it slip into bordering Kershaw County, west of the Wateree River. Even today no one really knows the exact boundaries of Longtown, which makes archival research tricky.

Immediately off the U-turn exit for Lugoff are two truck stop hotels. We always stayed in the Ramada Inn when we came down for funerals and summer vacations when we were young. Across the two-lane highway from the hotel is The Waffle House, which Sheria and I used to dodge traffic to get to. We'd eat breakfast and order takeout for everyone else.

The Piggly Wiggly was down the road in back of the parking lot for Western Sizzlin' Steak House. Mrs. White was waiting for me in the parking lot in a white Cadillac. She was mad. I was late and because I didn't believe in cell phones I wasn't able to let her know I was almost an hour behind. "I was getting ready to leave," she said.

"I am so happy you didn't, Mrs. White. I am very sorry to...."

"Well, come on then. Let's go see if Mrs. Jones is home." She pulled out of the parking lot and I followed.

We headed toward Mt. Joshua but at the last stop, instead of turning left to the church we kept straight. We both parked on the grass, near two magnolia trees with what looked like long strands of cotton hanging from the lower branches. Mrs. Jones' son Brother—that is what everyone called him—put Spanish moss on the trees fifteen years ago and had turned the front yard into something out of a Louisiana swamp movie, oddly stunning.

No one was home. At the front door, Mrs. White confessed that she had forgotten to call to let them know we were coming.

I stared at the moss while we sat on porch bench outside an empty house, deciding what to do. Mrs. White didn't want to come back again. I told her it would be okay if she didn't because now I knew where to go. As we sat fanning our hands in front of our faces to cool ourselves, a handicap van pulled up. Mrs. White and Mr. Brother had gone to a doctor appointment that morning and were just getting back.

Mr. Brother wheeled his mom to the ramp access in the back of the house. He got her settled in and then came around the front to open the door. Mrs. White told him we had taken a chance they would be home and asked if Mrs. Jones was up to having guests.

"You all come right on in." He held the screen door open.

Sitting in the wheelchair, Mrs. Jones had her legs propped up and several blankets over them to keep warm due to poor circulation. Her elbows rested on the arms of the chair, and her long, skinny, wrinkled fingers were clasped together resting under her chin.

I explained that I was one of Annie's granddaughters from Connecticut and that I was in town to learn more about the Butlers.

"How is Annie?"

"You know she died last year around this time?"

"You don't say?" She looked down at a string of the fringe on a blanket in her lap. "I didn't hear nothing. You left her up North?"

"No, she wanted to be buried back home. We buried her at Mt. Joshua."

"Up the road here?" I nodded. "Well, I just didn't know." She shook her head.

I asked if she remembered much about the Butlers and the Murphys and she said "Not that much" in a way I'd learned over the years is old-people-speak for: "It depends on what you want to know." I started asking what I wanted to know.

I explained how much I knew about the family and that I could only go back as far back as my great-great-grandfather Robert Murphy.

"You mean white colored Murphy?"

"Robert Murphy, yes."

"We used to call him white colored Murphy."

"You knew my great-great-grandfather, Robert Murphy?" She nodded. She knew him. I got chills. I didn't know she could go that far back. "Why did you call him white colored?"

"He was so light he looked white." She smiled, but it looked like she wanted to laugh.

"What was he like?"

"He was real old when I knew him. He was quiet, kept to himself most of the time. He didn't like being around a lot of people. But when his family didn't go to church on Sunday he would invite us over to his house Sunday afternoon for Bible study and singing."

"I hear they called his house the Big House."

"It was on an old plantation. There was a post in the front for visitors to hitch their horses."

It sounded like something out of the movies, but instead of Scarlett O'Hara and Rhett Butler, it was black folk.

"He owned all that farmland back in there." She raised her hand in the air, pointing in a circle in the direction of Longtown. "Him and the Roaches, they were the only blacks in the area who owned land like that."

"Did anyone talk about how he got all that land?"

"I don't know, but I think his father owned part of it."

"Did Annie ever mention the Martins?" she suddenly asked, changing the subject.

I didn't recognize the name, but the way Mrs. Jones asked it, I sensed that I should have. Dad's biological father was the only person she could be talking about. "You mean, my Dad's father? I never knew his name."

I explained to her that single women today who have children out of wedlock tend to give their children the father's last name. I was also impressed with Grandma that she didn't. Mrs. Jones didn't understand the logic of giving the child the father's last name if it wasn't the father who raised the child.

"Why do the mothers do that?" she asked. Back then the child had the mother's last name if she wasn't married.

I asked her what the locals said about Grandma when they heard rumors she was single and pregnant. "It wasn't like it is today with teenagers showing off their bellies. You were ashamed. Boys didn't touch girls until they got married. They weren't supposed to." She went on to say that when Grandma was pregnant she started walking behind her family on the way to church and was the last one in. Hearing that made me sad.

"But when Dad was born, Grandma said her parents raised him so she could move to Connecticut with Grandpa and get settled." My comment was a little defensive, because if the family was upset then why did they agree to raise him?

"Annie had a hard time with delivery," Mrs. Jones said, the pushing and pulling did something to her insides. "She went through a lot to have him. So when he came out, things changed." But she couldn't have any more children after that.

Mrs. Jones continued saying that everyone in Longtown who knew the Butler family, knew that "Her brothers and sisters were all close. You messed with one; you messed with all of them." Mrs. Jones told a story about Grandma that showed a side I had never seen—if it hadn't been confirmed later by cousin Junior, I wouldn't have believed it. When one of Grandma's brothers, Drummond, returned from World War II, his mind wasn't the same. He became spooked by the sounds that reminded him of the war. He checked himself into a mental facility, and when he got better the facility would only allow his wife to sign him out because they wanted to be sure he had a place to live. He and his wife were on the outs at the time, so she refused to sign him out. Though he planned to move back in with his parents, the wife, who lived in Longtown, was going to let him rot in the hospital. When Grandma heard Drummond's wife wouldn't sign for him, Grandma went to see her. "I wasn't there, so I don't know exactly what Annie said. But people got to talking and said that Annie told that woman right at her front door that if she didn't go to the hospital and sign out her brother today, she was going to come back and kill her."

"My grandma said what? Noooo." I couldn't believe it.

"Now that sounds like Annie!" chuckled Mrs. Jones.

"It does?"

"Her mouth was in her stomach."

What? Mrs. Jones repeated it. Her mouth was in her stomach.

I looked at Mrs. White and Mr. Brother for help. I was the only one who didn't get it.

Mr. Brother translated it for me. "Whatever she wanted to say, it came right out of her. She didn't hold anything back."

Mrs. White nodded that she was ready to go. Mrs. Jones wheeled as close to the door as she could without her feet hitting the screen. She had one last question for me. "Was Annie a big lady?"

"Do you want to know if my grandmother was fat? Yes, she was on the heavy side. Why?"

"I knew it. Those Butler women went up North and they all got big after they stopped working on the farm." I made a quick mental note to self: Go to the gym when you get back to NYC to fend off the fat gene.

I went to CVS pharmacy and bought the last red hot water bottle they had, then drove the half hour back to Mrs. Jones' house to give it to her. She had complained that her feet and legs were always cold when she got in the bed at night. A hot water bottle was a trick I learned in the mountains of Uganda, where it was freezing at night without electricity for a heat. "Fill it up with hot water and put it under the sheets a few minutes before you got to bed. Then when you go to lie down, the sheets will be warm so your feet won't be cold," I said, handing it to Mr. Brother and thanking her again for agreeing to spend the afternoon with her.

I pushed back plans to drive to see cousin Junior the next morning and told him I wouldn't get to Charleston until late evening. I had to visit Dad's grave. Stopping off at the store, I bought a bucket, sponge, soap, and garden gloves to take with me to clean off his stone and Grandma's and Grandpa's too. The church benevolent fund did this for the cemetery plots on a regular basis but I felt it was my responsibility while I was in town. I also bought a gallon of bottled water because I didn't know if I'd have access to a garden hose.

I went by the local florist in Lugoff to get some flowers. I asked for hydrangeas because we had them in Connecticut, and I couldn't think of the names of any of the flowers Dad planted in our backyard. "They aren't going to last in this heat. You might want to go with something like——," the florist started to point me to the fake section, which I actually felt insulted by.

"I don't do fake flowers, and neither did my dad. The flowers don't have to last. They only need to last as long as I am there." We went to this florist every time someone died, for the casket spray. She gave me a 5 percent discount.

For the first time ever driving to the church cemetery, I wasn't sad. I was looking forward to spending time cleaning off the graves in the 110-degree heat. I brought a change of clothes and put on a t-shirt and shorts and stayed for an hour, pulling weed grass, and removing branches, twigs, and rocks from the mounds. I poured the bottled water into the bucket, added soap, and washed the red dust and dirt from the tombstones. Then I poured clean water over them to rinse off the suds. When I was done I went to the car, which I'd left on to keep the air conditioner running so the flowers wouldn't wilt, and grabbed the white hydrangeas and placed two stems on his tombstone. Then I walked to Grandmas and Grandpa's and did the same.

I changed back into my clean clothes and headed to the Camden Archives and Museum, which had an excellent library for genealogical research, according to the brochure. A woman named Peggy behind the information desk welcomed me with a soft hello and asked if she could help. A staff archivist with grey hair, round glasses, and a Laura Ashley pink blouse, she knew her way around the collections for a family genealogy searches. From a shelf in the corner, she pulled out a spiral bound document with a teal cover titled, "The Murphy Family 1822-1994" by James Bernard Murphy of Orangeburg, South Carolina.

After reading a handful of pages, I assessed that James was writing about a different Murphy family tree from Longtown because I didn't see any reference to Robert. There were two other Murphys who lived in Longtown and I had then assumed that my Murphy line had to have come from one of those two.

Peggy walked around the library pulling books and volumes that mentioned the name Longtown. I looked at the stack of 10 maroon bound hardcovers on the table and dived in for three hours. After that I stopped. I'd forgotten how overwhelming and time-consuming this stuff could be. Family or not, I no longer had the patience to search blind like I did when I was 10 years younger. I gave Peggy a three-page handwritten memo detailing everything I knew and wanted to know and wrote a check out for $80 to the Archives & Museum. She told me she would look into everything and get back to me in a week.

I arrived in Charleston around 11 p.m. and proceeded to unload my luggage and produce from the back of the station wagon. Before going to the cemetery that morning I'd visited the Columbia Farmers' Market. It opened at 6 a.m. and I got there shortly afterward to stock up on six cantaloupes, three watermelons, a box of looseleaf lettuce, and a bushel of peaches from a black farmer who took the time to explain that all peaches look the same but don't taste the same, depending on the type of seeds used. I did a taste test.

Junior was still up, and when he saw all the fruit I was carrying into the house he plugged in an empty refrigerator stored in an addition to the house area. Hanging near the door was Dad's blue denim shirt bearing the logo for Pratt & Whitney, where he worked for 36 years. I stopped to touch it. Junior had taken Mom up on the family offer to come by the house and get what they wanted of his stuff before Goodwill hauled it away. I also saw a dark blue Pratt & Whitney baseball cap. It made me smile.

Junior showed me to my room upstairs. We made plans to go to dinner tomorrow. Before he went downstairs I asked him about the story of Uncle Drummond in the hospital and if he had heard it. "I remember myself this happening not long after the war, around 1946," he said. "I was about eight. Now I don't know where she talked to the woman, but Annie took her older sister Susie Mae with her. That was how all of the family was then. Family had to stick together. Don't let nothing come between blood."

For dinner, we went to a local restaurant known for its crabs. I put the tape recorder on the table and pressed play, and we stayed for hours. He talked about how the Butlers were called "Big Mouth Butlers" because they talked loud. That one of Grandpapa Murphy's sons didn't like his second wife, after his mom died, and tried to poison her. How Grandpapa Murphy wanted his children and grandchildren to go school and helped pay for them to enroll in Browning Home, a boarding grade school for blacks in Camden. "My mother credits him for her education. He'd tell her, 'Don't be like your dumb mammy.' They didn't say mother or mom back then. I sent her there to get an education and she didn't finish."

He laughed at the strained relationship Grandpapa Murphy was said to have had with his son-in-law Papa Butler. They had a falling out once though no one remembers over what. But Papa moved his family off his father-in-law's property to a white sharecropper's shack. "My mother was young at the time and she never could understand why her father moved out of his nice house to live in a shack." After a year, they moved back. "I guess Papa was saying he had to be his own man."

And when Grandpapa Murphy died in 1924, his white family buried him at Mt. Joshua. "My mother's words were that his uncles said that none of the blacks could touch him. From the time he died to when he was buried, they could have nothing to do with the body. All of the funeral preparations were done by the Murphy whites."

I asked if he knew anything about Grandpapa Murphy's parents. He didn't.

On our trip back to the house, there was a large thud behind us that neither of us could figure out. It turned out I had left the third watermelon in the back of the trunk. "You remind me so much of Annie," Junior told me, which surprised me. What did a watermelon say about me to remind you of Grandma? He explained that Grandma used to pack her car with vegetables and fruits from Longtown whenever she came South to visit. She never went home to Connecticut empty-handed. "Seeing you with all that food in the back of the car said Annie all over again."

About two weeks after I got back from Charleston I got an envelope in the mail from the Archives and Museum in Camden. Peggy had written a letter and provided all of the documents she could find on my great-grandfather. She found more than she was expecting; genealogy of slaves is hard to track because most of the records are not in public domain and were kept private by the slave owner. In the envelope were a will, death certificate, census records back to 1840, an 1853 clip from the local *Camden Weekly Journal*, and two maps. But the big discovery was that Grandpapa Murphy was the illegitimate son of a plantation owner Joseph Murphy and a slave named Eliza. Joseph owned 67 slaves in 1860.

The name Joseph sounded familiar because his will was mentioned in that teal spiral notebook I had looked at but dismissed when I was in the Archives and Museum last month. Peggy had made a copy of it for me and included it in the packet because the slave owner Joseph James written about in "The Murphy Family" binder and the Joseph that Peggy was now talking about was the same person. The difference was that James was a descendant of two slaves owned by Joseph so his book researched a different family tree starting with the Murphy slaves. On the other hand, my family is a descendant of a slave and Joseph himself.

I called James to hear about the 30 years' worth of research he had done on the Murphys.

He kept asking me if we were from the same Joseph. We compared the birth dates and names of the other illegitimate children Joseph, who never married, had. I explained I was a black person from one of his illegitimate sons by a slave. It all lined up.

I asked if he knew where Joseph, who first showed up in Longtown in 1790, was from. I remember Grandma saying he was from Ireland.

He didn't.

I asked if he knew anything about the Murphys running a slave trade from West Africa to South Carolina's east coast.

He didn't.

"After the war was over, Joseph Murphy gave his slaves some of his land. But it is all gone now. No one held on to theirs."

"We have ours," I said proudly, and explained the 80 acres owned by the Butlers from the Murphy line is still in my family. But just 80 acres. Apparently, not all of the nine children were paying taxes on the land, which was still under Grandpapa's name, and when the tax collector came to collect back taxes the hundreds of acres was forefeited to the state—all of it. On August 5, 1946, the Butlers bought back their part and divided it amongst their 10 children. Now it is divided up with his great-great-great grandchildren.

"Oh, I didn't know that."

He had to get off the phone. He was making barbecue sauce for a family reunion. Next year he was planning a Murphy reunion and was sending out 5,000 invitations later this year. I said that was beautiful.

"What's beautiful?"

"That two people 100 years ago could start a line that today is 5,000 strong."

"Yeah, I guess it is. I never saw it that way."

I suggested that I invite his line of Murphys to our next family reunion, which we plan to have in Longtown in a couple of years. We agreed to stay in contact.

Before he hung up, I asked if he knew anything about the white Murphy descendants. Everything I knew pointed me to a dead end.

"I found two descendants who are still living near the area.

"Are their names Murphy?"

"No, they've been married down the line, but they have Joseph's family Bible still. When I went to see them they told me that, and when I asked to see it they quickly said no."

"They wouldn't let you see it?"

"You know people down here still have this strong guilt about everything that happened. But I was disappointed when they took it back that they had the family Bible. Before I asked to see it they said it had a lot of information about the family and the plantation in it."

"Do you have their address? I would love to make a trip down there to introduce myself."

"I have it somewhere." I could tell he didn't want to tell me.

"Do you remember their first or last names?" I asked, humbly.

"Well, you can't just go knock on someone's door. You have to be invited."

Okay. "Would you mind calling them and telling them that a descendant of Joseph Murphy would like to meet them?"

"I plan on being in Longtown in two or three weeks and was thinking about dropping by their house. I'll give them your name and number and leave it up to them if they want to contact you."

I'm still waiting for that call.

ACKNOWLEDGMENTS

Thank you to the families who invited me in; people who didn't hang up the phone and those who did; patient drivers who continued to give directions from the car after the light turned green; B&B owners who feed me amazing breakfasts every morning that made me happy to start the day; the historians who laughed; state aging centers that listened; helpful genealogists who knew more; courthouse archivists who can read scribble; librarians who let me ramble monotonous details; interns who worked for little cash and a lot of take-out; Susan Greenberg for accepting my ideas; Tim Seldes for keeping me focused; Elyssa East for sharing; Merlin Chowkwanyun for being the history teacher; Wendy Paris for listening to and editing my thoughts; Joane Amay for the sample sales; the research assistants who found the Kentucky centenarian booklet, who transcribed the tape, who typed out the journal, and who found the Fisk University VHS tape; Kwanza for the rent; Sheria for picking me up; Mom for feeding me when I was on empty; family and friends who kept me motivated by asking the same, albeit annoying, question for almost a decade, "How is the book coming?" and God for holding my hand. I have been blessed.

Notes

Preface: Curiosity Kills the Cat

Page vii   "On the passenger seat of my rental car was a front page article from *The Charlotte Observer...*" Dave Baity, "Retire at 90? No Way from This Builder," *The Charlotte Observer*, Nov. 28, 2001, page 1L.

Page x   "The sentiment was so strong that U.S. Rep. Tony Hall, a white Democrat from Ohio, and eleven white co-sponsors..." Bill Nichols, "Slavery: Should the nation apologize? Critics argue substance is needed, not symbolism," *USA Today*, June 18, 1997, page A1.

2: California: Sipping on Dom Pérignon

Page 10   I use Crispus Attucks Wright's father's first name Warner so not to confuse with his son.

Page 12   "Everyone knows that 1865 was the year the Civil War ended and the Thirteenth Amendment abolishing slavery was ratified..." "Constitution of the United States," Thirteenth Amendment.

Page 12   "... Congress didn't vote on the Fourteenth Amendment granting black Americans citizenship until 1868....with inalienable rights to freedom." "Constitution of the United States," Fourteenth Amendment; Eric Foner, *Reconstruction: America's Unfinished Revolution*, New York, NY, Harper & Row, 1988, pages 251-61.

Page 12   "Harsh, restrictive state laws known as Black Codes....coerced the population to work as farmers for little or nothing." Rodney D. Coates, ed, *Race and Ethnicity: Across Time, Space, and Discipline*, Brill Academic Publishers, 2004, page 39.

Page 13   "...would organize similar dance performances...called the cakewalk..." Kwame Anthony Appiah and Henry Louis Gates Jr, eds., *Africana: The Encyclopedia of the African and African American Experience*, Basic Civitas Books, 1999, pages 350-51.

Page 14   "...the United States was moving toward the peak of a unique social and political movement the likes of which would never again be seen in this country." Eric Foner, *Freedom's Lawmakers: A Directory of Black Officeholders During Reconstruction*, revised edition; Baton Rouge, LA, Louisiana State University Press, 1996, pages xi, xxxi.

Page 14   "As early as 1866, there were more black students than whites enrolled in schools throughout the South." Stanley Lieberson, *A Piece of the Pie: Blacks and White Immigrants Since 1880,"* Berkeley: University of California Press, 1981, page 139.

Page 14   "...according to a Pugh family letter...parents started sending their children away to 'paying' schools." Letter from Willie T. Nichols to Thomas B. Pugh dated Aug. 11, 1867, courtesy Ellender Memorial Library at Nicholls State University in Thibodaux; Pugh Papers #2052.

Page 14   "...one Northern abolitionist observed the push to build schools.... 'Private schools for Negroes sprung up outside Bureau control. Enrollment in such schools grew from 150 in February to nearly 3,000 in December.'" Quoted in Howard Ashley White, *The Freedman's Bureau in Louisiana*, Baton Rouge, LA, Louisiana State University Press, 1970, page 177, as cited and quoted in York College Cuny, *Reconstruction and its Effects on African Americans*, Derell Kennedo, *The York Scholar*, Vol. 4 fall 2007.

Page 14   "By 1877, two thousand black men actively participated in local, state, and federal government..." Foner, *Freedom's Lawmakers*, pages xi, xxvi.

Page 15   "Louisiana alone employed more than two hundred officeholders..." Ibid, xiv.

Page 15   "...twenty-two blacks were elected to Congress, most just out of slavery..." Philip Sheldon Foner and Robert J. Branham, *Lift Every Voice: African American Oratory, 1787-1901*, University of Alabama Press, 1998, page 506.

Page 15   "This bitter resentment was epitomized by a Georgia Democrat... as he wrote, 'men who were but yesterday our slaves.'" E. Merton

Coulter, *Negro Legislators in Georgia During the Reconstruction Period*, Athens, GA, 1968, quoted in Foner, *Freedom's Lawmakers*, page xii.

Page 16   "Intimidation also reigned from Democratic rifle clubs, where members..." Heather Cox Richardson, *West from Appomattox: The Reconstruction of America After the Civil War*, New Haven: Yale University Press, 2007, page 177.

Page 16   "...cut voting population from over 90 percent during Reconstruction to less than 6 percent by 1892." *Race and Voting in the Segregated South*, Constitutional Rights Foundation (CRF).

Page 16   "In Louisiana, the number of voters fell from 130,334 in 1896 to 1,342 in 1904." Jack M. Bloom, *Class, Race, and the Civil Rights Movement: The Changing Political Economy of Southern Racism*, Indiana University Press, 1987, page 267.

Page 16   "Moses Sterrett, who served two consecutive terms in the Louisiana legislature, could only get work..." Foner, *Freedom's Lawmakers*, page xxx.

Page 16   "Because by the 1880s a majority were sharecroppers..." Ralph Shlomowitz, "The Origins of Southern Sharecropping," *Agriculture History*, 53, 3, July, 1979, pages 557-575; Department of the Interior, *Report on the Production of Agriculture, Tenth Census,* 1880.

Page 18   "The reference he made was to Proposition 209, the controversial 1996 referendum that barred public institutions in California..." CA Secretary of State-Proposition 209 on the November 1996 ballot.

Page 18   "'All these years we've been fighting to get into professional schools and now they want to turn back the clock.'" Betsy Peoples, "Taking a Stand Against Prop 209," *Emerge*, Rosslyn: Mar. 1998, Vol. 9, issue 5, page 34.

Page 19   "A year later after the law passed, the University of California (UC) reported an 80 percent drop in the admission of black students to law school...the first-year class had one." William Raspberry, "We Are Asking the Wrong Question," *The Washington Post*, May 11, 1988, page A23.

Page 19   "A headline in the Boston Globe in 1998..." Lynda Gorov, "UC's Fall
           Class Is White, Asian; 2 Campuses Report Effects of New Law,"
           Boston Globe, Apr. 1, 1998, page A3.

Page 19   "...with black enrollment at UCLA, where Mr. Wright went as an
           undergraduate, at its lowest level since the late 1960s." Jennifer
           Bihm, "Access Denied to Minorities in UC System," Sentinel, Los
           Angeles, CA, LXX, 12 (June 10-16, 2004), pageA1.

Page 19   "University presidents from Columbia, Harvard...their schools
           accepted a large number of white applicants with lower-than-
           average test scores..." Patrick McGee, "Texas Anticipates Effect of
           Supreme Court Affirmative Action Ruling," Fort Worth Star-Telegram,
           June 22, 2003; Linda Greenhouse, "Justices Look for Nuance in
           Race-Preference Case," The New York Times, Apr. 2, 2003.

Page 27   "During the 1956 presidential race, the New York congressman
           told a Republican dinner party..." "Powell Cites Gains Under
           Eisenhower," Los Angeles Times, Oct. 24, 1956.

Page 28   "The same year he won a bronze medal in the Berlin Olympics....
           Dr. Linus Pauling who later won the Nobel Prize in chemistry in
           1954 and the Nobel Peace Prize in 1962." Nobel Foundation.

Page 34   "Augustin and W. W. were two of the first four Americans to settle
           in Assumption Parish along the bayou in 1823." Federal Writers'
           Project, Writers' Program, Louisiana: A Guide to the State, U.S. History
           Publishers, 1947, page 575.

Page 34   "W. W. owned Woodlawn—800 acres of crop land, 1,550 acres
           of swamp, 162 slaves..." The Pughs of Bayou Lafourche, Plain View
           Press, 1985, pages 13-17.

Page 34   "Augustin had his seventy slaves build a small cottage...." Ibid.,
           page 30.

3: Virginia: One Life to Live

Page 39   I use Walter Scott's father's first name so not to confuse with his
           son. Use mother's first name to be consistent.

Page 39   "Born in 1838, Robert Henry was almost thirty when the Civil War ended." Confederate Pension Rolls, Veterans & Widows, Military pensions, United States, Prince Edward County, Virginia. Dept. of Accounts, Application Roll 111; 1925. Courtesy of the Scott-Carrington Family.

Page 39   "Mr. Scott's mother Alice was seven when the war ended," Gilliam will dated April 6, 1860, Prince Edward County Courthouse, Farmville, VA. & August 1860 Census in the County of Prince Edward filled out by Slave owner German Gilliam, Slave number 30, Prince Edward County Courthouse, Farmville, VA.

Page 40   "The Prince Edward County school board gained national attention because it refused to enforce the ruling..." Jeffrey A. Raffel, *Historical Dictionary of School Segregation and Desegregation: The American Experience*, Greenwood Publishing Group, 1998, page 115.

Page 40   "The county's eighteen hundred black students were locked out of an education ..." "A Few Negro Students Awarded Scholarships," *Farmville Herald*, Sept.11, 1959.

Page 40   "But with the help of emergency funds designated by the Virginia legislature..." "School Foundation Gifts Tax Deductible," *Farmville Herald*, Aug. 11, 1959, "Patrons, Inc., Is New Corporation to Aid Private School Foundation," "Football Pushed," Jaycees and editorial, "Books! Books!," *Farmville Herald*, Aug. 14, 1959. As cited in *American Tragedy: The Story of the Prince Edward County School Closings*, Stephen Day, Marshall University Graduate School, summer 2007.

Page 46   "...Mr. Scott's father was volunteered by his owner, Tom Treadway, to join a Colonel Carter with the Confederate Army of Northern Virginia in Richmond in 1864." Confederate Pension Rolls, Veterans & Widows 1925, Application Roll 111.

Page 46   "... 'volunteered to defend their homes against the new threat from the North.'" Charles Rice, "The Black Soldiers Who Served in the Confederate Army Are the Real Forgotten Men of the Civil War," *America's Civil War*, Nov. 1995.

Page 49   "Lynchings and torture of blacks by white Southerners, once limited to scare tactics..." Sig Synnestvedt, "Lynchings and torture of blacks by white Southerners: Citizenship in the United States Since Reconstruction," Macmillan, 1972, page 60.

Page 51   "...Owning this farm, we had the 'Big House' where the master once lived..."Washington and Scott, In Tuskegee & Its People, page 347 as cited by Christianburg Institute.

Page 51   "...Institute for Colored Youth...the oldest of the Historically Black Colleges ..." Cheyney Universities of Pennsylvania.

Page 58   "...Dorothy E. Davis v. County School Board of Prince Edward County." U.S. District Court for the Eastern District of Virginia Richmond Division, Filed May 23, 1951. Civil Action No. 1333.

Page 58   "The Virginia State Department of Education was not ashamed to play favorites..." "Prince Edward County: The Story Without An End," a report prepared for the U.S. Commission on Civil Rights, July 1963 found at Virginia Commonwealth University.

Page 63   "The slave quarters had been turned into public restrooms." Appomattox Court House, National Historic Park, Virginia; National Park Service; U.S. Dept of Interiors.

4: Kentucky: Master in the Family

Page 65   "... I barely made a dent in the twenty-page list of Department of Aging centers." fax from NASUA, National Association of State Units on Aging received Feb. 27, 1998.

Page 65   "He sent me a 1959 newspaper article from the Norfolk Journal & Guide about his great-grandmother..." "April 27 Is the Big Day, Mrs. Scott's Nearing 100," Norfolk Journal & Guide, April 11, 1959.

Page 66   "...the article in The Courier-Journal about one-hundred-and-two-year-old Charlie Hayden..." Byron Crawford, "Moving Right Along at 102: New Name on Sign Honors Long Life on Danville Avenue," The Courier-Journal, June 10, 1998.

Page 67   "...stuffed a fifty-one-page booklet of Kentucky centenarians put out by the state's Office of Aging Services in 1999," Kentucky centenarians with lives spanning three centuries 1800-1900-2000 and in conjunction with The International Year of Older Persons 1999, sponsored by The Kentucky Office of Aging Services.

Page 68   "The Bluegrass Region is home to an extensive collection of such structures....illegal to disassemble in public rights-of-way." Interview with Karl Raitz, Chair Department of Geography, University of Kentucky, on Oct. 6, 2008, and interview with Chris Harp, Executive Director, Dry Stone Conservancy, a Lexington-based non profit dedicated to the preservation of dry stone structures in Kentucky's Bluegrass landscape, Sept. 19, 2008.

Page 70   "Mr. Hayden's father, Austin, was thirteen when slavery ended.... Austin reportedly said. They had nowhere else to go." Interview with columnist Bryan Crawford.

Page 71   "...The breed, chiseled in shades of dark brown, graceful and tall, became popular during the Civil War as the mount of choice of Generals Lee, Grant, and Stonewall Jackson." American Saddlebred Horse Association.

Page 73   I use Ezra Hayden's father's first name, Austin, so not to confuse with his sons.

Page 74   "...the last public execution in the United States in 1938..." Perry T. Ryan, *The Last Public Execution* in America, 1992.

Page 74   "Whites were hanged only for murder, while blacks were hanged for murder, attempted murder, rape..." Charles J. Ogletree Jr. and Austin Sarat, *From Lynch Mobs to the Killing State: Race and the Death Penalty in America*, NYU Press, 2006, page 99.

Page 75   "...actually had fun cutting out a man's heart and..." Ashraf H. A. Rushdy, "Exquisite Corpse," Transition Issue 83 (Volume 9, Number 3), 2000, pages 70-77.

5: Indiana: "Black Man's Protection"

Page 82   "... 'The Colored people are Sending for us in Every Direction... they want Schools Started.'" Marion Brunson Lucas, *A History of Blacks in Kentucky: From Slavery to Segregation*, 1760-1891, University Press of Kentucky, 2003, page 229.

Page 82   "...Charlie begged to continue to following year, his father told him....'All you ever need to know is giddy up and whoa.'" Interview with columnist Bryan Crawford.

Page 84   "...slaughter of 5 million hogs when market prices had bottomed out to as low as two cents a pound..." "Hog Prices Decline in Chicago Market," New York Times, Aug. 30, 1933; "Hog Plan Dooms 5,000,000 Animals," New York Times, Aug.19, 1933; "30,000 Hogs Taken in Farm Aid Move," New York Times, Aug. 24, 1933.

Page 86-87 "Marion County was also the home of the whiskey-producing Maker's Mark Distillery, which is a National Historic Landmark." Marion County Chamber of Commerce, Lebanon, Kentucky.

Page 88   "When Kentucky was first settled, people like the Haydens brought white indentured servants with them from the Old World." Eric Williams, Capitalism and Slavery, University of North Carolina Press, 2007, page 9.

Page 89   "...It has been argued by Aristotle in The Politics that some people are born to be masters and others are born 'by nature' to be slaves." Richard Kraut, Aristotle: Political Philosophy, Oxford University Press, 2002, pages 277-297.

Page 90   "In her letter she wrote that Augustus died in 1888 and on his death certificate the family wrote the name Gus." Letter from Sister Donnelly in Ennis, Texas received around Dec. 30, 2002.

6: Kentucky: "I Found Ray Charles"

Page 95   I decided to use the first names of Alice and Robert Hopkins, reserving the right to use Mr. and Mrs. only when I had met someone in person.

Page 96   "Born around 1845, her mother Fannie was Cherokee Indian." Declaration for Widow's Pension, received Feb. 21, 1911 for Fannie Hopkins.

Page 96   "Her owner was James 'Hampton' Watts..." Author interview with Gertrude Grey, July 11, 2002.

Page 96   "...a stocky Virginian, from Halifax County...thirty-six-year-old
           Hampton..." *Graves County Kentucky: History & Families,* Turner Publish-
           ing Company, Paducah, KY, Graves County Genealogical Society,
           page 482.

Page 96   "In mid-1850, thirty-six-year-old Hampton left Old Dominion
           for Western Kentucky..." estimated date base on letter from Wil-
           liam H. Watts to James H. Watts dated Nov. 15, 1850, courtesy of
           Graves County Genealogical Society.

Page 96   "...the U.S. government was giving away land in the newly settled
           Indian territory." Michael Vincent O'Shea, Ellsworth D. Foster,
           George Herbert Locke, *The World Book: Organized Knowledge in Story and
           Picture,* Hanson-Roach-Fowler company, 1918, page 3308; Letter
           from William H. Watts to James H. Watts dated Nov. 15, 1850,
           courtesy of Graves County Genealogical Society.

Page 96   "Along with his first wife, Hampton built a new home around
           Baltimore in Graves County." *Graves County Kentucky: History & Families,*
           page 482.

Page 96   "...he owned so much virgin terrain that the family bragged he
           couldn't cover his land in one day on horseback." Author inter-
           view with Gertrude Grey, July 11, 2002.

Page 96   "...his brother William wrote a letter from Halifax County on
           November 15, 1850, agreeing to join him..." Letter from Wil-
           liam H. Watts to James H. Watts dated Nov. 15, 1850, courtesy of
           Graves County Genealogical Society.

Page 96   "...he couldn't travel 'this faul'....He had a family of twelve,
           including himself and his wife..." Ibid.

Page 96   "We had Drouth here this summer from the first of June to the
           first of September....Negro boys and girls is selling from $800
           to $1000. Men from $1000 to $1200." Ibid.

Page 97   "...his oldest son John Robert, nicknamed 'Bruzz'....and enough
           slaves to give each child one of his or her own." Author interview
           with Gertrude Grey. July 11, 2002.

Page 97   "...Congress banned the slave trade in 1808." U.S. Congress, "Act
           to Prohibit the Importation of Slaves," Section 4, 1807.

Page 97   "...there was also the fact that he was born around 1840." Declaration for Pension, received June 28, 1911, lists Wesley Hopkins as 71 years of age, Certificate No. 256685.

Page 97   "...citing excuses like bad weather conditions, or ship repairs or restocking of supplies. In fact, fifty thousand slaves were illegally smuggled into the United States from 1808 to 1860." Hugh Thomas, *The Slave Trade: The Story of the Atlantic Slave Trade*, 1440-1870, Simon and Schuster, 1997, page 616.

Page 97-98 "Wesley was then sold in Baltimore to W. W. Hopkins and his wife Lucy..." Molly Harper, "Area figures in rights film: Ex-slave's tales provide reality for interviews usable in schools," *The Paducah Sun*, Jan. 6, 2002.

Page 98   "Early in my research, I got a similar report from a family of three in D.C.—one son and two daughters—whose father had fought in the 45th Union Infantry Regiment. The fading, ninety-plus-year-old siblings....the answer was no." Author interview with John Johnson and Alice Vreen whose father was Private Alonzo Johnson of Company F 45th Infantry Regiment in Philadelphia, 1997.

Page 98   "...researchers who studied groups such as survivors of torture in Chile under the Pinochet regime and those imprisoned in Nazi camps..." David Shapiro, "The tortured, not the torturers, are ashamed" *Social Research*, winter 2003.

Page 98   "A former house slave in her nineties interviewed in North Carolina in 1937 was quoted as saying..." David W. Blight, *Race and Reunion: The Civil War in American Memory*, Harvard University Press, 200, page 315.

Page 100   "Wesley was one of approximately 40,000 black soldiers from the border states..." James W. Fraser, *A History of Hope: When Americans Have Dared to Dream of a Better Future*, Macmillan, 2002, page 88.

Page 100   "He was twenty-four when he was mustered in the summer of 1864." Appendix Company "B" Eighth U.S. Colored Artillery (Heavy) Mustered in Private Wesley Hopkins, Aug. 15, 1864 in Paducah, KY, page 139.

Page 103   "...'Cause love is soft. Love is sweet. Love is just a little baby.' " Lyrics to 1977
            Thankful album by Natalie Cole

Page 105   "Up until that point the state had taken a 'wait and see' approach
            to the Supreme Court decision." A. Lee Coleman, "Desegregation
            of Public Schools in Kentucky—One Year Afterward," *Journal of
            Negro Education*, Vol. 24, No. 3, Summer 1955, page 248-257.

Page 106   "Mrs. Wilson had her own moment in the spotlight in 1984
            when the local newspaper, *The Mayfield Messenger*..." Wendell Giv-
            ens, "For Mayfield's Mrs. Jennie Wilson: Life's Struggles Were
            Well Worth It," *The Mayfield Messenger*, Apr. 16, 1984.

Page 111   "In a county that once had three thousand slaves, Barry Blythe,
            known around Graves County as Uncle Burly, was the last one
            alive." *Graves County Kentucky: History & Families*, pages 10-11.

Page 111   "...'Zachariah Blythe turns out to be Bill Clinton's great-great
            uncle'...." Gary Boyd Roberts, in cooperation with New Eng-
            land Historic Genealogical Society, Boston Massachusetts, "Cal-
            loway's Two Colonels," Ancestors of American Presidents, *History
            of Calloway County-1931*, Santa Clarita, CA, 1995 pages 130-134;
            177-178; "Benton Paths" publication of the Benton County (MS)
            Historical and Genealogical Society, Vol. 2. #4, Dec. 1992 as cited
            in "Bits of Bark From the Family Tree" published by Batesville
            (AR) Genealogical Society, Vol. XVIII, June 1993, No.2, page 11,
            "Blythe (The Family Tree of President Clinton)."

7: Kentucky: Pit Stops

Page 116   "Rita Ridley's House Bed & Breakfast, a Victorian home ordered
            from a Sears and Roebuck catalog in 1907..." According to Rose-
            mary Thornton, *The Houses That Sears Built*, Gentle Beam Publica-
            tions, Feb. 25, 2004, each "kit home" "contained 30,000 pieces,
            including 750 pounds of nails and 27 gallons of paint and var-
            nish. A 75-page instruction book showed home buyers, step by
            step, how to assemble those 30,000 pieces of house."

Page 117   "Parts of Cave Spring at one point had been called at least five
            different names that are now spread out in different counties."
            Other names include Cave City, Cave Hill, Sinking Spring, Cove
            Spring.

Page 119   "...laughed that parents proudly tell their teenagers, 'I'll beat the
            black out of you,' as a way to keep them in line." Real Time with
            Bill Maher; Sept. 5, 2008.

Page 119   "...a Portland, Oregon defense attorney cited post-traumatic
            slave syndrome in defense of his client charged with the beating
            death of his two-year-old son." Holly Danks, "Judge Rejects Slave
            Trauma as Defense for Killing," The Oregonian, May 31, 2004, page
            E01.

Page 119   "The lawyer's argument even gained pseudo-credibility..." Ibid.

8: Tennessee: Interracial Adoption

Page 121   I use first name for Peter Vertrees so not to confuse with other
            Vertrees family members.

Page 121   "But mixed-race children from white women were not slaves but
            sold as servants until adulthood...designed to punish the mother
            for miscegenation." Naomi Zack, Race and Mixed Race, Temple Uni-
            versity Press, 1995, page 79-80.

Page 121   "This was the primary source of the increase in free black popu-
            lation in some states....one half of the mixed population lived in
            upper southern states around the Mason Dixon line, including
            Kentucky..." Ibid., page 80-81.

Page 123   "The law required Peter's white mother, Mary 'Polly' Elizabeth
            Skaggs to hand over her son to the courts when he turned five....
            The grandfather would rear his grandson as one of the family
            and 'provide the necessities of life.'" Indenture of Apprenticeship
            from Peter Skaggs to Jacob Vertrees; Edmonson County Court,
            June 8, 1846 to be carried out on Dec. 16, 1846 when Peter
            Skaggs was about five years old, courtesy of Kenneth Thomason.

Page 129   "...was of South Carolina senator Strom Thurmond and his illegitimate daughter with his housekeeper." "Strom's Secret," Ken Cummins, *The Black Commentator*, issue number 21, Dec.19, 2002.

Page 130-131   "...Peter's family tree as far back as 1716 during the reign of Louis XIV....two Vertrees brothers, Jacob and John, who belonged to a noble family, fled France to Holland and from there set sail for America." Hardin County Historical Society , *Who Was Who in Hardin County*, 1946. Reprint 2005, section "Captain John Vertrees."

Page 131   "When they arrived, they changed their last name, Van Tress, to Vertrees..." Ibid.

Page 131   "There is no record of the later life of Jacob, but his son, Isaac, was a private in the Pennsylvania Line during the Revolutionary War and was discharged in 1779 at Fort Pitt....In 1800 he deeded his land on the forks of Otter Creek near Vine Grove together with his home to his son Jacob." Ibid.

Page 131   "'Ms. Odom is related to the patriot Patrick Henry?'....The short answer was yes..." Mary W. Schaller, *Papa Was a Boy in Gray: Memories of Confederate Veterans Related by Their Living Daughters*, Thomas Publications, June 2001, page 111.

Page 132   "...1861-1862, Peter and his doctor uncle spent much of their time visiting sick soldiers in their infantry whose illness was listed in the medical records as 'nostalgia'..." Schaller, *Papa Was a Boy in Gray*, page 111-122.

10: Alabama: Lessons from the Grave

Page 143   I use Jackson's last name out of respect and to not confuse it with his daughter.

Page 146   "It grieves me to part with these papers....When other girls had rough times, they turned to their fathers. I couldn't turn to my father, but I'd think of him trudging to Huntsville..." Charlotte Fulton, "Daughter of Runaway Slave Celebrating 100th Birthday," *The News-Courier*, Mar. 15, 2001.

Page 147   "...original 'assignment notice,' dated the day before New Year's Eve in 1863 when he arrived at a Union army outpost at Pulaski..." Original Assignment, Dec. 30, 1863, notice courtesy of AAMU State Black Archives Research Center and Museum.

Page 147   "...Union scouts were paid $16 a month and $100 a head to recruit slaves to leave the plantations to join what would become one of the nation's first black fighting regiments." Robert Dunnavant Jr., *The Railroad War: N.B. Forrest's 1864 Raid through Northern Alabama and Middle Tennessee*, Pea Ridge Press, Athens, AL, 1994, page 43.

Page 147   "The Union Army had occupied Northern Alabama at the time, including northern Limestone County where Jackson was a slave." Ibid.

Page 147   "By Christmas Eve, the 110th U.S. Colored Infantry had 960 new recruits." Ibid., page 44.

Page 147   "He was recorded to be five-foot-six with a 'yellow complexion.'" Assignment notice, December 30, 1863 courtesy of AAMU Research Center and Museum.

Page 147-148   "...he was promoted to corporal just thirteen days after enlisting. Then a month later came another promotion to sergeant..." Selected Papers of John Jackson Dawson 1832-1905, as prepared by West Galley of the Museum at AAMU.

Page 148   "...the sergeant title was listed on his discharge papers three years later." Original discharge notice Feb. 6, 1866, courtesy of AAMU Research Center and Museum.

Page 148   "Part of his duty was to write daily reports to hand to superior officers." Charlotte Fulton, "Mason Donates Father's Civil War Documents," *Athens News Courier*, page 1.

Page 148   "...the state of Alabama prohibited such education, punishable with 33 lashes for the first offense and then to be sold for the second." John G. Atkin, "A Digest of the Laws of the State of Alabama, Containing all the Statutes of a Public and General Nature," Montgomery, Alabama, 1833, page 397.

Page 148   "On a September morning in Athens, Alabama, Jackson was captured by Confederates when his company was overrun while guarding Fort Henderson." A copy of the Morning Report of Captured Negroes by Confederate General Nathan Bedford Forrest from the National Archives, courtesy of AAMU Research Center and Museum.

Page 148 "...Confederate General Nathan Bedford Forrest, a former slave trader, was a vicious racist already under Congressional investigation for the mass slaughter of 450 black troops shot while surrendering." Dunnavant, *The Railroad War*, page 45.

Page 148 "Suffering from three gunshot wounds in his left thigh, left shoulder, and right hip, Jackson marched with other prisoners 60 miles to Cherokee where they were loaded onto a railroad cattle car..." Bob Dunnavant, "Saga of John Dawson: A Limestone slave chose to fight for freedom." *Athens News Courier*, Feb. 6, 1977, courtesy of AAMU.

Page 148 "'He said he was always hungry on that train,' ..." Ibid.

Page 149 "Another soldier from the 110th described their new lives in an affidavit, 'If we lagged or faltered or misunderstood an order we were whipped and abused. Some of our own men were detailed to whip the others.'" Ibid.

Page 149 "Mrs. Mason went to school, and even taught school in a building that was erected on the site where her father had been shot and captured during the war." Holly Hollman, "Trinity High School graduates planning reunion in Athens," *Decatur Daily News*, Aug. 9, 2006.

11: California: The Rental Market

Page 155 "Born in 1846 on the John Albright plantation in Holly Springs, Mississippi....At the age of 11, he saw his father auctioned, sold, and shipped to a man in Texas." Elizabeth Lawson interview with George Washington Albright in *Daily Worker* June 18, 1937.

Page 155 I use George Washington Albright's last name out of respect.

Page 155 "Risking the penalty of 39 lashes on a naked back and having his thumb cut off above the second joint..." Heather Andrea

Williams, *Self-Taught: African American Education in Slavery and Freedom*, UNC Press, 2005, page 18. Addresses exaggeration of the number of lashes mentioned by Albright in *Daily Worker* 1937 interview.

Page 155 "...Albright was taught by the owner's children in the plantation kitchen while his mother cooked and looked on." *Daily Worker*, 1937.

Page 155 "...1874, a twenty-eight-year-old Albright ran for state senator and won, serving one term, from 1874-1879," Senate of the State of Mississippi.

Page 156 "...a newly formed clandestine organization of slaves took it upon themselves to spread the word on their own, calling themselves Lincoln's Legal Loyal League." *Daily Worker*, 1937

Page 157 "...Albright introduced the first temperance bill which became law." "Former Slaves Will Review Old Times at A.M.E Church Tonight," *The Pueblo Chieftain*, Feb. 12, 1943.

Page 158 "At the peak of political power, black officials claimed 55 of the 115 seats in the house, 9 of 37 seats in the senate, and speaker of the house." Steven Hahn, *A Nation Under Our Feet: Black Political Struggles in the Rural South from Slavery to the Great Migration*, Harvard University Press, 2005, page 260.

Page 158 "The state already held the record for lynching more blacks than any other." William Fitzhugh Brundage, *Under Sentence of Death: Lynching in the South*, UNC Press, 1997, page 216.

Page 159 "...two sterling silver candlesticks he said he designed for Tiffany's while working for a silverware company in New London... Revere Silversmiths." Revere Silversmiths, Inc., Catalog No. 1103, Modern Swirl Candelabra Height 7" Length 9".

Page 160 "...less likely to brush their teeth..." David L. Ronis, "Preventive Oral Health Behaviors among African-Americans and Whites in Detroit." *Journal of Public Health Dentistry*, 1992, University of Michigan Study.

Page 160 "...their children are less likely to sleep properly." Maninder Kalra, MD, *Chest Journal*, April 2006, reported that black children are three times more likely to snore than other races.

Page 166 "...may sound, disadvantaged parents raise their children, let's just say, differently from what I've seen in the middle class." Betty Hart and Todd Risley, "Meaningful Differences in the Everyday Experience of Young American Children," 1995.

Page 169 "...purchased by one-time carpenter Winfield Scott Stratton, who traveled by foot with his dog all over the Colorado mountains, looking for gold and found it in 1891....became one of the country's first millionaires when he sold it a few years later." Sprague, Marshall, 1994. "The King of Cripple Creek: The Life and Times of Winfield Scott Stratton, First Millionaire from the Cripple Creek Gold Strike." Colorado Springs: Friends of the Pikes Peak Library District.

Page 173 "The CIA acknowledged that not only did the Loyal League exist, but membership included slaves who doubled as spies for the Union Army." P.K. Rose, "The Civil War: Black American Contributions to Union Intelligence," Stud. Intel. Winter 1998/99:73-80. Center for the Study of Intelligence, Central Intelligence Agency.

Page 173 "Perhaps as early as the start of the Civil War in 1861, slaves had banded together to track and leak Rebel movements..." Allan Pinkerton, *The Spy of the Rebellion*, G.W. Carleton & Co. Publishers, New York, 1883, page 355.

Page 173 "...get their hands on battle plans, and record meetings of Confederate officers who tended to dismiss their presence in the room when discussing tactical ops." "The Civil War: Black American Contributions to Union Intelligence." CIA.

Page 173 "...slaves were considered to be enemy number one by General Lee. In a letter in May 1863, he wrote: 'The chief source of information to the enemy is through our Negroes.'" U. S. War Department, *The War of the Rebellion: A Compilation of the Official Records of the Union and Confederate Armies*, Washington, D.C., Government Printing Office, 1880-1901, Vol. 25, Part 2, p. 826 (Lee to Critcher, 22 May 1863) as cited in "The Civil War: Black American Contributions to Union Intelligence." CIA.

Page 173   "... talks about how a 'trusty' Loyal League messenger had direct access to him and his office." Pinkerton, *The Spy of the Rebellion*, pages 355-357.

12: North Carolina: Driving While Black

Page 183   "...100 years following the end of slavery, I found that 80 percent of black households were headed by married, two parent families." Letha A. Lee, *Human Behavior in the Social Environment from an African-American Perspective*, Haworth Press, 2007, page 57.

13: South Africa: Reconciliation Hearings

Page 189   "...across a rebroadcast of Archbishop Desmond Tutu speaking at Fisk University on one of the public access stations." Jan. 14, 2000 at Fisk University.

Page 189   "...date back to the commission set up in 1974 by Ugandan dictator Idi Amin under pressure from human rights groups and the international community." Interview with Priscilla B. Hayner, program director of the International Centre for Transitional Justice by UNESCO, cited in the *Courier* in May 2001.

Page 190   "...the government was guaranteeing freedom from prosecution, in exchange for testimony." Section 20(1) of the Promotion of National Unity and Reconciliation Act, No 34 of 1995.

Page 191   "...September 25 to September 29. The three applicants involved were former operatives hired by the Civil Cooperation Bureau (CCB), a special-forces unit referred to as apartheid's death squad." Testimony included Wouter J. Basson, denied amnesty in 2001 for major offenses, Ferdinand Barnard, denied amnesty in 2001 for major offense, Leon Andre Maree, refused amnesty.

Page 192   "The first Truth and Reconciliation Commission in the United States was in Greensboro, North Carolina in July 2005.... to investigate a 1979 massacre..." Darryl Fears, "Seeking Closure on

'Greensboro Massacre'; Reconciliation Panel Convenes in N.C. to Address '79 Attack by Nazi Party, Klan," *The Washington Post*, Mar. 6, 2005, page A.03.

Page 193   "…'alternate way to create what never happened, and that is a major investigation.'" Fears, "Seeking Closure on 'Greensboro Massacre.'"

15: South Carolina: A Meeting at Piggly Wiggly

Page 207   "His family donated the land the Mt. Joshua United Methodist church is built on." Mt. Joshua AME Zion church letter and deed.

Page 210   "Longtown is the oldest part of Fairfield county and its early history is the least well-known...." Claude Henry Neuffer, *Names In South Carolina Volumes I-XII 1954-1965*, The Reprint Company, Spartanburg, SC, 1976, page 233.

Page 210   "...one cotton plantation house was said to have a 365-windows—one for every day of the year." Ibid.

Page 210   "When Sherman's army marched through Longtown in February 1865, soldiers set it on fire." Julian Stevenson Bolick copyright 1963 by Julian Bolick, Ltd. printed Clinton, SC, Jacobs Brothers.

Page 210   "Despite its wealth, the town which was once called Log-town for the large number of log cabins, was not mentioned on early maps prior to those created by the Confederates during the war." Ibid.

Page 210   "The heavily wooded land once supplied the fur trade for the Wateree Indians." Ibid.

Page 219   "...Peggy had written a letter and provided all of the documents she could find on my great-grandfather....descendant of a slave and Joseph himself." Letter from Peggy, Camden Archives and Museum, July 17, 2008.